Praise fo

"*Morning Fuel* is a masterclass in how to meet grief with grace. Written in the time-honored format of a book of days, each daily mini essay offers a shot of positivity in engaging and relatable bite size pieces that include reflective takeaway questions for the reader . . . Insightful and thought-provoking, Galli's new book provides profound lessons on how to live more mindfully."
—Liane Kupferberg Carter, author
of *Ketchup is My Favorite Vegetable:*
A Family Grows Up with Autism

"The stories in *Morning Fuel* serve as a convenient hand-book for those who wish to examine their own ways of thinking and acting in our challenging world, and as a guide to a more meaningful life."
—Luanne Castle, author of *Our Wolves*
and *Rooted and Winged*

"If you remember and loved *Simple Abundance*, you will welcome and embrace Rebecca Galli's daily reflection, *Morning Fuel*. Her eye for the detailed moments of everyday life enriches those moments and elevates them into reflections that lead to wisdom. Each day's entry is like reading a note written by a loved friend and left for you to read when you wake up after she's already left for work. What a way to start your day!"
—Martha Finney, co-author of *Healing at Work*
and *Any Dumbass Can Do It*

"Reading the day's *Morning Fuel* changes my experience from my dark thinking to divine light. This sets me on a new, possibility filled trajectory for my day."
—Hilary Burns, show host and best-selling author

morning
fuel

DAILY INSPIRATIONS TO STRETCH YOUR MIND BEFORE STARTING YOUR DAY

FROM WHERE I SIT

@CHAIRWRITER

REBECCA FAYE SMITH GALLI

SHE WRITES PRESS

Published 2024
Printed in the United States of America
Print ISBN: 978-1-64742-782-5
E-ISBN: 978-1-64742-783-2
Library of Congress Control Number: 2024913085

For information, address:
She Writes Press
1569 Solano Ave #546
Berkeley, CA 94707

Interior Design by Tabitha Lahr

She Writes Press is a division of SparkPoint Studio, LLC.

Portions of this work have been previously published in *The Baltimore Sun, The Towson Times, North County News, AutismAfter16.com, Nanahood.com, Thoughtful Thursdays, Rethinking Possible,* and *The Herald Dispatch.*

Names and identifying characteristics have been changed to protect the privacy of certain individuals.

This book is dedicated to my family:

Mom, Dad, and Forest;

Rachel, Brittany, Matthew, Madison and Peter—
their spouses and children,
and Joe, Cindy, and Zander.

I love you all—always and forever.

Thank you for keeping my life full and fueled.

Introduction

Some would say life has not been kind to me. At age twenty, I lost my seventeen-year-old brother. Two of my four children had special needs. One of my two sons died at age fifteen. And at thirty-eight, nine days after my divorce was finalized, I was paralyzed by transverse myelitis, a rare inflammation of the spinal cord that affects one in a million.

More than once, it's been hard to find the strength to power through and live fully in this life I did not choose.

But through the years, I've learned that how I start my day sets the tone for how I get through the day. So, I jumpstart each morning by leaning on the words of others and letting their strength help me find mine. I read. I write. I craft and ponder stories, old and new, that help me stretch my mind before starting my day.

We are shaped by our stories. From a young age, we hear them, tell them, and routinely use them to share our lives with one another. Some of these stories are told and then forgotten, all in the same day. Others become foundational and stay with us for a lifetime.

Many of the stories in this book are my foundational ones, the ones I've written or retold that continue to guide and strengthen me. Alongside them, I've offered up quotes, mantras, and other snippets of cherished words and phrases that have given me strength over the years. My goal is to meet you here daily and share a story or thought that promises to inspire, encourage, or make you think.

I hope you'll welcome me as part of your own "morning fuel."

JANUARY

January 1:

The Year of Sparkle

"How many of you make New Year's resolutions?" the career consultant asked us at the holiday luncheon.

Most hands, including mine, went up.

"And how many of you keep them?"

Only a few hands stayed raised. Mine was not one of them. Clearly, most of us needed to hear what Mary Ann Singer, our guest speaker, had to say.

"Instead of creating a list of resolutions," she suggested, "pick a theme. The theme becomes your focus, inspiring you to take actions in its support. You are moving toward something rather than denying yourself or relying on willpower."

Every year since that 2008 gathering, I've taken Singer's advice and chosen a theme word to anchor my mindset for the coming year. My all-time favorite was *sparkle*. After a year of paralysis-related limitations, I wanted to engage more fully in my social interactions, sharing bright and shiny parts of me wherever I could.

So instead of zooming through the doors at my local Sam's Club, I took the time to show my Southern roots—smiling, saying hello, and exchanging pleasantries with the greeters—before continuing on to do my shopping. I also splurged on a pair of gold sequined boots, a bold statement necklace, and two blingy jackets. As one of my wheelchair friends likes to say, "If you can't stand up, stand out!"

But "sparkle" wasn't just about making friends and standing out. In fact, the game-changing part of that year and its theme was looking for the sparkle *in others*.

Everyone sparkles somehow, right?

True, I still "blessed folks' hearts" with polite irritation when people I loved or perfect strangers failed to meet my expectations. But I also worked hard to find their unique sparkle, the gems they alone had to offer. And life became so much brighter.

Over time, seeking the sparkle became a foundational practice for me, fueling an intentional optimism with the power to brighten any day.

How about you? What theme word or phrase could anchor your mindset this year? What sparkle do you see today, both in yourself and in the next person you greet?

January 2:

Stuck or Struck

"Happiness," my father often told me, "lies in the difference between being struck by a challenge or being stuck in a challenge."

I thought about his words when my sister Rachel was preparing to return home to Georgia after a week-long visit. Both of us, now empty-nesters, had just enjoyed five agenda-less days peppered with shopping, makeovers, long lunches, and even longer conversations.

She planned to leave on Thursday. On Friday, I was scheduled to fly to Nashville for a writers' conference.

But Mother Nature had other ideas. A steady snow began Thursday morning, canceling Rachel's trip and then mine.

Undeterred, we started checking other flights, airlines, and departure cities. But after an hour, I realized we were wasting our efforts.

"Sissy," I said as she scrolled through the flights on her laptop, phone shouldered to her ear. "It's not safe. Let's just accept it—we're stuck!"

She looked up, nodded, and powered both off.

Then we smiled at each other.

I don't know if it was the nip in the air, the sight of falling snow—something we'd only dreamed about as kids raised in the South—or the excitement of more time together, but we did something we hadn't done in years.

We went outside and played.

"Watch this," I said, showing Rachel my new moves. The driveway was freshly covered with a new blast of snow. I scooted out onto the blank canvas, using my wheels to create "wheelchair snow art" by spinning, weaving, and making doughnuts and spirals.

"Go Sissy!" Rachel cheered. "Wait, I need to take a picture." And she ran in to grab her phone.

"Of course," I called after her. "Mom would be proud." Our mother was ahead of her time, a nonstop shutterbug who believed it didn't happen unless you had a photo of it, as our bookshelves of photo albums attest.

When the snow deepened, Rachel bundled up and plunked down on the far side of the driveway.

"What are you doing?" I hollered as she lay down and disappeared into the snow.

"I'm making a snow angel!" she hollered back, flapping her arms and legs.

"You're nuts, Sissy!"

"Yep, so are you. Wanna build a snowman?"

And there we were: two sisters—two empty-nester women embracing our moment—playing in the snow like kids.

Far from being stuck in our challenge, we were struck by it—and just as Dad predicted, that made all the difference.

꧁꧂

How about you? When's the last time you played?

January 3:

Filling the Empty

Maybe it was the lingering transition period between the holidays and the New Year, or my sad, undecorated Christmas tree, or the echoing silence in my home after my family left me with so many wonderful memories.

Whatever the cause, life felt extra empty.

I'd also made some bittersweet discoveries while cleaning up and clearing out some old files—divorce spreadsheets, letters from Mom and Dad, drawings from my children's toddler years, medical records from my illness and subsequent paralysis, and dozens of cards and letters I'd received during that time wishing me health and healing.

The evidence of loss was almost overwhelming. I had to dig deep during my morning readings to find comfort.

In his meditation, "Precious Human Birth," from *The Book of Awakening*, Mark Nepo writes:

> "Today you are precious and rare and awake.
> Ask what you need to know now. Say what
> you feel now. Love what you love now."

His words landed softly but solidly, reorienting me to the present. They helped me push aside the feelings of loss by remembering to focus on the things I still have, the things I still love. *Now* was the operative word, a great reminder to stay present and to give the past its proper place.

As my files so clearly showed me, I was not living the life I'd planned. I had to accept that fact, one more time, and get through it. Grief is never one and done, I've learned. It can pop up when we least expect it.

Life can be so hard sometimes, and feel so empty. Yet, there is still much good to be found and learned from our plans—even the ones that didn't work out.

Love what you love now.

And so I do.

Each day I try to give those things I love now an extra measure of attention, letting them grow and root out any emptiness that I may feel. From the first sip of my morning coffee to the evening's final snuggle from my aging puggle Tripp, I'm determined to cherish today's loves a little more so that what's tangible, present, and available now can lift my spirits.

How about you? What lifts your spirits when the emptiness of loss visits you? Does focusing on "the now" help?

January 4:

A Charging Rest

Today's inspiration comes from my wheelchair's battery indicator gauge. It's a useful device, giving power percentages as well as a color warning that ranges from green at 100 percent, through yellow, and down to red.

Rarely do I reach the red zone unless I'm super active or the overnight charger connection is loose and prevents a solid charge. The latter situation is a terrible way to start the day because it means I must park by my bedside charger and sit still until it's finished charging—not fun, and so not me!

I thought about my wheelchair's gauge as I slowly recovered from Christmas one year. Don't get me wrong, I'd *loved* our holiday celebrations, especially since I'd gotten to spend them with my first grandbaby, Blakely Faye. I wouldn't have given up a single minute of the *fifteen* days of family: dinners for ten, brunch for twelve, five trips to the airport, six trips to the mall, game nights, movie nights, take-out, and pizza ordered in—just once.

Every day my wheelchair reached the red zone. But on Christmas Eve, it was at 0 percent by 9:00 p.m.—and I still had stockings to do.

"I'm not sure what happens when I reach 0 percent and don't stop to charge," I told my son Peter. "Want to hang out with me? We might have a little adventure tonight."

"Sure, Ma. I'm up for it."

Home from college, Pete put on *Home Alone* while I scooted slowly back and forth between the gifts and stockings. Once finished, I stopped to watch the movie.

Then a strange thing happened. The gauge moved from 0 percent to 2 percent to 4 percent to 6 percent, despite not being plugged in. I guess "resting," even without charging, counted.

Wouldn't it be nice if we had battery indicator lights to show us our energy level to see how our "resting" was restoring us?

True, nothing fully restores us like the solid charge of a good night's sleep. But other things can recharge us as well; it's just a matter of figuring out what those things are.

In the post "Finding What Energizes You," blogger Sharla Kostelyk suggests we ask ourselves questions like:

- What could I talk about for hours?
- What do I feel passionately about?
- What do I do where I feel less tired afterwards than I did before I started?
- What do I get so excited about that I want to tell everyone I know?

Once you've discovered what energizes you, she suggests including it more regularly in your life. Especially if you need a boost.

Great questions! And the answers have given me some unexpected ideas on how to recharge more creatively.

How about you? What have you discovered that re-charges you?

January 5:

The Fabric of Friendship

It was supposed to be a week filled with "catching up" conversations. The holidays were tucked away, and I was excited to fill my empty calendar with time and tales with friends, including two out-of-town guests.

There's nothing quite like sharing a meal and swapping stories to cement stories into memories.

But a nagging cough turned out to be an upper respiratory infection, or "Miss URI," as my doctor labeled her, who grabbed every one of my Plan A's and twisted them into fragile Plan B's.

My friends, however, were undaunted.

One set of lunch plans turned into a take-out chicken noodle soup for me and a salad for her. Another overnight visitor's dinner became a delivered margherita pizza, served on tray tables for "boudoir dining" so I could continue to rest, heal, and sip on some hot tea in the comfort of my own room.

They brought my newspaper in, my dog out, my mail in, my trash out, and even shopped for medications for me. One friend bought a new coat for my daughter Madison, and another offered to deliver it to her for me.

As I rested in bed, my eyes landed on one of my favorite decorative pillows, which reads:

THE FABRIC OF FRIENDSHIP
IS STRONG BUT STRETCHY

Strong but stretchy, indeed. My friends didn't cancel their plans with me. No—they simply flexed and stretched themselves to accommodate my new situation. How lucky I am!

How about you? Have you experienced the flexibility of a strong but stretchy friendship?

January 6:

Living into the Unknown

Hours after my daughter's nearly twenty-hour labor in August of 2015, I got to hold my first grandchild, Blakely Faye. I also saw the precious little one in October for Halloween, and again for Thanksgiving, and yet again for her first Christmas.

That schedule may not appear unusual, but in our family, getting together is no small feat. Blakely Faye lived 3,000 miles away. And I am in a wheelchair.

Paralyzed from the waist down, I've used a wheelchair since 1997. Travel is doable but requires detailed planning and advance work, so I've learned to cherish every minute of family time together.

After Blakely Faye's December visit, I delighted in sharing as many photos and stories about her as my friends could stand. Until that question came—the one I had no answer for.

"When will you see her again?"

I smiled hard each time, but for the life of me I couldn't stop the tears. "I don't know," I would whisper and then quickly change the subject.

It was a hard truth. And for me, a person whose life is built on structure and schedules and plans, it was difficult to embrace the uncertainty.

What do you do when you don't know what's next? When you can't plan despite all best intentions? When your orbit of life is outside the spinning world of someone you love and care about?

A piece of advice from writer Susan Shapiro helped. Although the context is for those seeking clarity in their relationship status, her suggestion can be applied to any confusing situation, any time we're obsessed with something beyond our control:

"When in doubt, do your life."

So I did.

I committed to writing weekly and launched my Thoughtful Thursday email column. I increased my volunteer activities, joined a women's group, and scheduled more outings with friends.

Texting and FaceTime kept me connected to Blakely's firsts. But, instead of obsessing about the future of our next visit, I acted on doable tasks in front of me. Those life-redefining efforts helped fill the void of the unknown while reminding me how important it was to have a vital and busy life of my own.

***

How about you? What helps you get through times of uncertainty when you can't plan?

January 7:

The Nudge We Need

After my memoir *Rethinking Possible* was published, I learned firsthand about the power of encouragement. Although I'd written extensively about my paralysis and adjustments to life from the wheelchair, I'd never spoken publicly about it or answered questions from strangers about my crazy life.

As I told my email subscribers, I was "scared spitless."

They wrote back, encouraging me to press on and not let my fears slow me down. By the time the publicity cycle had finished, I'd spoken sixteen times to audiences ranging in number from 12 to 750. It wasn't easy, but I felt energized and strangely courageous because of my community's steadfast support. My confidence grew with each event, a result of their unwavering encouragement.

The next year I chose that word, *encouragement*, as my New Year's theme. I wanted to get better at giving it, to acknowledge it more fully when I received it, and to work harder at finding new ways to make it part of my daily life.

Life is hard. Encouragement helps.

Why?

Encouragement connects us in a positive way. It can be as simple as a compliment or an observation. At its core, it shows we are paying attention to someone we care about.

The word encouragement comes from the Old French word *encoragier*, meaning "make strong, hearten." We have the ability to give strength, heart, and courage to one another—pretty incredible. Let's go, right?

Encouragement is a difference-maker. It's the fuel we need to keep going in the face of hardship. We strive. We struggle. We fail. Sometimes we need a kind word or thoughtful comment to remind us to *just keep going*.

How about you? How will you use the powerful force of encouragement today? Can you give it? Or acknowledge receiving it?

January 8:

Root-Bound Realities

I raised an eyebrow when the young woman appeared, lugging two heavy hoses. She paused to drop one in front of a flowerbed, then hooked up the other and turned the sprinkler on.

I'd parked my wheelchair on the hotel porch, right behind several large sheltered planters. Realizing her plan included watering my porch companions, I asked if I was in the way.

"No, not yet. I'll probably get to that one last," she replied motioning to the one behind me. "It's so root-bound, it's hard to get water in it."

I nodded in acknowledgment and turned around to see my root-bound friend. It was a large evergreen, perfectly shaped in two tiers. Its twin framed the other side of the hotel's entrance. They both looked healthy to me.

"What do you mean when you say they're 'root-bound'?" I asked.

"Their roots are so large that the water just sits on top—it takes a long time for it to be absorbed," she explained. "They really need to be in bigger pots."

As I watched her methodical watering, I pondered my root-bound friends and wondered if the term applied to humanity as well.

Do we sometimes become so root-bound that we can't absorb the nutrients that help us grow?

Although comfortable, sometimes our routines, rituals, and traditions need to be altered to allow for growth.

The very thing that has housed and made possible our current success may limit our future possibilities.

With the New Year upon us, we may benefit from examining our root-bound lifestyles, ideas, and patterns.

And perhaps repot.

How about you? What areas of your life could expand if given more room to grow?

January 9:

Consider It an Honor

I couldn't remember her name. Even though I'd met the woman several times before, for the life of me I could not remember her name!

Of course, she remembered mine.

"Hi, Becky," she said. "I'm reading your book and coming to your next book talk."

I winced as I looked at her smiling face, deeply embarrassed by my memory failure. I took a deep breath, returned her smile as brightly as I could, and asked, "Would you remind me of your name?"

"Jean," she said, kindness deepening her smile. "It's Jean."

"I'm so sorry. I'm not very good with names."

"Oh, don't apologize," she said brightly. "I consider it an honor when someone asks my name."

My eyes widened. "Really? An honor?"

"Of course. You want to know my name. It's an honor."

"Oh my." I chuckled. "Well, you may be honored again a few more times in the future! I really am terrible with names."

She laughed a gentle laugh, one that said very clearly that indeed she would be honored.

Unlike my pastor father and my hostess-with-the-mostest mother, both of whom always seemed to remember names so easily, I struggle.

I try. Really try. I write them down. Try to associate each one with specific details. Even review my name list before I go to an event.

And still I fail.

But Jean inspired me. As I wheeled away from this lovely woman, it occurred to me that I'd experienced a shift in my thinking. I'd always felt awkward asking someone to repeat their name, especially when I thought I should know it. I thought they would somehow think less of me for not remembering.

But Jean's response gave me a new idea. Instead of embarrassment, what if I approached it as extending an honor? What a difference that would make in my habits, my attitude, and even my view of failure.

After all, my intent is sincere. Names are important; I know that. It's just really difficult for me to retain them.

Maybe this shift in perspective will give me the confidence to wince less and ask more. Hopefully, everyone will feel honored in the process.

⁓⦻⁓

How about you? Are you ever embarrassed to ask someone to repeat information you've been told previously? Would you feel differently if you thought they would consider it an honor?

January 10:

Fears and Risks

When my sixteen-year-old son Peter learned to drive a stick shift, I finally faced a nagging fear. I wanted to master the art of driving with only my hands.

Eighteen months after my paralysis, I completed the driver's training and received my license, trading in my sunroofed station wagon for an accessible van. But for years, the van's hand controls had just sat there, winking at me, taunting me with one thing I refused to do: drive.

The vehicle adaptation is simple. A spinner knob on the steering wheel enables the driver to maneuver the vehicle with one hand, while the other hand uses a lever to the left of the steering column to control the gas and brake pedals. Push it to stop; pull it to go. No feet required.

I understood it. I knew how to do it. I just wouldn't. I was scared.

For the twelve years since my paralysis, people had shuttled me around, never complaining or challenging my decision. Perhaps they understood my caution. I never was much of a risk-taker. Then I went to bed not feeling well and woke up paralyzed—that didn't help. Risk-taking was elevated to a whole new level of consideration.

But as I watched Pete hop into his Wrangler, I marveled at his determination. Undaunted by stalls, jerky stops, and uneven starts, he soaked up every bit of his father's instructions on how to shift gears—and soon succeeded.

His two-handed feat inspired me to attempt my own.

But first, I had to quiet the mental noise. What if I went too slow, pushed the wrong lever, or people honked at me? Left turns terrified me. With my limited abdominal muscles, I would have to lean hard into the steering wheel knob while turning in that direction or I would tip over and face-plant into the passenger seat.

Pete cheered me on, offering to help. He rode with me and held my right shoulder to prevent me from tipping as I got used to the mechanics.

People did honk at me. But I chose to see it as their problem, not mine, and stayed focused on my objective. And when I mastered a Starbucks drive-through that required three left turns, I knew I'd finally accomplished my goal.

How about you? What fears are worth facing for the sense of accomplishment doing so could bring? What risks are worth inviting into your world this year?

January 11:

Savor Your Sips

One of the ways I measure how I'm doing in life is by how quickly I drink my coffee.
—Stephanie May Wilson

Isn't that the truth?

I love to start the day with something warm that brings comfort to my body. Through the years, I've alternated between coffee and tea, caffeinated and decaf. Regardless of the beverage I choose, how I take that first morning sip of nourishment is a direct reflection of how I'm doing.

Do I sip and savor?

Or gulp and go?

Life is better when I have the time to sip, reflect, and ease myself into the demands of the day. But lately, I'd been gulping far more often than sipping.

Planning helped, of course. So did adding margins, a calendar technique I'd begun years earlier where I added extra buffer time on my calendar before and after activities. But when progress on a writing project stalled, I discovered I needed to take bolder measures.

One new friend and now mentor—James Barnes, the founder of JB Innovation—offered advice that helped: "Before you can make time for something you want to start, it helps to decide what you are going to stop."

Gulp.

As I looked at my calendar, I noticed some patterns. Rarely did I have a free morning (always my most productive writing time), much less a free day. No wonder I couldn't make progress: I hadn't allowed the time for it!

So, I made a "stop doing" list:

1. Stop morning appointments for at least three days a week. Mark "W" on the calendar for writing time.
2. Stop scheduling appointments every day of the week. Mark "HW" on the calendar for home writing days.
3. Stop writing projects, classes, or courses that don't help me with my next book.
4. Stop mindless television watching. Record what can be watched later.

It worked! I made huge progress on my writing projects (you are holding one of them!). More importantly, I'm sipping more than gulping—truly savoring a more balanced pace of life.

⤞⧠⤝

How about you? Did you sip or gulp your morning refreshment today? Does that reflect how you're living your life?

January 12:

The Strings That Connect Us

Today's inspiration comes from my friend Nancy and a story she shared during a gathering I attended.

As Nancy was preparing to leave her three-year-old grandson, who lives out of state, she told him how sorry she was that she had to say good-bye, how sad it made her, and how very much she was going to miss him.

"It's okay," the little fella assured her. "There are strings between our hearts."

I joined the collective "aww" from the audience, and tears began to well. How beautiful. How absolutely beautiful!

And how I hoped it was true for me, too. Did Blakely Faye, my precious granddaughter, feel that way? Had I done enough in her first three years of life that she, too, felt there were strings between our hearts?

I'd tried.

We both loved Disney princesses. Cinderella was our favorite, so she was mentioned in every conversation and featured in special gifts of dress-ups, jewelry, and anything that sparkled. Even though we lived twelve hours apart, I'd been a regular part of Blakely Faye's world ever since she'd figured out how to see my face during my FaceTimes with her mom. I often joined Blakely on her bed to look at a book or at her table to have tea and a cookie.

But during her Christmas visit, she stole my heart with a new holiday outfit complete with gold shoes, a gold purse, and a shirt that read, "I sparkle like my Nana." Inspired by her bling, I put on my gold sparkle boots and some new sequined pants. She hopped up on my lap, and we wheeled up and down the driveway, sparkling all the way—a joy ride memory we both still treasure.

It's hard to be family when distance separates us. Yet even when there is proximity, it still takes some "doin'," as my mother used to say, to be with one another.

Relationships don't just happen. It takes time, effort, and creativity to keep those strings between our hearts connected.

How about you? How can you strengthen the strings that connect you to those you care about?

January 13:

Unexpected Blessings

Madison, my daughter with autism, was eight years old. As a baby, she'd cried a lot, slept little, and had trouble engaging with anyone, even members of our family. Her verbal ability at age eight was minimal. What speech she did have—the product of years of specialized therapy—was scripted, and every response required repeated prompting.

Yet she was happy.

She loved to sing Mary Kate and Ashley songs, and she memorized every word of her Barney videos. Her rhythm was precise, whether jumping in time to the music or bending sideways at the waist and swinging her head of long shiny hair back and forth, adding drama to her dance.

She shied away from family activities with her siblings, even though they encouraged her to join. Sometimes she would. Most often, she would not. She preferred to play alone.

At meal time, though, she would come to the table and sit silently with us. Our family ritual was holding hands around the table and praying the children's blessing:

"God is great, God is good, let us thank him for

our food; by his hands we are fed, give us Lord our daily bread. Amen."

Madison was well-behaved in our circle but never seemed aware of what was happening or participated. She would consent to hold hands during the prayer, but when first syllable of "amen" was uttered, she would bolt upright and leave us to return to her singing and dancing.

Until one Friday night.

It was our family pizza night. We were seated and had joined hands. Head bowed and eyes closed, I was about to lead our prayer when Madison shocked us all.

"God is great," she began in her best Barney voice . . . and she didn't stop until she reached the "amen." She said the entire prayer, more words than I'd ever heard her say—solo, and with no prompting.

I was in shock! The only rationale I could imagine was that I was taking too long to pray and she wanted to get back to her dancing. Nevertheless, I gained a whole new respect for rituals and the power they have to teach—whether we are aware of it or not.

How about you? What have you learned through a ritual? Or taught unexpectedly by using one?

January 14:

The Gift of Saying No

During a morning catch-up call with my sister Rachel, I lamented the fact that I had declined an invitation to join a good friend for an upcoming event. It was a last-minute offer, but I knew I would have *loved* both the event and meeting the people who were attending.

"I really, really wanted to go," I told her, sighing. "But I decided against it."

"Well, Sissy," she began. "Just remember, saying no to one thing means you are saying yes to something else."

Her words hung in the air, then settled in deep, cutting through to the heart of the matter.

When had my younger sister become so wise?

As I thought about it, saying no to that invitation meant I was saying yes to taking care of my health. My paralyzed parts had been giving me extra trouble. As a T-8 paraplegic, the body below my waist has a mind of its own. I jokingly call her my "two-year-old," since she's hard to predict, control, or count on for good behavior.

Though I joke about her, life is hard when she's misbehaving. I often don't feel well and don't know exactly why. Leg spasms can mean anything from a urinary tract infection to a bowel blockage to a kidney stone to a hangnail on my big toe. I get grumpy and impatient with myself and others, especially when I have to cancel or alter my plans.

For the previous few weeks, my two-year-old had not minded me. Perhaps it was time to give her my undivided attention.

Rachel's approach grounded me, allowing me to shift my perspective. When I focused on the *yes* part of my decision, instead of the *no*, it brought not only relief from disappointing my friend, but also affirmed the positive benefits of tending to my health.

How about you? Is it hard for you to say no? Does looking for the yes in your answer help?

January 15:

The Doorway Effect

⌒⌇⌒

Have you ever walked into a room and forgotten why you were there?

As a child, I remember Mom entering a room with one index finger extended, as if she were making a point or getting ready to speak. When I asked her about it, she said, "Well, honey, when I raise my finger in one room and keep it up until I reach the other room, it helps me remember why I came into the room."

Midway into my January clean-out mode, as I was traipsing all over my house, gathering and sorting files, closets, and clothing, I noticed I was having Mom's problem. I'd come into a room and then forget why I was there.

Was it another sign of aging?

Apparently not.

Scientists call this phenomenon the "doorway effect." It occurs because we change both our physical and mental environments when we move into a different room. When the context changes, we think about different things and our goal is forgotten. Or, as Melissa Dahl at *New York Magazine*'s Science of Us sums it up: "What happens in the kitchen, stays in the kitchen." And, according to the researchers who have studied the doorway effect, the more thresholds crossed, the greater the memory lapse.

Yikes!

I have a *lot* of doorways in my home. In fact, in order to get from my desktop computer (where I research and edit) to my sunroom (where I read and compose), I pass through four doorways.

It's a wonder I remember anything!

Yet I am encouraged. It's not age or illness that's causing this phenomenon. It's simply my brain doing its thing—as it's wired to do.

In all my research, I've never found an "official" solution to this problem. But Mom's simple way of remembering works for me. I look at doorways differently now—challenging myself to stay on task as I pass through each one with my index finder defiantly raised.

How about you? Have you experienced the "doorway effect"? What helps you stay focused as you move through your day?

January 16:

The Denial Blanket

In her book *The Language of Letting Go*, Melody Beattie describes denial as a warm blanket that we wrap around ourselves to protect us from cold truths or a reality we are not ready to accept. And it is not our job, she says, to rip others' blankets off or shame them for using one. "Shaming makes them colder," she writes. "It makes them wrap themselves more tightly."

Instead, Beattie asserts, our job is to make others feel warm and safe. Then, in time, they may let go of the blanket—but only when they are ready.

Her imagery reminded me of the Aesop fable about the North Wind and the Sun and their competition to see who could strip a traveler of his cloak. The Wind blew hard, and the traveler clung even harder to his cloak to shield himself from the cold. But when the Sun shone brightly and warmed him, he readily took it off.

As I mulled over Beattie's words and the fable, I suddenly felt overwhelmed with gratitude for all those in my life who have chosen to warm me with understanding, encouragement, and patience as I've worked through so many challenges that were hard for me to accept: My brother's death. My children's disabilities. My divorce. And the long three years it took me to finally accept my paralysis.

No one ever shamed me. Or criticized me. Or tried to rip my blanket off.

They only loved me through it, giving me a safe space to work through and accept what I very much wanted to deny. In those dark, cold days, they chose to shine brightly. They warmed me so I could let go of my blanket.

I only hope I can be as loving to those I encounter who are wrapped in their own blanket of denial.

How about you? What blankets of denial have you wrapped yourself in? Did feeling safe and warm help you through it?

January 17:

A Mindful Season

The static crackled, but the irritated voice came through clearly on my end of the phone. "I have one more store to try," my friend said. "I'm hoping Walmart won't disappoint me."

We pushed back our lunch plans another half hour. I had to snicker as I hung up. She was a woman on a mission, determined to find that perfect storage box—today.

What is it about January that brings out the clutter-conquering spirit to lump, label, and organize with such zeal? My friend had been to two stores already. She reported empty shelves—or, worse yet, lid-less containers.

After the holidays, January gives us time to be mindful. Perhaps it begins when we take the tree down.

We drag the unadorned evergreen down and out, and its trailing needles shift us into a mandatory cleanup mode. Inclement weather often puts us home with our projects and promises of what we hope to accomplish in the coming year. The time is ripe to reorder our world and reorganize with the future in mind.

Those shiny new storage containers have their purpose. They encourage us to organize the old so we can begin the mindful placement of the new.

How about you? How can reorganizing help you prepare for this year's goals?

January 18:

Shortcut Misses

A young artist was searching for a good location to set his easel, hoping to capture nature's majesty on canvas. As he walked through the woods, he noticed dozens of trees with circles drawn on them and bullet holes precisely in the center of each circle.

"This must be some kind of marksman," he whispered to himself. "He hasn't missed the bull's-eye yet!"

He continued on, and soon spotted a young mountaineer with a gun.

"Are you the one shooting holes in the trees?" he asked.

"Yep," replied the lad as he leaned against a tree.

"How do you do it? You haven't missed the center of a circle yet."

"Nothing to it." He reached into his pocket and pulled out a piece of chalk. "I just shoot the hole then draw the circle around it."

We smile at the antics of the young mountaineer—and then wonder about his motives. Was he trying to impress others while kidding himself? Or was he just too lazy to practice his marksmanship?

It may be more efficient, but where's the sport in that effort?

It reminds me of my attempt to explain putt-putt golf to my five-year-old friend Zander.

"The object of the game," I instructed, "is to get the golf ball in the hole."

He looked at the ball on the ground and then sized up the hole at the end of the turf.

"Oh, that's easy, Aunt Becky." He put down his putter, picked up the ball, walked to the hole, and dropped it in. "See? What's so hard about that?"

Just like our bull's-eye buddy.

But what if our young marksman's motives were a bit more complex? Unlike the innocence of my five-year-old friend, perhaps he was a savvy perfectionist, afraid of risking an off-center shot. Or maybe he was just lazy, so he played it safe, focusing on the result rather than the skill needed to achieve it.

Regardless of motive, results-driven living—shooting first, then drawing the circle—shortcuts the process that makes us true marksmen. When we omit hard work, discipline, and the opportunity to learn, we can set ourselves up for empty accomplishments. Sustained fulfillment comes not only from reaching our goals but also from the lasting lessons learned in the process.

How about you? Have you ever taken a shortcut that affected how you felt about your success?

January 19:

Planning Possibilities

During my IBM career, January planning sessions were mandatory for all sales reps. Account reviews culminated in detailed plans, complete with action items and due dates. In the years after, I participated in both church and charity planning events and even added a family planning session with my kids and their dad.

Why not? I reasoned. *Let's agree on what's important in the upcoming year—school, church, sports, vacation, as well as personal goals—and then make a plan.*

"What is planned is possible," my father used to say.

But what really needled me was my imagined corollary of, "What is not planned is darn near impossible."

Ideas without plans often stay that way, I've learned. Projects without timelines can fail to progress. And even the best of intentions without commitments may never be realized.

Plans give us the ability to harness the potential of possibilities.

How about you? Is January a time of planning for what's important to you? Should it be?

January 20:

The Friend in the Mirror

"Be your own best friend," my sister Rachel advises, particularly when I'm hard on myself for not meeting my own expectations.

When my inner critic's voice gets too loud and I find myself repeating its words out loud, she'll ask, "Would you say that to a good friend?"

Even if I would, most often I wouldn't say it as harshly as I say it to myself. So, I reframe that self-talk with kinder, gentler words.

She also reminds me, "You know, you better like yourself because you are stuck with you the rest of your life." Yikes!

Sometimes I take a peek in the mirror and pause to study my reflection, realizing that the choices I make daily contribute not only to who I am but also to who I am *becoming*—the Becky of the future.

I can decide what kind of mom I want to be.

What kind of ex-wife I want to be.

What kind of friend I want to be—to others and to myself.

When I shift my perspective to this angle, how my behaviors reflect who I am, it's easier to make the kinder, more loving choice—to take the "high road," as author Scott Peck would say. I've never regretted taking the high road—with others and with myself. And that choice always lifts my spirits.

How about you? What kind of friend are you to the person in the mirror?

January 21:

Both Beauty and Beast

Thirty-two-and-a-half inches of snow graced my deck in less than thirty hours. It was a personal record for me, a

Southerner by birth, and for most of the Baltimore-Washington metro area.

"Prepare for the unexpected," the local authorities had warned. *Just my style*, I'd thought as I put together my plan. I had water, meals, auxiliary heat, and a confirmed snow-plow service in place. My power wheelchair, phone, and laptop—and their respective backup batteries—were charged and easily accessible. A magnetic flashlight clung to my bed's wrought-iron headboard.

My biggest fear was losing power. Even with my backup generator, a prolonged outage—which they were predicting—would be difficult for me.

But strangely, I was looking forward to the experience. I'd lined up a bunch of got-to-get-around-to-it-sometime projects and was prepared to dive in—either to catch up or get ahead.

I was ready to be blizzard-bound.

As I walked the dog one final time on Friday afternoon, I could tell this was going to be a different storm. The first flurries felt like slivers of ice, stinging my face like sleet but sticking quickly to the ground. By the evening news hour, those who were live-reporting were using ski goggles to protect their eyes.

Saturday, I awakened to a dense white fog and the whistle of thirty-five-mile-per-hour winds. Hours later, every door to my house was snow-packed. I used a dustpan to scoop out a spot for Tripp to use the bathroom that was—well, let's just say, "Good enough."

We were iglooed in.

Sunday morning, the beauty of the storm arrived. Sunshine lit up my blanketed lawn, making it dance with blinding white crystals.

Twenty-four hours later, a plow, a bulldozer, and a three-man crew spent hours digging us out.

Then the beauty became the beast.

The weight of the snow, or the effort to remove it, knocked my garage door off track. It opened, and then wouldn't close. The repairman could not get to me until the following day, so my garage door stayed open all night—which made the garage freezer stop working, which made all the food in the freezer thaw, which made me throw away all the food.

But I didn't lose power. Or run out of food or water. And after three long days, I was able to let Tripp outside. We were happy and relieved to have survived and enjoyed both the beauty and the beast.

How about you? Have you ever been confronted by the unexpected and found it to be both a beauty and a beast?

January 22:

Two Words of Comfort

My favorite encouraging phrase comes from my mother. Throughout my life, whenever I fretted about falling short of a goal, she would tell me, "BB, honey, I think you are doing mighty well."

Mighty well.

Something about those words would make me pause—and allow me to stop striving so hard for a moment, relax, and assess the progress I'd made.

When perfection eluded me, "mighty well" encouraged me.

How about you? How can you use the phrase "mighty well" for your own self-assessment or for someone else who could benefit? Do you have a favorite encouraging phrase?

January 23:

The Art of an Empty Shelf

Somewhere, keep an empty shelf. An empty shelf means possibility; space to expand; and luxurious waste of something useful for the sheer elegance of it.
—Gretchen Rubin

Love that!

But, I must admit, it is hard for me to do. I've made a lot of memories in my life and have managed to hang on to most of them. Instead of adopting a clean desk policy, I like to borrow a phrase from one of my favorite people and politely describe my mess as "piles of interests."

Nevertheless, I'm discovering there is power in cleaning up, clearing out, and leaving empty spaces. It feels good, even encouraging, to have a place ready to receive whatever is next in my mission to try new things in the new year.

When we empty a shelf, we clear out what is no longer relevant so that we can invite in new possibilities. We create a vivid visual reminder that letting go is part of growing.

In fact, the notion that this open space, this "luxurious waste of something useful," existing "for the sheer elegance of it," seems to elevate the end product to an art form.

Like art, we can let it speak to us uniquely—and powerfully.

How about you? Have you found satisfaction, encouragement, or even inspiration in leaving a shelf empty? What does it invite you to explore?

January 24:

Redefining Stress

Dr. Wilkie Wilson, professor of pharmacology at Duke University, asked a group of high school parents to define "stress."

"Anxiety. Worry. Tension. Pressure," several of us called out.

"And how does stress make you feel?" Wilson asked.

"Frustrated. Edgy. Physically ill," others replied.

Then Wilson pointed to the screen to reveal his definition: "Stress is the effort of the brain to adapt to a change in the environment."

The parents collectively paused at that new thought, keenly aware of its contrast to our definitions.

He went on to define acute stress and chronic stress, noting how our bodies were built to handle the ups and downs of acute stresses, where we respond to sudden changes and then recover. But chronic stress, he warned, could be dangerous; when changes are not resolved before another change takes place, there is no time for the body to recover, and the effects steadily accumulate.

I listened, yet my mind was still stuck on his definition—its simplicity, neutrality, and truth:

Stress is the effort of the brain to adapt to a change in the environment.

As I reflected on the hubbub of the holidays, I recalled times of stress where I felt overwhelmed and tense and became frustrated and edgy: an emergency trip to the vet, spoiled meat, pneumonia, a power outage, and a migraine had all made unplanned appearances at my home during the holidays. And yes, I'd felt stressed. As I reviewed each circumstance, I realized I had been reacting to an unplanned change. In a strange way, though, it was comforting to think that my reactions were caused biologically; they were my brain's effort to respond to change.

I wasn't being irrational, grumpy, or rude—my brain just needed a moment to adjust to a new circumstance.

So often we're told how to manage, avoid, or overcome stress. Wilson's definition doesn't do any of that; it simply grants us a new freedom to embrace that part of daily living that is inevitable.

Perhaps it is worth remembering that both the changes we experience and those we impose on others will inevitably cause stress.

But, no worries.

We simply need to acknowledge the science at work, give our brains (and theirs) a moment to adapt, and press on.

⁓⦉⦊⁓

How about you? Might redefining stress change your perspective on how to manage it?

January 25:

The Great Simplifier

⁓⦉⦊⁓

Unlike the beast of a snow that left me with a garage door stuck open for three days, this snow was far less treacherous. Still, it wreaked havoc. Why?

This time around, the forecast had the widest range of predictions I've ever experienced—anywhere from one to nine inches. If you can call that a prediction.

I can't recall the exact variables, but it had to do with fronts and pressures and clipper systems and temperatures and a tremendous number of unqualified "ifs."

So how do you plan for that?

I wasn't the only one confused. Many schools started out with delays before deciding to close. I stared at my booked calendar and wrestled with all the ramifications. What could be rescheduled? What could not?

Then, in the middle of all the indecision, I recalled a quote that I'd read during a recent morning quiet time. It was from Hans Hofmann, abstract artist and teacher: "The ability to simplify means to eliminate the unnecessary so that the necessary may speak."

At this thought, I smiled. Yes! Snow is the great simplifier. The more we have of it, the simpler life becomes. At one inch of snow, quite a few things are possible. But at nine? The necessary can become unnecessary very quickly. Maybe that's what a snow day can teach us. If we're overwhelmed, we can just imagine nine inches of snow outside our front door.

Slow down, take note, and let the necessary speak.

How about you? Short of a nine-inch snowfall, what simplifies your life?

January 26:

The Joy of Wasting Time

It's a topic we don't like to talk about—wasting time. Even writing the words causes me to wince. Who likes to waste time? And who would ever admit it if they do?

We like to be efficient and productive, and often feel particularly accomplished if we figure out a faster way to complete a task.

Yet, whether we admit it or not, we do waste time. Our mind darts off topic, reminiscing or dreaming about anything but the present task. One project reveals another, and our curiosity hijacks our schedule. Or perhaps we get stuck, failing to progress—taking a break that never ends.

Philosopher Bertrand Russell offers a thought that both inspires and comforts me:

"The time you enjoy wasting is not wasted time."

Thank goodness!

I discovered Russell's words about the same time that winter made its first official appearance with a round of snow. I had great plans for the day but decided to pitch them and watch Mother Nature's handiwork instead.

As the tiny flakes blanketed my world, I took extra time with my coffee and morning readings. Later, I snapped a few photos of my yard's transformation.

My father called these kinds of days—days where you meander through the day with no set agenda—LID days, or "Let It Develop" days. He cherished these purposely unplanned days, which he used to piddle in his workshop, putter around the garden, or otherwise do whatever the day revealed as its opportunities.

No to-do lists. No schedule. No clock watching or timers. Let. It. Develop. And, Bertrand Russell would add, "Enjoy it!"

Although I wasn't expecting any benefits on my snow day, I discovered several. By the day's end, I felt restored—more content, centered, and ready to face the hectic week that lay ahead. Perhaps my yard wasn't the only one transformed that day.

And I wonder, would it be oxymoronic to *schedule* a LID day?

Maybe. But I'll bet it would be worth it!

❧

How about you? Have you ever experienced the benefits of "wasting time"? What do you think about scheduling a LID day for yourself?

January 27:

My Oprah Dilemma

A new friend Paul and I were having lunch. He was from out of town and in the process of writing his first book. I offered to share with him what I'd learned from my publishing experience.

He admitted that he hadn't read my book yet but said he was eager to learn all about my life story.

First, he asked about my paralysis.

Yes, it happened in six hours, nine days after my divorce was final. Yes, the incidence is one in a million. Yes, two-thirds of people diagnosed with transverse myelitis have some kind of recovery, but no, I didn't.

Then he asked about my family.

Yes, I had four children. Yes, one had autism. Yes, one had a rare blood disorder. And, yes, one had epilepsy and later died at age fifteen.

And then he asked about my siblings.

Yes, I have a sister. I had a brother, but he died when I was twenty. He was seventeen.

"Oh, I'm so sorry to hear," he said, pausing to absorb it all. Then the thought struck him: "Wait, isn't Oprah from Baltimore?"

"Yes."

"Don't you think she might be interested in your story?"

"I've always hoped so."

"Well, have you tried to approach her?"

"Yes, I have. For about fifteen years."

"Really? And you got no response?"

No response. I thought about that phrase, letting it seep into those many years of disappointed efforts. Finally, I took a deep breath, smiled, and said, "You know, she's just not interested."

We both laughed out loud and finished our lunch.

Later, I thought about my response.

Obviously, I knew by this point that Oprah wasn't interested—but for some reason, saying it out loud to another person filled me with an enormous sense of freedom. Stating it so clearly allowed me to stop wondering why she's not interested and get on with the pursuit of anyone who is.

Why was it so freeing to me? It meant the problem wasn't mine anymore. The pressure and responsibility shifted off of me and onto her or other forces beyond my control. (But if she calls me someday, rest assured, I'll answer!)

Sometimes we need to give persistence a rest and enjoy the freedom of accepting reality.

How about you? Have you ever decided to stop chasing a dream that was draining you? Was it a relief to give persistence a rest?

January 28:

Taking Compliments

The boutique owner's blue-jeweled necklace sparkled as she held the shop door open so I could wheel though.

"I love your necklace," I told her. "It's so beautiful!"

"This old thing?" she hastily replied. "It's tarnished. I really need to get it dipped again."

I smiled back, then winced. My father's words came flooding back, their truth undeniable now. "Always express gratitude for a compliment; never discount it," he said. "When you belittle the compliment, you also belittle the one giving it."

He was right.

Her words stung. Embarrassed, I looked around to see if anyone else had witnessed our exchange. I felt like my opinion was flawed. My definition of beauty fell short of her standards. I'd offered a compliment, and instead of being met with gratitude, I'd been judged.

Although the incident made me think twice before offering her another compliment, it also made me think even harder about how I receive compliments given to me.

Do I discount them by not acknowledging the thoughtfulness behind the comment?

When you think about it, giving a compliment requires observation, valuation, and the effort (and risk!) to convey that thought. Who are we to dismiss all that?

Maybe a simple "thank you" is all that's needed.

How about you? How have you experienced giving and receiving compliments?

January 29:

Who's in Your Boat?

Today's inspiration comes from a favorite visual artist, BB LaMartina, and her painting *Staying Steady . . . Navigating Through Turbulent Times*. The large impressionistic work features the bow of a boat cresting a powerful wave. I love the stormy blue, green, and grey colors, the tinges of gold (love that bling!), and the hint of hopeful aqua misting in the background.

"Brighter, clearer days are ahead," it whispers to me.

"Thank heavens," I exhale back.

But as I studied BB LaMartina's piece more closely one day, I was reminded of the most important question

I've learned to ask while going through stormy seas. From the death of my brother to managing my special needs children to adjusting to life with paralysis, the question I've long found to be most useful is a simple one:

Who is in my boat?

That image of a worn but triumphant bow brought to mind each circumstance and its crew while emphasizing the importance of figuring out what was needed to keep steady. With each challenge, I always consider:

- Who has expertise that is helpful?
- Who can listen with compassion and objectivity to clarify options for the next steps?
- Who can be counted on for support, comfort, and an encouraging word?

Compassionate listeners, objective friends, medical professionals, faith advisors, and family and friends who brought comfort and laughter at any hour—these are the folks who helped me figure out how to stay steady amidst terrible swells.

With the right crew, I'm confident I can stay steady, no matter how stormy the sea.

How about you? If you are experiencing a challenging time, who can you ask to be in your boat?

January 30:

Creative Penalties

My younger siblings were at it again. Rachel had called Forest a name, and he wanted her to pay for it.

"I want her to write this fifty times," Forest, then eleven, requested. "Then maybe she'll think twice before she calls me that name again."

The paper he thrust toward my parents read:

In the future, far or near, I will not under any circumstance of any kind call my brother, Robert Forest Smith III, any bad names for any period of time or do anything of any kind to insult my brother in front of company of any kind, because it is not a good habit or a good thing to do to anyone or anything. But if I do this ugly and cruel thing to Robert Forest Smith III again, I will copy this statement twice the number of times I did this time.

Our parents agreed—and the creative penalty was effective. After copying Forest's words fifty times, Rachel never had to write them again.

Even though I was only a bystander, this incident taught me something too. Words have power. So do consequences. And sometimes the victim is the only person who can say how justice will best be served.

What about you? Was there a time you stood up for yourself? How did it feel—and did it work?

January 31:

The Power of the Reset

For weeks I'd lived with one malfunctioning sports channel that would not switch to high-definition mode.

Its images were grainy and blurred and filled only part of my TV's high-resolution screen.

I first tried fixing the problem on my own. My "smart" TV prompted me through its protocol—pushing one button, rebooting, waiting, pushing another button—before giving an error code and instructing me to call customer service.

After eight minutes of holding music, a polite but efficient gentleman asked me for every piece of identifying information possible (except for my blood type) before suggesting I unplug my device, wait a few minutes, and plug it back in.

I followed his advice—and magically, my full screen came to life in pristine high definition.

Ugh, I knew that trick! I wasn't sure why I hadn't tried it.

Feeling stupid, I figured I might as well learn from this moment, so I asked, "Why did I have to unplug for this channel? None of the other channels had this issue."

His explanation surprised me: "Some channels require more signal strength than others. A total reset by unplugging is necessary to restore it, especially after the recent storms."

After I hung up, I started thinking. Maybe that happens to us too. Life hurls some storms our way that knock us out of our "high-definition" mode. Some parts of us recover fully, but maybe there is a channel or two that's still lagging.

Maybe we need to unplug to restore completely.

Now I take my cable guy's advice and "unplug" when I feel like I'm functioning but not at full capacity. I'll clear some white space on my calendar. Take extra time to observe a morning sunrise. Cherish an extra snuggle with Tripp. Or maybe get lost in binge-watching a new show.

Life may be meant to be lived "high definition." But sometimes we don't have the signal strength to sustain it, especially after a storm. Sometimes we need to reset—with a little self-care and compassion.

How about you? How do you reset after stormy weather in your life? When have you experienced the need for a total "unplug" to restore completely?

FEBRUARY

February 1:

Keeping Our Hearts Light

February is a tender month for me. My divorce was finalized in February. My son Matthew, who died at age fifteen, was born in February. And it's the anniversary month of my bout with transverse myelitis, that malicious inflammation of the spinal cord that paralyzed me when I was thirty-eight years old.

It's also my birthday month.

So February is a celebratory time, but it's also a time for reflection on the dreams I had, now shadowed by a reality I never could have imagined.

Yet I'm happy.

Mark Nepo's words describe best what I've discovered:

"The heart is very much like a miraculous balloon. Its lightness comes from staying full."

Isn't that so true?

Those words and the image they create in my mind—a large heart, composed of many colorful balloons—offer both a symbol and a road map. To keep my heart full, I'm intentional about cultivating new and varied interests and I work hard to strengthen and build relationships. I make sure my calendar is punctuated with time not only for doing but also for just being with people who enrich and expand my life.

My heart is full because my life is full.

When we let our capacity to love fuel our capacity to grow and flourish, I truly believe our hearts can always feel full.

How about you? Do you find your heart is lighter when it is full?

February 2:

Open to Receive

Although my mother had many strengths, using electronics was not one of them.

An aging but still useful intercom system linked Dad's downstairs study and the upstairs kitchen. It saved a lot of stair-climbing and hollering.

Sometimes Mom would call down on the intercom with a message for Dad. She'd usually end with, "I love you, Tweety." (That was their pet name for one another.)

In order to hear Dad's response, she needed to flip the switch on her intercom unit. Sometimes she'd forget to do that and then playfully ask, "Don't you love me?"

Dad had said it, but she couldn't hear it because she hadn't positioned her receiver to receive it. Sometimes he'd have to yell—through several doors and an entire floor—"I said I love you too, Tweety. Flip your switch and you'll hear me!"

In our relationships, our failure to feel and experience love can sometimes be traceable to being unreceptive. We may have forgotten, or chosen, not to flip the switch of our own hearts. Others may want to show us love, but we can't experience it because we've closed ourselves off to it.

We alone control how receptive we are to the love around us. If we flip our switch, who knows how our lives may be enriched by what we hear and experience?

How about you? Are you open to receiving love? Is your switch flipped on?

February 3:

Hard Good-Byes

My cousin Robin had flown in from South Carolina to stay with me for a few days. Although we Snapchat, Face-Time, and text regularly, we both were looking forward to an in-person visit to really catch up.

Robin's mom was my one-of-a-kind-but-everyone-needs-one Aunt Pearl. She was my mom's younger sister. Together, they were two of the strongest women I've ever known. They lost their father at a young age, spent their childhood in an orphanage, and each lost a child due to an accident.

They had both experienced so much hardship—and yet they both delighted in life, planting love and laughter wherever they went.

Robin and I played hard during her visit. We shopped, dined out, and shared more than a few family stories over coffee and a dessert or two.

We also worked hard. My home had misbehaved, allowing Mother Nature to intrude where she didn't belong. Water had found its way inside in unwanted places, resulting in damage that required a full-blown remodeling project.

"Recycle, reorganize, or pitch," was our triage mantra as my home exhaled everything from paperwork to furniture. It was exhaustingly productive—but fun!

Before I knew it, it was time for Robin to head home. It was hard to say good-bye. But the quote she sent once she arrived back home gave me an unexpected perspective, prompting both a smile and a few tears:

"How lucky I am to have something that makes saying good-bye so hard" (Winnie the Pooh).

A knot swelled in my throat as I considered that thought. Yes, I was lucky it was hard to say good-bye. Lucky and grateful for my cousin, for who she is to me and for how she shows her love for me.

Hosting our loved ones invites hard good-byes. We carve out special time for special people, creating memories that may last a lifetime. When that time ends, it can be difficult to accept.

But the truth is, the harder it is to say good-bye, the luckier we are.

How about you? Have you been lucky enough to have had to say any hard good-byes lately?

February 4:

Wired for Friendship

The more friends you have, the healthier, happier, and more mentally acute you will be, now and in your later years, I learned in a book talk given by Barbara Bradley Hagerty, former National Public Radio correspondent and author of *Life Reimagined*.

"We are wired for friends," says Hagerty. And she had the brain scans to prove it.

As a participant in University of Virginia Professor Jim Coan's "hand-holding study," Hagerty found herself in an MRI machine with one ankle strapped with shock-producing electrodes while other sensors recorded her brain's response.

Once settled inside the machine, an "O" or "X" was flashed before her eyes. She was told no shock would be delivered with the "O," but when the "X" flashed there was a one-in-five chance she'd be shocked.

Her responses were tested when she was alone, with a stranger holding her hand, and then with a good friend holding her hand.

When alone or holding a stranger's hand, the regions of the brain that process danger "lit up like a Christmas tree" when the "X" flashed. But when holding a friend's hand, her brain grew quiet.

Why?

"What we think happens," Professor Coan reported, "is having a friend with you alters the perception of that threat." In other words, our brain is telling us that even if something dangerous happens, it will be okay because we have help from a trusted source.

Studies show that those with a network of friends live longer, recover faster from serious illnesses, and even preserve their memories better than those with few or no friends. In short, friendships matter.

I experienced the value of friendship firsthand during a seventeen-day hospital stay battling sepsis. The presence of friends and family not only comforted me, it gave me strength to endure the treatments.

More importantly, their involvement gave me the confidence to challenge the medical community when they tried to discharge me too quickly. With their support, I made the case for a delay, a critical element in my complete recovery.

Bottom line? Cultivate friendships. Your health may depend on it—and your happiness certainly does.

How about you? When have you experienced of the benefit of friendship when going through a difficult time?

February 5:

Strong-Willed and Spectacular

My sister Rachel was my parents' strong-willed child, a relentless limit-tester who gave them their "parenting stripes," they joked.

She often stirred things up, from raiding my closet to speaking her mind at the darndest times. Unbridled by fear or consequences, she regularly challenged our parents. Yet, this defiant and confident behavior served her well as she grew up and we plowed through adversity together.

I never saw it clearly until well into adulthood, when my life was turned upside down from an injury I'd sustained while transferring from my wheelchair. The scrape was small, but initially went unnoticed because of my paralysis. It became a wound. Once discovered, specialized treatments and nursing care seemed to be working—until I reinjured it and one wound became two.

And then, eighty-nine days after sustaining the initial scrap, I had two open wounds that just wouldn't heal.

Five hundred miles away, Rachel had listened calmly to each update for the first seventy-five days. But when she learned of the second wound, her tone changed.

"I'm coming up, Sissy," she said simply.

I protested, but she was insistent.

Confidently defiant.

For seven days, she waited on me, serving me breakfast, lunch, and dinner. She made sure I was in bed twenty-three hours a day relieving the pressure on the wound—a key element in healing, we were told.

She talked to the nurses, questioned the doctors, googled, texted, and emailed on my behalf. But mostly she sat on my bedroom couch and kept me company while I healed.

Three days after she left, both wounds had closed!

Limit-testing strong-willed kids can be a parental challenge. It's comforting to know they can turn into spectacular adults. I am grateful that Rachel's confident defiance matured into steadfast and spectacular caring.

And I'm guessing she's not the only child whose persistent limit-testing has revealed, and perhaps even built, positive grown-up character traits that can last a lifetime.

How about you? Have you ever looked at a "spectacular" adult and wondered what they were like to parent?

February 6:

The Hard Work of Remembering

The conversation had been light during my birthday dinner, with mutual updates on work, family, and friends. Then my son's fiancée (now wife) took a sip of water, cleared her throat, and delivered a question I'd never been asked before:

"What words of wisdom can you share about what you learned from the past year?"

"Words of wisdom?" I stammered back.

Meredith's soft blue eyes were earnest, wide with interest. I glanced at my son Peter and shook my head, smiling back at both of them.

"That's a great question, Mer," I began, buying more time to consider my answer. "Well, I know I've learned a lot in the last twelve months, that's for sure. But have I become any wiser?" I muttered the last sentence more to myself than to my dinner mates.

As my mind ticked through the months and experiences, I thought of the research I'd done on our ability to remember (and forget), especially when we cross through doorways. Now I was perched on the edge of another type of threshold: my birthday.

What was worth remembering?

As I considered the year's peaks and valleys, the lesson became clear. With the support of friends and family and a long enough healthy stretch with my body, it was okay for me to strive beyond what I thought I could do.

I never imagined that my publicly speaking about my book, something I'd initially feared and resisted, could loosen the limitations that paralysis had imposed on my life and connect me in a meaningful way to so many.

The wisdom?

Perhaps I should consider my perceived limitations as written "in pencil" and fair game for changing.

Although managing expectations is a delicate balance—what's challenging can easily become overwhelming—that year, all the effort was worth it.

And worth remembering.

How about you? Think about your last twelve months. What lessons are worth the hard work of remembering? What wisdom have you gained?

February 7:

Staying Charged

⌒

While my power wheelchair was being repaired, I had to rely on my back-up one, a ten-year-old battered beauty with a broken chassis that made me lean sideways.

Although it was safe to use, the ol' gal's battery couldn't hold a charge for long.

The trip from my bedroom to the back door to let the dog out used 22 percent of the battery. From the back door to the kitchen for a cup of coffee took another 20 percent. Even the short jaunt from the kitchen to my sunroom for my morning reading time cost me 18 percent. I didn't dare attempt taking the dog for a walk down the driveway. So no getting the newspaper at dawn. No getting the mail at noon.

When the battery indicator entered the red zone, I had to go back to my bedside wheelchair charger, plug in, and wait until I had enough charge to venture out again.

After a while, I began to chuckle at my new lifestyle. Before I chose to do *anything*, I had to assess the task.

Was the effort worth the energy expenditure?

I began to wonder—what if we had our own energy indicators, an instrument that could tell us exactly how much energy a task took and notified us when we were depleted? Would we make different choices? Look at life differently?

Mom used to say that we only have twenty-four buckets of energy a day, and we should choose carefully how we use each one. She weighed activities based not only on the time commitment but also on the energy required to participate.

How wise she was!

We budget our money. We budget our time. Maybe we should also budget our energy. We might be happier and more robust if we did!

How about you? How do you assess and manage your energy requirements?

February 8:

Recovering Nicely

She remembered my birthday. And she wasn't even one of my girlfriends. Marie was my mom's girlfriend, and she continued to send me birthday cards for over twenty years after my mother's death.

Each birthday card included a handwritten note. One year she updated me with a short timeline on some major events on her life:

- **October 2012:** Blacked out and fell, fracturing pelvis. Nice recovery after being hospitalized and therapy.
- **December 2013:** Began living alone after [husband] Raymond's death.
- **December 2014:** Fell and broke femur. Spent January and February in nursing home. Lots of therapy.
- **March 2015:** Back home. Another nice recovery and living alone. Began driving again, short trips around town and to church.

Yes, she *fractured her pelvis* and *broke her femur* and then spent *two months* in a nursing home before coming back to her home to *live alone*.

Amazing.

Even more amazing were her comments. Most of us say that we survive our challenges. We get through our difficulties. We may grin and bear it, slog through, or get it over with. But do we ever take the time to say that we recover—*nicely*?

I marvel at Marie's grit. Her acceptance of the highs and lows of life. Her positive attitude. She made me smile from deep within.

I want to be more like Marie.

So often we go through life's challenges and fail to give ourselves credit for the times we've moved with grace through those hardships. Marie taught me that it can be energizing to pause, reflect, and acknowledge each achievement.

In fact, I think it can be a powerful ingredient in living resiliently.

When we choose to declare that we have recovered nicely, we put a bow on that "gift" of experience—and that can make us feel more confident that whatever comes next, we can handle that too.

How about you? When have you experienced a "nice recovery" from a challenge?

February 9:

What Doesn't Change

Six-year-old Ashley gently placed her latest stuffed animal, a jet-black Labrador puppy, into her girlfriend's arms. "His name is Sharpie," she told her friend. "I named it after my cousin's mom's ex-boyfriend's dog." She smiled brightly, proud of the pup's heritage.

"It's ex-husband, Ashley," her mom corrected. "Aunt Becky's ex-husband."

"Oh yeah, ex-husband," Ashley repeated. Then, after a minute, she asked, "Mom, does that make Brittany my ex-cousin? Is Aunt Becky her ex-mom?"

Ashley's mom sat down and carefully explained to her daughter that you can never be an ex-mom. "Once you are a mom, you are always a mom," she said tenderly to her youngest child. "Divorce may change a lot of things, but it doesn't change that."

Honestly and innocently, my niece Ashley was looking for definitions in the haze of divorce and the resulting blurred relationships.

Divorce confuses kids—and, sometimes, adults. Often, we are so busy letting go, ending and finalizing, and getting ready for life-after-divorce that we forget that the relationships created before the divorce continue to exist. We may not have ex-moms and ex-dads, but we may very well have ex-uncles and ex-aunts—if we choose to relabel those relationships in that way.

But kids are the center of their own universe. They want to know how things relate to them—*Who are they to me?* The experts tell us that children need clarity and consistency. There is life after divorce, but there was life before divorce, too, especially when children are involved.

At one point in time, there was love in a divorced relationship. Enough love to create a home; enough love to merge two worlds for a common future; enough love to birth a child.

And if that child is lucky, maybe there is still enough love, if only for the child, for us divorced adults to be mindful of their view of the world and our role in it when life-after-divorce begins to redefine their reality.

After all, there are no ex-moms or ex-dads. Parenting, mindful or not, continues.

⤙⧓⤚

How about you? What experiences have you had in clarifying relationships affected by divorce?

February 10:

Everything in Its Own Time

During my childhood years, a good friend would send our family an amaryllis every November. The bulb arrived in the mail, packaged with instructions as to how it should be treated. We removed the foam pad from its top, placed the pre-planted pot on a saucer, and watered daily, just as instructed.

There wasn't much to see in the beginning—just a blade tip peering through dirt in a pot. It hosted no beauty and not much promise of the season's celebration. Yet it always grew and bloomed just in time for Christmas, mirroring the crescendo of excitement that season brings.

One December, however, our amaryllis didn't bloom by Christmas. We held out hope, but by February she still had not bloomed. While we waited, she became a fixture of stymied growth on our breakfast room table. We called her Miss Amaryllis and hypothesized her issues—too much water, not enough sun, or maybe she'd been damaged.

Finally, mid-February, Miss Amaryllis bloomed, sporting the richest, reddest blossoms the likes of which we'd never seen on any of her forbears in the previous ten years. She refreshed the meaning of the term "late bloomer" for our family, brilliantly illustrating both nature's wonder and steadfast persistence.

Sometimes our schedules are not our own, we learned.

Like Miss Amaryllis, perhaps we sometimes need a little sustenance and patience in a nurturing environment before our beauty can mature.

Thank you, Miss Amaryllis, for your magnificent witness to a new grasp of an old truth: all creatures and creations are different and will, with the right care, blossom and bloom in their own time.

How about you? What pre-planted treasures are you harboring inside that could bloom this year? How would your package instructions read?

February 11:

Age-Defying Philosophy

Mr. Joe was eighty. Both feet turned in until his toes met. He walked with two canes but could outwalk most teenagers. He loved life and everybody. And everybody loved him.

One day he banged on my father's church office door.

"Have you got a typing book I could borrow, Pastor?" he asked in an urgent tone.

Dad squinted at him. "A what?"

"You know, a book you learn how to type from."

"No," Dad said. "But you can probably get one over at the high school."

Mr. Joe shuffled closer. "Would you call over there for me and ask?"

"Yes," Dad promised, "but may I ask what you want with a typing book?"

"I want to learn how to type."

My father sat amazed. Mr. Joe had fingers that reflected all eighty years of life lived, knobby and arthritic; it would be hard for him to learn a skill like typing. But Dad called anyway.

Yes, they would loan Mr. Joe a book.

"So, tell me, Mr. Joe, why do you want to learn to type?" Dad asked, placing the phone back in its cradle.

"You just never know when you'll need it," Mr. Joe quipped—and with that, he breezed out the door toward the high school.

Six months later, a small pulpwood company opened an office in town. They needed someone to answer the phone and do some typing.

Mr. Joe got the job.

At eighty.

I'm amazed how "young" some "old" people are.

I love the golf stories about those who can shoot their age and do so three times a week. I smile at the holiday memory of my Rock Band video-gaming, guitar-playing, seventy-two-year-old aunt, and the memory of my mother's dear friend "Uncle Charlie," who'd remind her every Sunday morning at church that although he was ninety-something, "I still have all my own teeth!"

We all love those stories of folks who have grabbed life, pushed back at Mother Nature, and engaged Father Time—probably because we hope to be them one day. Perhaps aging takes its toll on people in direct proportion to how well they have prepared themselves to keep growing and learning and living.

How about you? What are you doing to keep growing as you age and change?

February 12:

Unchosen Paths

On February 12, 1997, nine days after my divorce became final, I awakened in the early-morning hours with a dull ache in my lower back. Strange shooting sensations ripped through my legs, firing like electrical currents. Within six hours, the jagged bolts of pain had twisted their way up to my waist, permanently relaxing every muscle along the way.

In the intensive care unit, as I fought the pain with a morphine drip, I said to my father, "It's going to be okay, Dad. I just know it's going to be okay. I've been in the wilderness before. Fact is, I've been here so many times I have paths down here!" I managed to smile as the drugs lifted hope above the haze of the grim reality.

Paths in the wilderness—I've learned to seek them out as I have dealt with the difficulties that have come my way. I sought them in my twenties, when my seventeen-year-old brother died in a water-skiing accident. I sought them in my thirties, when I became mother of four children, two of whom had special needs—cerebral palsy, epilepsy, and autism. And now that divorce and paralysis had been added to the picture, it was time to seek them again.

Unwillingly, I'd become a veteran of "unchosen paths."

Unchosen or not, we all have paths in our wildernesses created by our patterns of coping. Once we figure out what those patterns are, it's easier to be patient with ourselves as we move through our next steps.

For me, I know I'm a process thinker—I need a lot of time to make decisions, often see too many possibilities, and have a hard time accepting "good enough." I also know I am a fighter, don't like to lose, and take a long time to give up unrealistic hope. To stay strong, I need to feel connected, supported, and find a way to speak my mind when life hurts.

Although paralysis has taken so much from me, each year on this day I remember the horror of the paralysis onset, how the ripples of its wake changed my life and those of others who care about me. Then I ask myself:

What can't it take from me?

It can't take my ability to love, my capacity to grow, my willingness to learn and problem-solve. It may limit me, but it can't limit my ability to manage, to focus, to accept what I can't change and get on with rethinking what *is* possible, despite paralysis.

Strengthened by what I still have and can still do, I keep moving on this unchosen path.

❧

How about you? What are your patterns of coping on unchosen paths?

February 13:

Wordless Comfort

When we honestly ask ourselves which people in our lives mean the most to us, we often find that it is those who, instead of giving advice, solutions, or cures, have chosen rather to share our pain and touch our wounds with a warm and tender hand.
—Henri Nouwen.

When we experience loss, we gain two unwanted companions—grief over what we've lost and also the continued presence of the absence of our loved one.

Sometimes the best comfort is feeling the nearness of others who have come alongside us in small but sustained ways. When we feel supported and loved, we're strengthened to keep moving and coping.

❧

How about you? What wordless comfort have you experienced or given during times of loss?

February 14:

The Shape of Love

Valentine's Day is a rather skimpy holiday for me. I'm divorced and have no love interest at the moment. My kids are grown and have their own lives and loves.

Don't get me wrong: I have people who love me. It's just that I'm no one's number one.

Skimpy or not, Valentine's Day is the holiday that honors the most powerful force we possess—the ability to love. It's the perfect day to reflect on all the love we have experienced, both as givers and receivers. The way we love and have been loved shapes the tone and texture of our lives, I've learned. Or, as Goethe says so beautifully:

"We are shaped and fashioned by what we love."

Love not only affects the substance of our lives, it also fuels and refines us. Each relationship laced with love prompts growth while also distilling down what's important, even vital, in future yet-to-be-developed relationships.

How about you? How has love shaped who you are and what you look for in relationships?

February 15:

Big Toe Moments

The ambulance's arrival had interrupted our conversation. Pat, my children's longtime caregiver, peered out my bedroom window.

"They're here," she said simply.

We'd waited to call 911 until the children had left for school. I thought I was having a kidney stone attack, but then the numbness began.

I couldn't move my legs.

Two paramedics ran up the steps, lifted me out of bed onto a folding stretcher, and carried me back down. The lights and sirens started, but I focused only on my big toe—my left big toe, freshly manicured with a sparkly snowflake. It was the only part of my lower body that I could still move.

"That's good, right?" I said to the paramedics, as they watched me wiggle the glittery toe.

"Very good," they said.

Then I could no longer move it. And the excruciating pain began.

Three days later, the pain stopped. I'd lost vision in one eye and was paralyzed from the waist down.

One third of those affected by transverse myelitis recovered fully within a year, I was told. Although my vision was restored within days, as the weeks went by I remained unable to wiggle my left toe, my daily test for recovery.

It was an odd sensation, trying to mentally will a body part to work. I would think the thought—*Move, toe, move!*—and shut my eyes hard and imagine my toe going up and down. Sometimes I thought I felt an impulse going down through my thigh, knee, shin, and foot, and then out through my toe, and I'd be sure I'd done it.

Then I'd open my eyes and find I was wrong. Again. Everything below my belly button just lay there, stupid and disobedient.

For nineteen months I tried and failed, chasing down all known options for recovery. I did not want to live my life from a wheelchair.

But eventually, life moved on. My children were growing. I needed to let go of the burden to somehow return things "to normal." I needed to accept my life as it was so I could embrace fully the life I could still have.

So I did. With great intention and a surprising sense of relief, I stopped trying to wiggle my left big toe.

How about you? Do you need to embrace any "big toe" moments that would allow you to live more fully in the life you have?

February 16:

Periods vs. Commas

It's an old story my father loved to tell. A man lived by the side of the road and sold hot dogs. He didn't hear well, so he had no radio. He didn't see well, so he read no newspapers.

But he sold hot dogs.

He put signs on the highway advertising how good they were. He stood roadside and cried, "Buy a hot dog, mister!"

People bought.

He increased his meat and roll orders. Bought a bigger stove. Business boomed and his son came home from college to help.

"Father, haven't you been listening to the radio?" the son asked. "There's a depression coming. The European situation is terrible. The domestic situation is worse."

That made the father think, *Well, my son's been to college. He reads the papers and listens to the radio. He ought to know.*

So, he reduced his meat and roll orders, took down his signs, and no longer stood by the highway to sell his good hot dogs.

Sales fell fast, almost overnight.

"You're right, son," he said. "We certainly are in a great depression. There just isn't any business to speak of."

"Positive thinking cannot hold back a depression—but negative thinking can produce one," my father concluded each time he told this classic tale.

In trying times, we are measured not by what the circumstances are but by how we react to them. A negative mindset faces reality and puts a period. A positive mindset faces the same reality and puts a comma on it, a purposeful pause to indicate there's more thinking (and perhaps problem-solving) to do—and then looks ahead toward what's to come.

How about you? When have you seen the benefit of a comma mindset?

February 17:

Can I Get Back to You?

I'd asked my visiting fourteen-year-old nephew if he'd like to have lunch before his golf game. I wanted to allow enough time for meal preparation.

He paused, then said, "Aunt Becky, can I get back to you on that?"

I slowly turned around to look at him. He was sitting behind me in the van, as we'd just pulled into the driveway after running errands. I had to see his face. Surely, he was laughing.

But he wasn't. Those penetrating blue eyes peeking from underneath his signature bangs met my curious look with a disarming sincerity.

"Sure, Adam," I replied, turning back around while trying to absorb his meaning. As I wheeled out of the van, I realized I still didn't know how to plan for lunch. Plus, I'd given him permission to delay his decision.

Had I just been managed?

With that simple reply, my momentum had been put on hold. I was no longer in charge. Instead, I was puzzled. What did Adam need to consider before answering? He was staying in my home with no other friends or family nearby. He couldn't drive.

Nevertheless, he wasn't ready to answer.

I soon discovered that this was my sister's fault.

Rachel had long ago instituted "Can I get back to you?" replies to address her children's requests for instant answers when she wasn't ready to say yes or no. The latter word maybe only invited more pleading. So she'd learned ask for time to get back to them.

With this response, urgency evaporated. It also put her clearly back in charge, a role hard to sustain during those demanding teenage years.

But now Adam had adopted her technique and used it on me.

Maybe that's not a bad thing. Sometimes we need permission to stop and think. In fact, "getting back to you" may be a great tool for teenagers to know, especially when those impulsive stages emerge. It's often best for kids to pause before acting, and "getting back to you" may buy them time to make a wise choice.

Adam and I did have lunch that day. But he didn't get back to me in time for any special preparation, so we shared a simple sandwich.

❧

How about you? How do you manage requests for instant answers or deal with the delay of answers from others? Are there times you need to pause before answering, just so you know how you really feel?

February 18:

Unexpected Promise

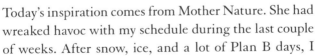

Today's inspiration comes from Mother Nature. She had wreaked havoc with my schedule during the last couple of weeks. After snow, ice, and a lot of Plan B days, I found myself with extra time to look out on my deck and consider her handiwork.

The words of the ancient Greek philosopher Heraclitus, considered by some to be the world's first creativity teacher, came to mind:

"The sun is new each day."

I must say, I'd missed that member of Mother Nature's family and was grateful for her return, along with the "newness" she offered.

With her shadows, she can cut fresh patterns into the ruts of our thinking.

With her intensity, she can turn black ice into a mirror of beauty.

Even frozen crystals, once the glaze of overhead trees, can now sparkle with life when her brilliance stretches to touch them.

Her unexpected promise to transform and bring a fresh look to the ordinary inspires me.

How about you? How does the sun affect your mood?

February 19:

How Many Bites?

My father watched the young man gather his tools after installing carpet in our home.

"You've done a good job," Dad said.

"Thank you, sir."

"Bet you've laid a lot of carpet."

"Yes, sir, I have."

"So, how long does a piece of carpet like this last?" Dad asked, more for conversation than information.

"Well, sir," the fellow said, smiling, "I don't mean to sound sassy, but let me put it this way: How many bites are in a sandwich?"

Dad laughed. "Enough said. I get your point."

Life is full of unanswerable questions. Some of them, like how many bites there are in a sandwich, don't matter that much.

Other unanswerable questions are more difficult.

How long does it take to get through the grief of a death or a divorce or the loss of a job?

How long does one keep trying to make a troubled marriage work?

How long do we push our children when we see them stuck in the shadow of their potential?

How long does it take to get through empty-nest syndrome and reinvent our reconfigured lives?

How long do we keep forgiving family members or friends before we become worn out or too callused to love?

It's different for different people.

Some losses are acute, with quick endings and formal farewells. Others are more chronic, requiring small yet painful daily adjustments that continually remind us of what could have been.

The answers to hard questions are often negotiable. Although our pain may be unavoidable, we can choose how long we tolerate, suffer, or delay moving through a difficult situation.

It's our choice when we give up, when we press on, when we accept, and even when we heal, I've learned. Our pace and our mindset are choices we can make.

We get to decide how many "bites" it will take.

How about you? Have you questioned how long a loss will linger? Have you found relief or strength in considering it a choice?

February 20:

The Company We Keep

It's the kind of statement that I like, one that makes me stop, think, and take a quick snapshot of my life:

> "You're the average of the five people you spend the most time with" (Jim Rohn).

Yep, that's a showstopper.

Who *do* I spend the most time with? More importantly, does my dog count?

Seriously, as I considered who those five people are for me, I thought about our interactions. What parts of their personalities and approaches to life had influenced me? Had their strengths become mine?

Then I wondered: Was physical presence required for an individual to qualify for one's top five? What about long-distance relationships? Or people we don't know personally but whose work we study? Or even the storied memories of those we've loved and lost?

I'm sure if I researched it a bit more I would find that Mr. Rohn has his own criteria. But I've found that simply stopping to consider the idea of a "top five" has tremendous merit.

Sometimes it's enlightening to stop the routines, step back, and take a moment to observe:

- Where do we spend our time?
- Who is with us, physically and otherwise?
- How does that influence who we are?

As I searched my inventory of recent interactions, I remembered that one of my top five showed me how to be patient and loving during another's struggle with the complications of aging and memory loss. Another showed me how to be generous by not responding to sharp criticism. And another demonstrated an extraordinary sensitivity to an awkward situation, choosing to handle it with grace and a smile.

Patient, loving, generous, sensitive, graceful, smiling —I hope those attributes were instilled in me.

Indeed, our relationship orbits become our influencer orbits. What a great reminder to be thoughtful about the company we keep.

How about you? Consider your top five at this moment. How have they influenced you?

February 21:

Lessons in Kindness

My daughter had two fender-benders within weeks of getting her driver's license. One of her girlfriends was with her in both accidents. After the second accident, my phone rang, lighting up with that friend's mother's phone number.

I braced myself for a tirade.

"Becky," she began, "I just wanted to let you know how thankful I am that Brittany is such a good driver. Those accidents could have been far worse. I am glad my daughter was with such a good driver."

Stunned, I babbled back my gratitude and apologies.

She insisted I had nothing to apologize about. Instead of being critical or judgmental, this fellow parent was generous with her approach to the incidents and to me.

As I hung up the phone, I wondered: If the situations were reversed, would I have been that understanding, that gentle, or that kind?

Parents aren't just adults with children, I realized. We are mentors, coaches, and colleagues with one another too. Our responses are more than adult reactions. They are lessons we give each other that can help us grow alongside our kids.

What we say and what we do matters to children— and to fellow adults too.

How about you? Have you been surprised by the unexpected kindness of a fellow parent or colleague?

February 22:

The Stress We Need

In her lecture on stress, resilience, and spirituality, Dr. Patricia Fosarelli offered a description of stress that confounded me. She said there were two ways to experience it: as dis-stress or as eu-stress.

Dis-stress implies all the negative qualities that we typically associate with stress: anxiety, worry, pain.

The term "eu-stress" was new to me. The prefix "eu," meaning good (as in euphoric), introduces the concept of "good stress."

I've got to admit, I scratched my head on that one. What could possibly be good about stress?

As I listened to Dr. Fosarelli (and then as I subsequently researched more on my own), I realized that these terms are less about defining stress and more about how we handle stress. We can become dis-stressed or eu-stressed about the same event.

The difference is in how we perceive the situation.

In dis-stress, we interpret the stressor as "bad," a negative threat, and out of our control. We approach it with our instinctive "reptilian brain" function, where our fight or flight response resides.

With eu-stress, we respond with higher brain functioning and see the stressor as a challenge. We feel we will be able to rise to the occasion and manage it.

So how do we move from dis-stress to eu-stress? There's no easy answer, but Dr. Fosarelli suggests considering the situation from a few different angles:

Physical—Are we caring for our bodies, getting appropriate rest, nutrition, and exercise?

Emotional—Do we have someone to confide in? Do we know what music or activities comfort us?

Cognitive—Can we reframe the stressor by its relative importance or as an opportunity to learn?

Spiritual—Can we recite a meditation or prayer? Can we name something that gives us meaning, joy, or sustaining hope?

If we are strong in these areas, then perhaps we will be more likely to view life's inevitable bumps as welcome challenges—opportunities to learn.

How about you? What could help you move from dis-stress to eu-stress?

February 23:

The Roundness of the World

In the early stages of the COVID-19 pandemic, hand washing, social distancing, and the "don't touch your face" mantra were the only defenses we had against a treacherous virus that indiscriminately left death in its wake.

In the midst of all the bleak news, Blakely Faye, my four-year-old granddaughter, asked a question that sent me pondering: "Why can't I feel the roundness of the Earth?"

What? (So glad she asked her father and not me!)

As I let the depth of that question settle in, I began to marvel at her profound curiosity, her attempt to understand things beyond herself, and her effort to personalize an abstract concept to her own experience.

Her simple question ushered in a new perspective for me. Maybe we were starting to feel the "roundness" of the world as the pandemic connected us in ways we never imagined. We were together in our isolation, united in our efforts to survive, and equally astounded by the virus's guile and lethal agility.

Yet fear, anxiety, and unanswered questions permeated our daily lives.

But maybe, dear Blakely Faye, if the roundness of the world were felt more, we would fear less and rest in the assurance that only our connectedness can provide: we are not alone.

How about you? Did you long for the feeling of con-nectedness during the pandemic or have you in other hard times?

February 24:

Beauty in the Pause

He wasn't very big—maybe three inches long, tops. But he was stubborn. This steadfast icicle had been hanging on the door of my son's Jeep for weeks, so long that I gave him a name: Sam.

Tucked in the shade of my driveway, Sam didn't have access to the sun that would have freed him or the driving trip that would have made him melt. My son was in college, 3,000 miles away. So Sam hung there—lonely, isolated. Even in his seclusion, however, he sparkled among the last remnants of snow, brightening the mud that slid under his pristine point.

I wondered about his fate just before we received the latest blast of snow/sleet/ice "wintry mix." I don't like that term, "wintry mix." It means unknown, fickle weather. Thanks to wintry mix, I've been forced to reschedule more than I've scheduled, and that's tough for a gal who believes that not much is possible without a plan.

Sam is the perfect example of a thwarted plan. I'm sure his intention was to melt with the rest of the snow and ease his way down my driveway into the mulch bed that hosts my spring bulbs. But there he was, frozen in time.

Sam was more than just frozen water, though.

"An icicle," my father once wrote, "is working water stymied in its pursuit by a hostile environment."

Now that's a dramatic definition! But it makes sense if we consider Sam's journey. As he moved through his life cycle, he worked through all sorts of obstacles—thick rocks, hard ground, trees with strong roots—before finally arriving at man's creation. Then something bigger grabbed him, slowed him, and finally stopped him by making him solid.

The "something bigger" was his environment—freezing temperatures. Something he had absolutely no control over. Something he couldn't defeat, but merely react to.

Perhaps Sam is a frozen reminder that there are some things in life over which we have absolutely no control. We may work our way through all sorts of obstacles with some degree of accomplishment. But then some unruly "wintry mix" stops our pursuit and freezes us.

Plans change in an instant. All we can do is react the best we know how.

Then we can remember Sam. Even though the pursuit of his purpose had been halted, he gave beauty. Eventually, he would be freed from nature's hold. Meanwhile, he coped with his hostile environment, inspiring patience and wonder in those lucky enough to see him.

How about you? Is a wintry mix in life thwarting your plans? Can you still find beauty in the pause or patience as you wait?

February 25:

Keeping Ink Pens Full

The children gathered around the pastor as he arranged the props for his story: paper, a ruler, and an ink pen.

"If I need these items to take a test, how will I do if the ink pen has no ink?" he asked the group.

"Terrible! Awful! You're going to fail!" they responded.

He nodded sagely. "You're right. With an empty ink pen, my efforts are wasted. The pen can't mark the paper."

Then he shifted the youngsters' attention to their church setting. "So, I'd like you to imagine this pen as the church. Then think of the ink as love." He reminded both child and parishioner that without love, the church's best intentions, programs, and plans would fall short of the greater goals.

How true it is with parenting too. Without love, our best intentions, plans, and programming for our children are bound to fail.

When our children are young, we have far more control of the design of their lives. We can choose their schools and sports; we can heavily shape the selection of their friends and free-time activities. For a brief time, our ink pens have final editing privileges.

Then the teenage years hit, and we find our ink pens drawing new designs: boundaries. This boundary-making adventure becomes more complex as our control of their lives slips away. We must creatively manufacture rules that protect yet allow room for learning and growth.

During this awkward time of emerging independence, our ink reserves can become depleted. It's easy for good night kisses to disappear, while good morning hugs are reduced to hand waves as they bolt out the door. Dinner time can become a round of musical chairs where the music stops to eject our beloveds to school, athletics, and social activities.

And love can leave in little ways.

Yet love can be restored in little ways too.

We can enter their world and send a text or even just an emoji that lets them know we care. We can help them stay in our world by inviting a pre-departure hug or kiss.

And, of course, we can emphasize the words that span all worlds, replenishing inkwells no matter what the age or stage: "I love you."

How about you? How do you keep your ink pen "full" for the important relationships in your life?

February 26:

Loving Beyond Boundaries

I was so surprised I think I damaged brain cells.

I'd wondered why my girlfriends were being so evasive about celebrating my milestone birthday. But an eightieth birthday celebration trumped my fiftieth, sports schedules outranked mine, and my well-meaning but slightly disorganized sister would not make airline reservations confirming her promised birthday visit.

No one would commit to plans for my special birthday. So, I made my own.

I scheduled time with my son to bake my own birthday cake—my favorite, red velvet. And I gladly said yes when my ex-husband and his wife invited me out for a birthday dinner. I'd asked my daughter to fly home from college to join us, but she had plans to visit her boyfriend.

So I focused on what I had, instead of what I was missing, and prepared for a good evening. I'd worked hard over the last ten years to create a good rapport with my ex-husband and his wife and was proud of the relationships we maintained. *I do enjoy spending time with them*, I thought as I waited for them to pick me up. I was looking forward to a quiet evening of fine dining and good conversation.

But there was nothing quiet about this birthday celebration. When we arrived at the restaurant, forty-seven voices yelled, "Surprise!"

I nearly fell out of my wheelchair.

My sister greeted me first, then my daughter and her boyfriend. My North Carolina college buddies had driven in; one had even flown in from London. Fabulous hors d'oeuvres, a five-course sit-down dinner, and a DJ spinning '70s music awaited. The grand finale? One huge red velvet cake!

What a night to remember—given to me by my ex-husband and his amazing wife. It was a powerful gift of love and its creative expression—one that reached far beyond the boundaries of divorce.

How about you? Have you experienced or witnessed love beyond divorce's boundaries?

February 27:

Life After Loss

After our mother's death, my sister and I sold the family home in West Virginia. In three short years, we'd lost both parents, propelling us into the deep waters of grief and the complex legal world of life after the loss of parents.

Tears and paperwork consumed our days. At its best, the paperwork forced us to push back the tears to focus on the business matters of the day. Bills needed to be paid, insurance statements checked, and papers filed.

Attorneys explained and re-explained estate matters. Grief numbed my mind—or at least coated it with a layer of haze. Email became my new friend to document the recurring questions and repeated answers.

We leaned on professionals. An appraiser helped us decide what to keep. A family friend became our real estate agent. Another friend connected us to a trusted mover.

Our parents created many memories and kept compelling evidence of most of them. Tom and his moving crew unloaded three thousand pounds' worth of those memories to my home. When my spreadsheet calculations of space were off, they quickly offered suggestions and repositioned several pieces.

"We don't move furniture," Tom told me when I thanked him for his efforts. "We move families."

Grief welled up again at his words. I was witnessing the descent of my past into my present. My parents' furniture now graced my dining room and completed my den. And its presence signaled the end of one era and the beginning of another—an uncomfortable transition.

"In three words, I can sum up everything I've learned about life: It goes on," Robert Frost says succinctly, almost passively.

Although Frost is accurate, life in transition—whether after death, divorce, job loss, or any significant, life-changing event—seethes with struggle. It's where we sort out what we keep and what we let go. What we cherish and what we forget. What we honor and what we lay to rest.

Transition is the time we redefine who we are by what we choose to do with what we have experienced.

Life indeed may "go on," but we actively choose what we take with us. We decide what has value and what moves both with us—and in us.

How about you? In times after significant loss, what has helped you keep moving as you decide what to keep and what to let go?

February 28:

Parallel Paths

❧

"It hurts to hope," I told Trish before I even sat down in her office. I couldn't stop the tears. As the hospital's psychologist, Trish supported families dealing with chronically ill children. My eighteen-month-old son Matthew was struggling with seizures, and I was a wreck.

She offered me a tissue and urged me to continue.

"I get so many mixed signals about Matthew's future," I explained. "First the seizures are nonstop and no one can make them go away and he is unresponsive to me. Then the seizures stop for no apparent reason and he starts to smile."

Since he was three months old, seizures had plagued Matthew, resulting in multiple hospital stays. His fluctuating progress had begun to overwhelm me, blurring my focus—the very thing I could usually count on to keep me stable and moving forward. I couldn't see the future or the path to it. I was drowning in uncertainty.

Trish listened to my account of each extreme and my attempts to address them and took a few notes. When I took a breath, she said simply, "It may help you to pursue parallel paths."

"What?" A different part of my mind latched on to those odd words. "Parallel paths?"

"Yes," she said. "Think of the future with the possibility of two paths. One path preserves the hope that Matthew will outgrow these medical complexities; the other incorporates the reality that he may not."

The strange notion settled like a calming spa mist in the room. I dried my eyes and inhaled it. "Pursue parallel paths," I wrote down.

Hope is a tricky emotion, I learned. It can be wonderfully sustaining or equally exhausting. Trish's parallel-paths concept gave me permission to hope *and* acknowledge reality by pursuing two outcomes at once.

This paradigm continues to help me navigate through uncertainty, especially when I have very little control over either outcome.

How about you? Could the parallel-path concept help you in holding on to hope when facing uncertainty?

February 29:

When Ignorance Helps

One of the best and fastest ways of acquiring knowledge is to insist on remaining ignorant about things that aren't worth knowing.
—Sydney Harris

From time to time, I've found the above thought helpful, especially when I'm trying to focus on a task that requires me to learn something new or difficult. Or when I'm on a tight deadline.

Stay focused, I tell myself. *Minimize distractions*.

Every interest doesn't have to be pursued. Every question doesn't have to be answered, at least right that minute.

Why is Pluto no longer considered a planet? How does Bitcoin investing work? Do black holes exist or not?

Nope—I don't have a pressing need to know the answers to any of these questions.

At least for now, I'll choose to be ignorant. I'm on a deadline and need to reserve my brain capacity and curiosity for what's most important.

How about you? What techniques help you avoid distractions when you need to acquire knowledge quickly or meet a deadline?

MARCH

March 1:

Spacious Living

I made it through February, a month that's filled with tender matters of the heart for me.

What helped?

Author Wayne Muller's thought captures it best:

"The more spacious and larger our fundamental nature, the more bearable the pains in living."

It's not easy keeping our fundamental natures "large and spacious," as Muller suggests. Sometimes we are limited by the demands of home and work responsibilities or fluctuating health concerns. Circumstances beyond our control confine us, and we don't get to live our life on our own terms.

Life feels small and limited—and when that happens, pain is amplified.

Yet living a "large and spacious life" requires intentional effort. Time with family and friends brings the warmth of companionship, reminding us that we are not alone while giving us the evidence that others care. More importantly, though, time with others gives us an opportunity to enlarge our life view in two specific ways: by being interested and interesting.

When we are *interested* in others and listen closely to what's important to them, we broaden our frame of reference. In fact, what keeps our friends' hearts full may buoy our own.

And when we share with them our stories, we have the chance to be *interesting*, even surprisingly creative.

Have you ever noticed that you tell the same story in different ways to different people? It may depend on the person or the circumstance, but when we change up our stories, we expand our thinking about the same event. We can think more widely, or deeply. Maybe even swap the play-by-play for the highlight reel.

All expansive pursuits can elevate us to a larger perspective—and perspective is the great minimizer of pain.

How about you? How do you keep your life spacious and large? What's easier: being interested or being interesting?

March 2:

Half a Stick

My mother loved chewing gum but would always tear it into two pieces, only chewing half of a stick at a time.

Oddly, chewing gum had a prominent place in our otherwise traditionally appointed homes. As a pastor's wife, Mom strived for a welcoming foyer. She cherished a special washstand Dad discovered at a flea market that he'd had refinished when we resided in one of his North Carolina pastorates. It became a fixture in our foyers, hosting Mom's sticks of gum in a silver-plated bowl perched beside a leather-bound guest book.

I never understood—and, amazingly, never asked her while she was still alive—why she tore each piece in half.

Thankfully, Aunt Pearl came to the rescue.

Aunt Pearl. Everyone should have one.

She is just as you might imagine: A refined woman of the South. Big hair, big eyes, big personality—and an even bigger heart. They called her "Miss Hollywood" in her assisted-living home, and the name was fitting; she practically invented statement necklaces. And bracelets. And rings.

The day after a family wedding, I parked my wheelchair beside her and we chatted in the hotel lobby. Then Aunt Pearl decided to powder her nose.

Her bejeweled fingers opened her shimmering gold purse to pull out her compact and lipstick—"Orange Flip" by Revlon, her favorite, she said. She dabbed and blotted, then tucked both back in their respective pouches. She paused and then dug in once more, searching for something at the bottom of the tiny purse. She pulled out her hand and opened it.

And there it was: a half-stick of gum.

"So Aunt Pearl," I said, watching her manicured fingers peel the small wrapping off the gum, "why do you tear your gum in half? Mom did the exact same thing."

I'd often wondered if the habit was a result of their upbringing, the time they spent in an orphanage after their father died. I braced myself for a big story, filled with details and drama.

"Well," she said, showing me the little stub of gum, "it's enough."

I shook my head and smiled.

"It's enough." What a great perspective. The one who loves bling and sparkles and the largeness of life still knows when something is enough.

The next day's morning readings offered this gem from Euripides:

"Enough is abundance to the wise."

My love and respect for Aunt Pearl and Mom grew richer and deeper that day. I can't imagine what it must have been like to live in an orphanage. I guess they learned then, and never forgot after, what was enough.

As for myself—when I think life is lacking or I'm falling short of my goals, I'm going to remember that half-stick of gum. Maybe what I have is enough.

How about you? How do you determine what's "enough"?

March 3:

Be the Mood You Want to See

After the birth of my first child, I began to meet with other mothers for playgroup.

"How are the kids?" I asked one veteran mom.

"Oh, they're in a tailspin, fighting and picking on each other. It's my fault. I was in a lousy mood this morning, and I let them see it. My mood is a lightning rod for them." She sighed and shook her head with resignation.

I'm not sure what I said in reply, but the comment put my thoughts into overdrive. I'd never considered that my mood could affect my child's behavior.

Over the next few days, I began to notice that when I hurried, my daughter whined. My impatience triggered her defiance. My stress provoked her upsets.

After my friend's lightning-rod comment, I became mindful of my attitude and its effect on my child. Self-awareness, some call it. Being mindful of who we are and how we affect others is another way to state it.

But it's hard to be in a stellar mood all the time. So I began to cheat.

I knew the things that could put me in a good mood:

Flowers always boosted my spirits, so they became fixtures on my weekly grocery list.

Music changes my mood too. So I began to play music during dinner. Classical, country, and '70s disco funk tunes rotated through our setting for supper. No mood was ever too dark that couldn't be brightened by the Commodores, Marvin Gaye, or Earth, Wind & Fire. And the kids got a bonus: a lesson in music appreciation.

Coffee always invigorates me too. Although I gave it up for Lent one year (What was I thinking?), one thoughtful friend gave me a coffee-scented candle that acted as an acceptable substitute.

In essence, I tried to create the environment for good moods, setting the tone for positive things to happen. If I'm going to be a lightning rod, I might as well be a good one!

How about you? Have you noticed your mood's effect on others? How could you be a better lightning rod?

March 4:

How Many, Really?

A good friend joined my father for coffee at a local diner. Midway through their second round, the friend asked, "How many friends do you have?"

"Oh, I don't know," Dad replied, noting the depth of his friend's gaze.

"Give me a number," the friend urged, acting smug, like he knew the exact answer and my father didn't. "Ten, five, three?"

"Oh, you know me better than that. I've got a lot of friends."

"Seriously, how many real friends do you have? I mean, people who relate to you because of *you*, not because of your role or position in life?"

The question hung there, Dad recalled. They both sugared and stirred fresh coffees in silence.

Finally, the friend concluded, "Most of us can count on our fingers, on one hand only, the number of real friends who would be our friends regardless of our position in life."

As I thought about Dad's friend's question, I, too, sipped my morning coffee in deep thought. The man had a point. Who were my "real friends"? The ones who had been there for me through the years? The ones I could call right that minute and know they would answer?

I sipped some more and then opened one hand and began counting, smiling as I remembered each friend and our storied history. We may have started our friendship as classmates, roommates, colleagues, or neighbors, but our relationship had evolved into much more than that.

Real friends? Yes, I'm lucky to have a few. Maybe today I should let them know just how much they mean to me.

How about you? Who do you consider your real friends? Is today a good day to tell them what they mean to you?

March 5:

Unspoken Words

During World War II, my father's story goes, a kind-hearted English couple adopted a six-month-old Polish baby girl. Shortly thereafter, they enrolled in a course to study the Polish language.

When asked why they were taking a class, they replied, "Little Sonya will soon be starting to talk, and we'll want to know what she is saying!"

Although we smile at that tale, the dedication of Sonya's parents is admirable. But what's truly impressive is the logic in their approach: they equipped themselves to enter their child's world, expanding their world to include hers.

I thought about their efforts when I visited with my granddaughter. At eighteen months of age, Blakely Faye was highly "verbal." Although I didn't understand her unique, nonstop gibberish, the one word she said clearly (and with great gusto and frequency) was, "No!"

I watched with amusement one evening when she put her parents through the paces. "No!" was the answer to every question. It was one of those special grandparenting circle-of-life moments. The memory of what you've lived through with your child floods back full force as you watch that child live through it with their own child. And you smile a sneaky smile inside, welcoming them to the parenting club and secretly hoping they appreciate you just a little more.

I tried to help. "Tell Nana what you want, Blakely Faye."

Without a word, she walked over and reached out her arms.

"You want to sit in my lap?"

She grinned.

"Hang on. Nana has to figure this out."

She was already trying to climb up my wheelchair's footplates. But I knew she would need one final lift to land in my lap, something my paralyzed abdominal muscles could not easily manage.

"Step here." I guided her to the side of my wheelchair, where I could lean on my armrest for leverage. "One, two, three, go!" I lifted her up and into my lap.

She beamed.

So did I.

"I guess she wanted a ride in Nana's wheelchair," I told her parents.

It's easy to forget that children have strong feelings long before they have language. The terrible twos aren't terrible because of the age, but because children are often communicating in ways we don't yet understand.

Like Sonya's parents, we have to be willing to equip ourselves to enter their world.

⤳⧡⤳

How about you? Have you ever had to decipher the unspoken words of a child—or adult?

March 6:

Refreshing

⌒⧳⌒

Mom and I sipped our soup, enjoying time alone before her trip back to West Virginia. As she began sorting out her schedule, we discovered a shared philosophy of "having something to look forward to" as a good remedy for tough transitions. She included lunch with friends as part of her plan.

"What friends do you find refreshing?" she asked, stirring her soup to cool it.

"Refreshing?" Surprised at the question, I put my next bite back in the bowl as I thought about it. "I've never described my friends with that term before, but it's a good thought." I named a couple of friends, and then asked her to tell me about her favorite refreshing friend.

Again, it surprised me. It wasn't her get-up-and-go, do-anything-anytime friends or even the friends she saw most regularly. It was Maxine, a friend who had limited availability because of the intensity of her responsibilities at home, caring for a husband who had been battling Alzheimer's for ten years.

"Why Maxine?" I asked.

"She's in a difficult situation but still makes the time for outings with friends," Mom explained. "She doesn't dwell on the hardship but enjoys the time we spend together. We talk, see movies, and laugh."

I smiled, thinking of the girl talk two seventy-year-old women might have. "How is that refreshing?"

"When you are with Maxine, her worries are behind her. She's made a point to have enough help at home so she can get out." Mom smiled. "It's refreshing to see someone with such a heavy load be so positive and enthused about life."

As I pondered my list of refreshing friends, I realized that they, too, were people with the ability to transcend their situation to make time for friendship. All knew how to manage their challenges in life—whether a high-profile career, a sixty-hour workweek, demanding kids, needy parents, intense spouses, or overbooked schedules—to create time for sharing a cup of coffee. I always found my time with them refreshing.

One Webster definition of the word *refresh* is "to restore strength and animation."

Indeed, after time with a refreshing friend, I often feel supercharged, inspired to revisit projects hanging in the neutral zone. With a refreshing friend, something always seems to be going right, as opposed to wrong. Positives filter up to the top of the conversation, framing the visit with a warm glow of possibilities.

How fortunate we are to have refreshing friends.

How about you? Do you have a refreshing friend? Are you one?

March 7:

Prompting Potential

He weighed in at 52 pounds, well under the 55-pound entry-level weight class. At age seven, my son Peter was scheduled to wrestle in the B tournament since he'd only competed in two matches. But Coach said the A team needed a 55-pounder to avoid a forfeit.

"Okay," I said. "Just don't let him get mauled."

Immediately, the opponent took Peter to his back with a big-scoring move, and I knew we'd made a mistake.

"Oh no," I whispered—then yelled, "C'mon, Pete!"

Other parents joined me as they realized the extreme imbalance of the match.

This wrestler dominated Peter. Single-leg take-down. Double-leg. Half-nelson. And the menacing "cradle." When performed correctly, this move results in a pin, wins the match, and awards extra team points.

Peter was cradled three times. Three times he escaped. What amazed me, though, was how he escaped. Just as Peter was about to be pinned, Coach shouted, "Straighten your leg!"

Pete did—and broke the hold.

Again, he got caught in the move; this time Coach yelled, "Grab his hand, Pete!"

Pete did and broke the grip.

Other moves put Pete on his back.

"Head up! Bridge! Turn!" Coach directed.

Done. Done. Done.

In the final seconds, Peter was faced down, and his opponent was trying another move. Pete peeked up and met my eyes. He was looking to me for help.

"Stand up, Pete!" I cried. "Lean into him!" I'd watched that drill so many times the words tumbled out.

Pete stood up. The buzzer sounded. The crowd cheered.

Peter lost but was not pinned.

"That match took a lot of courage," one parent consoled me.

But what struck me most was the teachability of the moment. Clearly outmatched, he'd held his own—with the help of some coaching. Pete was one 52-pound package of potential just waiting to be developed.

Parenthood's purpose became a little clearer to me. We

start with these 5- to 10-pound bundles of joy that quickly show us how different life can be with one small addition. From time to time, they peek up at us, looking for help. And if we're lucky, we know the right thing to say or do.

And as they grow, we grow too, discovering that we aren't the only ones who can help them develop their potential.

"Peter was terrific," Coach told me later. "He faced an experienced opponent and did well. Although he lost, he avoided being pinned and helped us win. You should be proud."

And I was—proud, scared, excited—but most of all, inspired to include more people in Peter's life who would help him reach his potential, on and off the mat.

⚬⚭⚬

How about you? Who in your life prompts you to reach your potential? Who can you help to achieve theirs?

March 8:

Active Loving

"Love isn't a perfect state of caring," said Fred Rogers. "It is an active noun, like 'struggle.'"

Sometimes love is easy and other times it's not. In the difficult moments, love navigates rough terrain by choice: We can let go. We can give up. Or we can settle in to work through difficult periods in our relationships.

Love isn't a silk flower arrangement that we dust occasionally. It's a living, breathing entity that requires ongoing attention. In some seasons of life, it may be easier to care for than in others. But we choose to tend to our loving relationships, to nurture their growth.

How about you? How have you handled a difficult season of loving? How have you experienced love as an active noun?

March 9:

Happiness Boost

It was a first for me—and for many others. Our public library hosted their first ever local author showcase event. Twenty-six authors were invited to share their books one Sunday afternoon. Our book reading could be no longer than five minutes, we were told. We would be timed.

Although I mastered the timing down to the second, I was still uneasy. The format was new to me, as was the podium and microphone accessibility. Thankfully, one librarian arrived early and problem-solved each issue so my reading, and my wheelchair, fit in seamlessly.

We heard from first-time authors and veteran authors; novelists, poets, memoirists, and life coaches; cancer survivors, abuse survivors, a police detective, an English teacher, a dog lover, and—my personal favorite—a former pastor who charmed us all with his imagined tale of a movie agent's hot pursuit of his book (a dream most of us have but would never admit).

The crowd was sparse but loyal, staying through three rounds of readings and two breaks sweetened by chocolate chip, peanut butter, and oatmeal raisin cookies.

Although we concluded promptly at 4:00 p.m., everyone lingered afterward to mingle.

Then the magic began.

Several audience members introduced themselves as writers with their own upcoming books. One librarian spoke about the event planning and promotion process, noting the need for libraries to reinvent themselves to serve their readers' interests. Then my fellow showcase participants started sharing their behind-the-book stories—what surprised them most in the book publishing journey, what they enjoyed, and what they found difficult.

I should have been exhausted when I finally made it home three hours later, but instead, I felt energized and surprisingly uplifted.

Why the happiness boost?

Gretchen Rubin, author of *The Happiness Project*, may have one explanation: "Challenging yourself to learn something new brings happiness because it allows you to expand your self-definition. You become larger."

Indeed, this debut event created firsts for everyone involved—the audience as well as the library staff and authors—and gave us the opportunity to expand our self-definition.

I'd gone to the event concerned about my reading and its logistics but left feeling happy and enriched. The happiness boost lasted for days.

❧

How about you? Have you learned something new that created happiness by expanding your self-definition?

March 10:

Light Bulb Moments

My friend Al and I had just shared a meal and were updating one another on our lives. He had a friend whose health was declining. I had a friend who was struggling with a difficult work environment. We had a common friend who was going through a tough downsizing transition.

"It's hard," Al said, "but you have to accept what you can't change."

I've always been a fan of the serenity prayer, but Al netted it out nicely, straight to its core.

I met Al in my IBM days, a decade before my paralysis. He was a Mensa-brilliant systems engineer, and I was a rookie marketing rep. I quickly learned the value of aligning my sales goals with his technical analysis of our customers' needs.

The friendship that grew from our IBM work remained steadfast over multiple decades, long after our careers diverged and my paralysis occurred. Our get-togethers often included a light dinner with sometimes heavy conversations on anything from history to politics to religion. He always helped me with a chore or two as well.

He'd been changing a lot of light bulbs lately. I'd had to ask him to change one more that night.

In our acceptance discussion, we concluded that the challenge is getting to the point of acceptance: *How do we decide what to accept?*

Toleration and moods are often my indicators of an issue I need to accept, I confided to Al. Such was the case with my burnt-out bulb, especially since it was the expensive kind that was supposed to last fifteen years.

I'd tolerated the darkened area, miffed that the bulb burned out before its time while secretly lamenting that I'd have to ask for help to change it. That bulb was undeniable evidence I couldn't do what I once did. It hit me in that vulnerable spot, the one that can lead me into a dark mood of victimhood thinking.

Yet a light was out, and I couldn't change it. I had to accept that fact. Plus, why let a burnt-out bulb remind me of my limitations? That was silly, especially when Al was there to give me his signature response: "I'm happy to help."

And he did.

Although life gives us plenty of inevitable realities that we must accept, we often have a choice about what we'll tolerate.

Thanks to Al, I had one less toleration to brood about.

How about you? Do your moody tolerations ever point to something you need to accept?

March 11:

The Inevitability of Discomfort

It'd been a week.

In separate non-weather-related incidents, I lost power for twelve hours and my plumbing backed up, causing a thunderstorm of "rain" to fall from my basement ceiling.

Then the door to my van refused to shut, forcing me to cancel two important meetings as I waited for its repair.

That same day, I learned that my daughter Madison had just been diagnosed with pneumonia.

A few hours later, one of my caregivers announced her resignation.

I felt the ground shifting under me, and I did not like it.

As one of my colleagues admitted in a recent strategy session: "I hate change."

I agree.

Although we may like to say we love to embrace the new, the truth is it is a chore. Habits are comfortable.

Traditions are predictable. Life is just plain easier when it keeps rolling along without the bumps.

Yet, they come. Big bumps, little bumps, and every size in between intrude on our daily living and remind us how vulnerable we are to forces outside of our control.

In his meditation "The Discomfort of Newness," Mark Nepo describes the disorientation that we must first feel when we are learning how to walk and dare to move away from a parent's hand to take our first steps, and then the dizziness we experience when we first fall in love and move beyond our own walls to include others. Each time we reach beyond the familiar, he says, there is a necessary acclimation to newness. But, he insists, "We needn't be afraid of it or give it too much power."

Then he notes how small birds fly—how sudden winds cause them to dip and swerve, and how they must adjust to keep flying.

"Breathe deeply," he writes, "and know that your heart is such a bird, and that its dips and swerves create a discomfort of newness that you have no choice but to experience, if you are to keep flying."

No wonder change is hard; its companion is discomfort!

Accepting discomfort's role fortifies my resolve to adjust and dip and swerve my way through tough adjustments. And the thought of a bird's grace in flight inspires me.

֍

How about you? How do you fortify yourself during flights through the inevitable discomfort of change?

March 12:

Always Have a Plan B

For years, my massage therapist Max came to my home to stretch my legs and use a special ointment that helped energize my paralyzed legs while soothing my overused shoulders and back.

One day Max forgot the ointment. On the next visit, he brought a small ointment-filled container and placed it on a nearby shelf in case he forgot again.

"So, is that your Plan B, Max?" I teased him.

He grinned. "Yes, I guess it is."

At each session, I noticed that Max retrieved the backup container, used it, and replaced it with another.

"Why do you always use the backup?" I asked him.

"I don't want it to become stale," he replied.

"So, you're keeping your Plan B fresh?"

He chuckled, nodding in agreement.

Fresh Plan Bs. That's a good strategy beyond the shelf-life of a massage cream. For many, early spring is a special season of Plan Bs for those applying to college.

High school counselors have educated us on the value of "reach" schools and "safe" schools. Yet we hope at this moment in our children's lives that their reach will be within their grasp and those safe Plan Bs will stay Plan Bs.

We've weathered campus visits, interviews, essays, and applications designed to reveal options for this life-changing next step. But if the wrong response comes, we, too, are devastated. Life's logic can baffle us, throwing us into that awkward but far too common experience of helping our child accept a situation we ourselves do not understand.

Yet, it can be a fine moment for teaching. Our response may become their blueprint.

Fresh Plan Bs help. In fact, keeping well-examined alternatives on hand at all times is a worthy lifelong pursuit.

Preparedness inspires confident living.

As we meet life's challenges head on, fresh Plan Bs can be just the thing we need to keep our lives filled with possibilities.

How about you? Have you experienced the benefit of a fresh Plan B?

March 13:

Generativity

One evening while watching an episode of the television series *Bull*, I was bewildered by a word that the trial consultant Dr. Jason Bull used to describe the kind of jurors he preferred.

He wanted jurors with "generativity."

What?

Thankfully his team of experts needed a definition too.

"Generativity," Bull explained, "is the concern for, and belief in, the future. It's a commitment to the idea that no matter how bad things may be at any given moment, you can persevere and redeem yourself."

Prospective jurors were asked questions designed to reveal their outlook on life: "What would you do if you lost your job today?" "Would you trade in your life for anyone else's?"

Those with generativity gave answers that displayed a confidence that things were ultimately going to be alright. Their tone and attitude indicated they would not be defined by a given circumstance but would instead strive to handle it and maybe even leave the world a better place because of it.

Although one critic called the show's generativity reference a "fancy word for optimism," I traced its origins to the seventh (Generativity versus Stagnation) of eight stages in Erik Erikson's theory of psychosocial development. In this stage we choose to discover our purpose, make our mark, learn from what we are experiencing, and leave the world a better place for future generations—or not.

Energized by my new vocabulary word, I couldn't help but wonder: Would Dr. Bull have chosen me for his jury? Did I have generativity?

The question helped me see everyday trials in a new light, renewing my confidence that I can get through any tough times if I only focus on the learning and growth that will come from the experience.

How about you? Do you have generativity? Does your approach to life reveal it?

March 14:

Because I Can

When life gets messy, chaotic, or uncertain, I need one clear, uplifting thought, to pierce through the hubbub. This quote from Martin Luther nails it:

> "Even if I knew that tomorrow the world would go to pieces, I would still plant my apple tree."

Yes! Although I know so much of our mental outlook is based on how we choose to respond to life's inevitable stress, sometimes I think we need to do more than brace for impact. We need to act directly in contradiction to our fears.

Despite the dark news, the negative tones, the fragility of life, I can still take a positive action. My "apple tree" can be simple—a kind word, a thoughtful deed, an unexpected hug, or a kiss of love. I may not see its long-term impact, but it's still a worthy action.

I will use the best of my humanity to rise above the worst.

I will—because I can.

How about you? How can you "plant an apple tree" today, by words or actions?

March 15:

Affirming Reflections

It was clean-up day in the church attic. The insurance company had concerns about "all that junk" causing a fire in one of my father's early pastorates.

"What do you want me to do with this thing?" a teenager hollered as he wrestled a funny-shaped mirror taller than his own frame.

"Kiss it good-bye and throw it in the truck," someone yelled back.

"Hold it," my father countermanded. "Take it to my office. I need something to look at myself in," he half-teased.

For months, the old, oblong mirror stood in my father's office, towering about six feet and creaking in its awkward cradle. It was alternately criticized and complimented by his visitors.

One day a friend whose antique expertise my father respected dropped in and spotted the mirror.

"Do you know what this is?" he gasped, caressing the mirror as if it were a loved one.

"No," Dad admitted.

"This is a cheval mirror. It's valuable and hard to find. Name your price and you've got it," he added, attempting to seal the deal.

But Dad declined his offer. Instead, he took the mirror home and put it in his master bedroom, where such mirrors belong. He and Mom pampered it properly for years before passing it along to Rachel, who continues to cherish its value and storied history today.

A basic life principle was at work in that incident, Dad concluded: "Praise puts possession in perspective!"

Sometimes we don't know what we have until someone affirms it.

That principle holds true for people too.

When we praise a person, we acknowledge who they are and what they have to offer the world. It's an affirmation that helps the receiver know what skills they can reflect back into the world, ones that can sometimes last a lifetime.

How about you? Can you offer someone an affirmation today?

March 16:

Catching Our Days

On writing days, I wear the same thing: black pants and a black fleece pullover, even in the summer. Uniforms reduce decision-making, I've discovered. They give us one less thing to adapt to or remember.

When I began my career at IBM in 1980, I was hired as a recruiter to help staff a new plant and laboratory facility in Charlotte, North Carolina. Our start time was 7:42 a.m., and the day ended at 4:24 p.m. Yep, I've never forgotten it. Although I was salaried, those times blueprinted my day; I knew what was expected.

Routines and structure not only give consistency, they also save time and energy and protect us from distraction. Author Annie Dillard offers this poetic reminder:

> "How we spend our days is, of course, how we spend our lives. What we do with this hour, and that one, is what we are doing. A schedule defends from chaos and whim. It is a net for catching days."

How about you? How can you improve your net for catching your day today?

March 17:

Slowing Down

For fast-acting relief, try slowing down.
—Lily Tomlin

I was tired. And tired of being tired. I couldn't figure it out until I looked back at my calendar and reviewed all my appointments.

In seven days, I'd had thirty-nine interactions!

Granted, some were Zoom meetings or brief appointments in my home, but still, no wonder I was exhausted! Each one had required scheduling, preparation, interaction, and follow-up.

Tomlin's statement above was right. I needed to slow down. My calendar didn't lie—and what it was telling me was that I'd overestimated my capacity.

For the next few weeks, I marked sections of my calendar in the most calming color I could find, sky blue, with my new slowing-down symbol: BT, which stood for Becky's Time (for rest and recovery).

How about you? Do you need fast-acting relief from an overbooked calendar?

March 18:

Happy, Sad, Mixed-Up, Mad

Although always a strong-willed child, my daughter Brittany's limit-testing escalated at age six, an apparent response to the special attention given to her siblings. Trish, a pediatric psychologist, had helped me in dealing with Matthew's seizures, Madison's autism, and newborn Peter's blood disorder, which had put him in the NICU for sixteen days. I decided it could be helpful for Brittany to start seeing Trish as well.

We soon implemented weekly "Behavior Charts" to target six good behaviors, monitored daily with stickers and rewards, and began a special nighttime routine.

"Okay, Britty, it's time for prayers," I said one night as I tucked her into bed.

"Aren't we doing happy-sad-mixed-up-mad first?" she asked.

"Oh yes, honey," I said. "I almost forgot."

Trish had recommended that I spend extra time with Brittany at bedtime every night to encourage her to share her feelings, using "happy, sad, mixed up, and mad" as a prompt. The hardest one for her was always the mixed-up one.

"So what was your mixed-up experience today, Britty?"

She scrunched up her face. "I don't know, Mom. What's yours?"

"Well, let's see. I'm happy that it rained today because we needed it. But sad because it caused your soccer game to be canceled."

It was a great prompt, leading to an extended discussion of rain, why it was needed, and what our yard looked like when there wasn't enough of it, as well as the soccer team, the coach, her playing time, and her feelings about all of it.

That exercise became a cherished part of our nightly routine, enabling us to take stock of the day and consider how we felt about its events. It also forced us to look at a single event from multiple perspectives—a valuable analytical life skill.

Life is filled with mixed emotions. Giving voice to confusing feelings helped us talk more honestly about complex situations.

Unknowingly, I think I also planted seeds of optimism for my daughter while nurturing my own. When we look at a situation in its entirety, searching for the positives despite the negatives, we create an expectation of a bright side, no matter what.

How about you? When you take stock of today, what are your happy, sad, mixed-up, and mad feelings?

March 19:

Counting On Spring

Every year I can count on it. By the time Easter Sunday arrives, the sun is in just the right place in the sky to awaken me each morning. Its bright sliver of light pierces through my bedroom window and beams right into my eyes.

I don't need an alarm clock.

The sunlight used to annoy me. Now it comforts me.

After nearly twenty years in this home, it reminds me that no matter the circumstances of my life, whether my house is filled with children and guests and celebrations or I am home alone with my dog, the sun will rise and wake me. Easter will come.

I can count on it.

How about you? Have you experienced the comfort of spring's predictable nature?

March 20:

Laughing Matters

Mom was a great note writer. Every Wednesday during her 8:00 a.m. hair appointment at the beauty parlor, she would use her time under the hair dryer to write what she called her "bread-and-butter notes." I grew up with her routine and that ritual. For me, it meant thanking people for anything and everything, which she did faithfully and with great heart.

Every week Mom came to the salon with her list, address book, stamps, stationery, and her favorite letter-writing pen. She was prepared to share her warmth and gratitude with everyone on her mind that week.

One year, I decided to "be like Mom" and send hand-written notes to those who'd given to Madison's birthday fundraiser for Pathfinders for Autism. I crafted custom notecards and return address labels, got a gold glitter pen, and even found sparkly hearts with which to seal each note.

Just like Mom, I prepared to be grateful.

But as I began to write my notes, two unlike-Mom things happened.

First, I forgot to keep a list of the notes I'd written. I wrote a few cards when the initial donations came in, but when Pathfinders later sent the master list, I couldn't remember who I'd thanked. Embarrassed, I had to contact those early donors and ask if they had received my note.

Then, the unthinkable happened: I wrote half of the next batch of notes upside-down. In my effort to be efficient, I'd stacked twenty unfolded notecards in a pile and written them all in quick succession. As I folded them, I realized I'd written on the wrong portion of the card for half of them.

I was mortified.

Now, perfectionist Becky (from my pre-paralysis days) would have rewritten every one of those notes.

But she wasn't around anymore.

What that's-the-way-it-is-deal-with-it Becky did was pause and take a deep breath—and then laugh so loud she woke up the dog.

I took my glitter pen, drew a big sparkly heart and an arrow to the note's upside-down text, and wrote, "Sorry, it's been one of those days!"

Mom would have laughed hard too. I can still hear her encouraging voice comforting me: "B-B honey, it's okay. We all make mistakes." Then she'd add with that classic Southern charm, "I think you're doing mighty well."

I'm trying, Mom!

Thanks for teaching me to be grateful, prepared, and willing to laugh when life doesn't go exactly as planned.

How about you? When is the last time you laughed out loud when you made a mistake?

March 21:

Letting Things Perk

I love author Melanie Beattie's unique description of procrastination:

"Not acting when the time is right."

This fluid definition allows for the possibility that we sometimes procrastinate for *good* reason. Beattie contends that doing something before the time is right can be as detrimental as waiting too long.

Waiting often gives clarity and perspective, I've learned.

And strength.

Before we act, we may need to take some time and percolate, just like my grandfather's first pot of coffee. Some of us remember a time when it took at least twenty minutes for the coffee to perk. You just didn't push the brew button; you "put on a pot of coffee," placing a pitcher-shaped pot filled with coffee and water on the stove so it could perk.

I loved watching the little glass top on the metal coffee pot. The water would first simmer with that steamy, buzzing sound; then suddenly pause; and then burst forth with the first perk.

It was just a flash at first. The caramel-colored water would be forced into the glass top, perking with no particular rhythm. As it heated up, the speed would pick up and the cadence would set in. One of my jobs as a little girl was watch the pot and yell for Granddaddy if the coffee started to boil over.

"Is the coffee ready yet?" he'd call.

"Just perking," I'd answer.

With each perk, the coffee got stronger, until it was pronounced "ready" by those in the know. What a talent that was, to know when the coffee was ready—when it had perked long enough. Not too strong. Not too weak. Just right. It was a sincere compliment to be told you made good coffee.

Procrastination may signal that an issue needs more time to fully form. Sometimes we may need to perk on what we're putting off to strengthen our resolve to act.

How about you? When have you experienced the benefits of procrastination with good reason?

March 22:

Pathfinding While Waiting

After ten days in intensive care and a month in rehab, I finally came home, paralyzed but hopeful of a full recovery. At age thirty-eight, with kids ages three, four, six, and nine, I had no idea what was next for me or my family so I just kept moving through life.

Within a few weeks, I received a yellow flyer in Madison's backpack inviting me to the home of Polly and B. J. Surhoff. They wanted to share information about a new autism therapy that was helping their son Mason, one of Madison's classmates.

Like many children with autism, Madison had very limited communication skills. At age five, she did not speak. My job as her mom was to be the master interpreter of her gestures, cries, tantrums, and moods.

It was exhausting.

At the Surhoff meeting, we learned about a new therapy and tried it with Madison. Unbelievably, she responded and started to speak, mastering her name, address, phone number, colors, and shapes within weeks.

I wasn't the only parent to have these happenstance stories. Soon a small group of parents met regularly. We wanted to help each other learn all the useful things we had discovered for ourselves.

I thought about what mattered in the frustrating search for help and information. What was it that we needed to be good parents?

One night, seated at my kitchen table, I took three coffee cans and traced their circles. I named each one—Resources, Referrals, and Research—and intersected them, then wrote "Pathfinders" in the middle. That's what we all needed: paths to find our way through the maze of information, not unlike the paths in the wilderness I'd experienced so many times before.

That theme and coffee-can creation became the beginning of our first logo and the start of our parent-crafted tagline: "Our mission is to find a path for our children."

Within three years, in February 2000, our small group founded Pathfinders for Autism, a nonprofit directed at improving the lives of individuals with autism and their families that regularly serves more than 20,000 individuals each year.

Looking back, I now see that the three-year effort to found Pathfinders gave me purpose while I was waiting for clarity about the permanence of my paralysis. It felt good to accomplish something positive and helpful for my child that also benefited others.

How about you? Have you witnessed or engaged in similar pursuits while waiting for clarity?

March 23:

Something to Look Forward To

"What's planned is possible," my father said often.

"Got to get my ducks in a row," Mom said almost daily.

I grew up with these mantras, so it's no surprise that my calendar is organized (like Mom) and always has something in it that I'm looking forward to (like Dad).

I review it daily after my morning reading time to make sure I have something scheduled besides transactional chores and obligations. If I don't, I pick up the phone, call a friend, and make plans.

As a family, we book our vacations a year in advance. It's the only way we can coordinate schedules that span the East Coast, West Coast, and a lot of global travel.

For me, there is tremendous joy in anticipating a planned activity, and that feeling can buoy me through almost any low period.

How about you? What plans are you looking forward to today?

March 24:

When You Can't Be There

It's the phone call you don't want to get: Your loved one is on the way to the ER. The person on the other end of the phone explains that they are not sure what's wrong, but the hospital is the next step.

What happened? slips out of your mouth, as if understanding the why of the situation will somehow take away your fear and shorten the distance between you. For whatever reason, you can't be there, so you enter this odd zone of hopeful trust. You trust that the professionals know what to do. You hope it will be enough.

Madison had been hospitalized. At age twenty-five, she still had limited speech and a high threshold for pain—not a good combination for assessing illness or injury. She could tell you the names of colors, shapes, numbers, and her family members when prompted, but she still couldn't say, "That hurts."

We relied on evidence. An observant caregiver had noticed that Madison would not lift her left hand to give her a "high five." Then she discovered the swelling. The staff nurse had advised a trip to the ER.

"I'll keep you updated," the kind voice on the phone assured me.

Even though the caregiver texted regularly over the next few hours, I still could not quite envision it—the bright lights, beeping machines. The pokes, the prods, the sticks.

"How's she doing?" I texted back. "Is she having any behaviors?" Long waits and noisy settings often provoked Madison's upsets. She'd become loud and unruly, sometimes hitting herself or others.

Then my phone lit up with a photo: Madison's cheerful face beaming from her hospital bed. What a relief to see her engaging eyes, her smile! To know she was where she needed to be and was tolerating it.

After a few tests, she left the ER with a treatment plan to address a suspected over-use condition.

And I was left with a deep, abiding gratitude for the professionals who took good care of my daughter—and for that spirit-lifting picture, which had provided such relief and shortened the distance between our worlds.

How about you? Have you ever received one of those phone calls? What helped you if you couldn't be there with your loved one?

March 25:

Letting the Future In

The executive was being interviewed about his company's extraordinary success. Seemingly stunned by the organization's sustained double-digit growth over the last ten years, the commentator paused, looked at the young exec, and asked, "How future-proofed is your company?"

I can't recall his exact response—something about being prepared with business plans in multiple areas, positioned for growth through innovation—but the question baffled me.

How can you *future-proof* anything? Your company? Your life?

And if you can, may I please buy a bottle of it?

Seriously. What does that mean, anyway? Our "waterproof" boots don't let water in. Our "childproof" locks don't let our children into areas we think they shouldn't access. We try to protect, to limit contact with harmful or dangerous things.

Is that how we should view the future—as something harmful, dangerous, or to be avoided?

What a negative way to look at an inevitable experience!

True, the future can hold scary things. But it is going to come whether we like it or not. So, instead of fearing it, perhaps we should consider the above company's approach and focus on being *prepared* for it.

I'll never forget when my power wheelchair was damaged beyond safe use and I realized my extreme reliance on it for my independence. But in the end, although the adjustment was tough, it was manageable. I'd kept an old backup one, regularly recharging it so that it could be suitable for limited use. I'd also maintained a good relationship with the same wheelchair provider for over twenty years so I could confidently rely on them to help me problem-solve through the situation—which they did.

Future-proofing? I don't think it's possible. Instead of trying to guard ourselves against the future, I've learned that it's better to simply let its possibilities in— and prepare for them as best we can.

How about you? How do you look at the future? Is it something to be guarded against or prepared for?

March 26:

Listen to Your Heart

Sometimes when life gets so busy that I'm on the verge of overwhelm, I have to give myself a time-out. I shut my eyes, take a deep breath, and exhale slowly. Then I ask myself:

What's the first thing that is coming to mind?
What's on your heart?

And for the next sixty seconds, I let those thoughts fill the empty breath, one at a time. I give them my undivided attention.

They deserve it.

Most often, what comes up first is the most important. Those pressing thoughts can be our best guide for recalibration. I may have other urgent matters at hand, but those first thoughts usually represent something deeper, and of more lasting importance.

The superficial noise of daily living can often muffle what our hearts want to say, what needs our attention. Shakespeare may have said it best: "Go to your bosom; / Knock there, and ask your heart what it doth know."

What does your heart know? In order to find out, you may need to stop, take a breath, and let it speak.

How about you? Take a deep breath and listen. What's on your heart today?

March 27:

Making Your Problems Your Friends

For weeks, I'd been wrestling with house issues, health issues, and some unexpected schedule changes—nothing serious, thankfully, but that steady stream of speed bumps had worn me down, and I was in a bit of a funk.

Then I stumbled upon this quote from Sarah Young:

"Make friends with the problems in your life."

What? I thought. *Are you kidding me? Why on earth would I want to do that?*

Weren't problems the enemy? Weren't they the glaring "fix-its" on my to-do lists, waiting to be attacked and checked off? Why would I want to make them my friends?

But just as I was about to mark that quote as "not applicable to me," I stopped to consider the process of developing a friendship. What is my mindset when I want to make new friends?

I am open, willing, and interested in learning about them. And, if I'm on my game, I listen more than I talk, probing with thoughtful questions. I'm steadfastly curious in my effort to get to know them.

Is there value in using that approach with problems? Problems invite drama. The attitude of "it's always something," along with its sidekick "and then it's something else," creates an inflammatory cloud of angst, shock, anger, and even self-pity. Reality is distorted, slowing the process of understanding.

But if I approach the problem as if I am preparing for a new friendship instead of an uninvited battle, maybe I'll be able to cut through the drama and instead be open to what the problem has to teach. What can I learn from this problem so that I can understand it better? Could that help me solve it more quickly?

Granted, some problems can't be fixed; we have to learn to live with them. But perhaps we can still treat them as a friend, inviting them into relationship as we enlarge our lives to include what we can learn.

After all, friends enrich our lives. Maybe with the right mindset, our problems can too.

How about you? What could you learn if you treated a problem as a friend?

March 28:

Focus with Care

Today's inspiration comes from my conversation with Kim Acedo, who once interviewed me for her *Me Time* podcast. During that interview, she shared a simple thought that has stayed with me:

"What you focus on expands."

When we focus on eating healthy, our knowledge of nutrition expands. When we focus on decluttering, our attention to different methods of organizing expands. Even our everyday outlook, our attitude toward life, expands according to what we focus on. When I look for the negatives in life, for example, I find more negatives. And when I look for the positives, I see more positives.

What a great reminder to be aware of our focus.

I had the chance to witness three dear friends "walk that talk" when they were helping to plan weddings for their children. The children's range and degree of "non-traditional" approaches amazed me. Even more amazing, though, was how my friends handled it.

They looked for the positives.

Instead of focusing on how "different" the weddings were from their own (or any other they had ever experienced!), my friends chose to focus on the creativity, independence, and uniqueness of their children and their ideas. Instead of questioning or judging those choices, they chose to embrace them and learn more about them, and in doing so learned more about their children and their spouses-to-be.

Granted, more than once, my friends shared their honest thoughts with me as they tried to process it all. (After all, what are girlfriends for?) But each would always end their confidences with that phrase that always keeps the peace in delicate situations: "But I kept my mouth shut." (And so we do, when something matters more than our opinions.)

Indeed, what you focus on expands. And so was the case for my three friends who chose to focus on their love for their children.

Three beautiful weddings. Three happy couples. Three bright futures, with no regrets over opinions expressed that were best left unsaid.

How about you? Have you noticed that what you focus on expands? How will you use this approach to fuel your day?

March 29:

Don't Be a Surprise

"Perseverance" was the NCAA wrestling champion's subject as he addressed the room of athletes and their families. Jarrod King, the speaker, had encountered more than his share of adversity, including four shoulder surgeries and a knee infection that left him in bed for seven weeks during the season.

Nevertheless, he'd become a NCAA champ.

"I'm not going to be surprised when you win a NCAA title," his coach had told him one morning during a six o'clock solo workout. And now "Don't be a surprise" had become King's message. Work hard. Work more. Show your work and let your work show, he advised. Expect to succeed and others will expect it of you too.

Persevere.

I thought about King's words as I looked back on my publishing journey for my first book. Although I'd been a columnist for years, writing a full-length book was another beast entirely—one that included a straight-up learning curve and massive doses of rejection.

To keep my spirits ups, I used my *Thoughtful Thursdays* column to share what had inspired me that week, along with any publishing challenges I'd bumped up against. As I mulled over King's words, I realized that "showing my work" had helped me keep going. Even though writing weekly was a difficult and time-consuming commitment, that work became the evidence of my progress and a great source of encouragement.

The solo journey, when shared, helped me gain an unexpected momentum. It helped me persevere.

How about you? Have you benefited from sharing your hard work?

March 30:

Sister Structure

Nine weeks after kidney cancer surgery, my father prepared for his return to the pulpit. Daily, I'd observed his progress and heard about his alliterative siblings of healing: Sister Strength and Sister Structure.

Sister Strength appeared to have set up residence, he'd reported. Thankfully, Dad had invited her sibling, Sister Structure, to join the healing process.

Sister Structure had never strayed far from our family. Over the years, she had served us well in weathering some of life's toughest storms.

Writer Brooks Adams said it best:

"What difference does it make how much honey the honeybee makes if the power

of the honeycomb fails? The honeycomb
falls and becomes a formless mass in the
beehive and the honeybee drowns in his
own product."

Structure is the honeycomb that supports the honey
we produce. It is the set of nails upon which we hang our
daily living chores and challenges.

Appropriately, Dad honored Sister Structure with
S's:

1. Study in the library
2. Sweat in the workshop
3. Shower in the bathroom
4. Sleep on the sofa

A simple plan, but a strong one. Through it, mind,
body, and soul were nurtured.

I, too, found the healing nature of structure throughout my adjustments to paralysis. Initially, though, Sister
Structure was absent. In the ER, blistering pain shattered
through any semblance of order, taking on a life of its
own as I waited for it and its cause to "run its course" as
it attacked my spine.

Chaos ruled.

But on the third day, the pain subsided, and my life
in intensive care assumed a rhythm with nursing shifts,
doctors' rounds, and medication schedules. Every day,
seven o'clock wake-up calls from my hospital bed to my
children connected me to their world. Meals bookmarked
the day into "after breakfast" and "before dinner" periods.
Physical and occupational therapies began. Goals were set.

Sister Structure quieted the chaos, but more importantly, she created the opportunity for a cycle of success.

When achieved regularly, routines gave me a sense
of accomplishment. Those accomplishments gave me
confidence. And that confidence became a foundation
for creating even more challenging routines.

Sister Structure meets you where you are. She demands no promise of success, nor is she selective about your attitude or circumstance. She waits patiently to assist in the need for order as we heal.

How about you? How has Sister Structure helped you get through a challenging period?

March 31:

Wake Up Elroy

It's one of my favorite tales from my father.

Elroy and Leroy are brothers, born and raised in the backwoods. One day they decide they want to learn to drive one of those big eighteen-wheel rigs.

So they make their way down the mountains to a trucking headquarters. They tell the man in charge what they want. He indicates they must take a test. Leroy, the older brother, volunteers.

"So, Leroy," says the trucking manager, "what you would do in this case? It's a dark night. Elroy is asleep in the bed behind the driver's seat. You're coming down a mountain that has a 100-foot bank on the right and a 200-foot drop on the left. As you come around a curve, you see another truck jackknifed, blocking the road. What's the first thing you'd do?"

"Well, the first thing I'd do," said Leroy, "is wake up Elroy."

"Why would you wake up Elroy?"

"Well, you see, Elroy ain't never seen no real bad wreck."

I smile each time I recall this story, no matter what frame of mind I'm in. There are times when most of us can identify with Leroy. Often, when bad things happen, about all we can do is brace for the crash.

The road sign "Look for Falling Rocks" also invited Dad's reflection. "There's not a whole lot we can do about falling rocks," he told me. "Rocks tumble down hillsides so fast we don't have time to look, let alone get out of the way."

Yet "falling rocks" happen. Disease, job loss, death—these things happen, and, like falling rocks, there's not much we can do about that.

But not all crashes are disastrous. Some are predictable, even welcomed. Our kids go to college, get married, move away for jobs, or expand their families with children. These are crashes too; their changes change us. We can see it coming, the loss of what was.

Sometimes all we can do is brace for impact and "wake up Elroy," reaching out to those who know us and love us. And then, pressing on, we reconfigure our lives to embrace change, ever thankful for the Elroys of the world who are there for us to help us make it through.

❧

How about you? Who are you grateful for that's helped you make it through a difficult adjustment?

APRIL

April 1:

Huge Small Steps

Today's inspiration comes from my daughter Madison. April is Autism Awareness Month. One year, the good folks at Pathfinders for Autism shared stories that highlighted "steps to independence" with their campaign, #ItsTheSmallSteps. And Madison had just made a huge small step!

When Rachel and I visited Madison to celebrate her twenty-sixth birthday, I was surprised—no, shocked—at her ability to "chill." For most of Madison's life, detailed schedules had helped structure her day. Knowing what was next kept her focused and engaged, often preventing upsets and aggressive or sometimes self-injurious behaviors.

"Schedule, please," was one of the few unprompted phrases she had mastered. She used it repeatedly, almost obsessively. It worked well for years—but as she moved into adulthood, her behaviors escalated. After several rough patches, she was admitted into a specialized in-patient program where her behaviors were studied, her medications adjusted, and a different way of directing Madison was devised and later implemented.

I knew she was doing well in the new programming. But when I learned we had almost an hour to wait between skating time and pizza at her birthday party, I was stunned by her new skill.

She chilled.

She sat calmly with Rachel. She jammed to her music, nodding her head and tapping her toes to the beat. Then she perched beside me, perfectly content to hang out and munch on a fresh bag of Cheetos.

She didn't pace. She didn't pull my hand to take me where she wanted to go. She didn't raise her voice or pound on the table. She didn't even request, "Schedule, please."

I couldn't believe it. My Madison had learned to wait patiently. What a huge small step! And how wise of Pathfinders to remind us to celebrate these kinds of achievements!

So often we grind so intensely through our daily lives—checking lists, solving problems, and anticipating new ones—that we forget to celebrate those "small steps" that can lift us up above our circumstances. That day with Madison, I was reminded to give them their due.

How about you? What small steps can you celebrate today?

April 2:

Nominating Friends

A friend joined my father for breakfast at a local café.

"Years ago I heard you say that we nominate people to be our friends but they must elect whether or not they become our friends," he said after sitting down. "Right?"

Dad nodded. "Something like that," he mumbled, stirring his coffee.

"Well, I have a friend who has become a really good friend," his friend said. "And that's exactly what he did. He nominated me for his friend—but he didn't stop there. Know what else he did?"

Dad shook his head.

"He campaigned for election!" A big smile creased his friend's face. "I'm glad he did, and I'm glad he won the election."

"So, how did he campaign?" Dad asked.

"Oh, in many ways. He invited me for golf, took me to his civic club, and invited us over for dinner. He even took us on an overnight trip for a weekend of relaxation."

"That's good campaigning," Dad said. "You liked that, huh?"

"You'd better believe it." His friend chuckled. "But he wasn't pushy. When we were invited to something but couldn't accept, he and his wife didn't seem hurt. They just gave us rain checks and we went later."

I smile at that story, considering my own nomination, campaigning, and election efforts. Friendships don't just happen, for sure. Although "campaigning" sounds a bit contrived, we do have to find opportunities to get to know our "nominated" friends. And not only does finding and pursuing mutual interests foster new friendships—it also encourages our own personal growth.

How about you? Do you have a person you've nominated to be a friend? How's the campaign going?

April 3:

Diamonds in the Rough

I'll admit it. I can be a pack rat. But not the can't-throw-away-anything, hoarding kind. I'm a well-intended person who makes stacks of to-dos that never quite get done—and then those stacks multiply and multiply.

I know in general where things are—I just can't tell someone else exactly where to find them. Locating an errant piece of paper is an almost spiritual experience in which I close my eyes and envision the paper, then recreate the setting where I last saw it.

I've tried to motivate myself with fancy labelers and designer folders. Yet the piles remain—a bit more festive and easier to spot, to be sure, but still there, mocking me. Beautified clutter.

I've tried inboxes, outboxes, and action, urgent, and pending folders, all with the same result: more piles.

Labeled clutter.

Each year, tax time challenges me, sending me into the jungle of my paperwork in search of all the records that "must be around here somewhere."

Eventually, as always, I track down all the necessary documents and submit them with time to spare. However, one year, the time-consuming process needled me. Was there a way to avoid this yearly stress? Would a clean desk help?

As I began to declutter my workspace, I stumbled on a few clever quotes I must have saved to justify my weakness:

"Creativity often resides in clutter."
"The mark of a genius is a messy desk."

I smiled at the affirmations as I dug further into a pile beside my keyboard and discovered some returned Christmas cards with incorrect addresses. I googled one friend's new workplace and found he had a website and a schedule of podcasts. Three days later, I watched one. I hadn't seen him for thirty years. He responded to my handwritten note with one of his own. Thank goodness I hadn't "filed" that envelope; I might never have renewed that friendship.

Then I found another quote that really got me thinking:

"An orderly desk reflects an orderly mind."

Did I want an orderly mind? Was a rote life, void of spontaneity-sparked insight and tangential escapades, right for me? Would an empty desk result in an empty mind?

Suddenly, my stacks of clutter gained a new glow of purpose. My steadfast piles were not albatrosses to bear—they were mountains of inspiration to be mined.

Precious discoveries await.

❧

How about you? What does your desk reveal about you?

April 4:

One Stubborn Mule

There was once a farmer who owned an old mule. One day the mule fell into the farmer's well. When the farmer heard the mule braying in distress, he felt sympathy but decided that neither the mule nor the well was worth the trouble of saving.

So the farmer rallied his neighbors to help shovel dirt into the well to bury the mule and put him out of his misery.

Initially, the mule was hysterical; but as the shoveling ensued and the dirt hit his back, a thought came to mind . . . each time a load landed on him, he could shake it off and step up.

And he did just that, blow after blow, repeating his mantra to encourage himself. No matter how painful the blows, or how distressing the situation seemed, he fought panic and instead focused solely on his goal. As a result, it wasn't long before the battered and exhausted mule stepped triumphantly over the wall of the well. What seemed like it would bury him had actually blessed him—all because of how he handled his adversity.

Late one night several months after my paralysis, my former IBM manager Ken Miller forwarded this story to me, with no author to credit. Somehow the mental image of a stubborn mule refusing to be a victim put some starch in my will that day.

I was not living the life I had planned. Yet, that stubborn mule intrigued me. He was panicked, but determined to not be buried.

Although I still find it hard to consider myself "blessed" by my adversities—just not that highly evolved, yet—I stole that mantra as my own theme song over twenty years ago and use it whenever pity threatens to take up residence in my mind.

Shake it off. Step up.

It makes sense.

It helps.

How about you? What burden can you "shake off and step up" to get through today?

April 5:

Victim No More

It can be easy and sometimes even pleasurable to play the victim—woe is me, and all that. But after many years, I've learned there's more strength in "shaking off and stepping up" like my stubborn mule friend. It's a choice I've made over and over as I've bumped into life's inevitable problems.

How?

To keep it simple, I've borrowed the basics from our friends in fire safety: Stop, drop, and roll.

1. **Stop.** And acknowledge what's happened. Accept it. Like our friend the mule, you've fallen into a hole and are feeling dirt hit your back. You may not be sure how

you got there or why you feel this way, but you know you aren't at your best. Nothing good can happen until you admit where you are and that you are struggling.

2. **Drop.** And decide. Do you want to do anything about it? Some folks enjoy misery. Whining comes naturally for them, and they like the attention their hysterics attract. Others ignore their predicament, overlooking the obvious because it is too painful or too difficult to face reality. Still others may not be ready to act. They want to wait it out, hoping for change that may be unlikely. They need time to absorb the situation. You can stay in this step as long as you like—but know that you are choosing to be there, even though there is an option to proceed.

3. **Roll.** And act. Once you've accepted the situation and are willing to address it, make a plan. What resources do you have? What do you need? Who can help you? Determine what is under your control and focus on your strengths to achieve it. Let go of the rest.

This is my coping cycle, the way I refuse to become a victim. I have used it for all sorts of struggles, sadness, and even deep grief. These simple steps remind me of the choices I always have and keep me moving through, instead of dwelling in, the latest challenge.

How about you? What can you do today to refuse to be a victim of a circumstance?

April 6:

A Fresh Start

*I love that this morning's sunrise does
not define itself by last night's sunset.*
—Steve Maraboli

What an encouraging thought!

I love the idea of a fresh start to every day. I begin mine by raising the blinds in my room and taking in all that nature has to offer that morning before taking the dog for our adventure up and down the driveway. We call it a "sniff-ari," where Tripp sniffs every flower, insect, and foreign animal scent he encounters during our expedition.

Nudged by nature's evidence, we return, energized to begin the rest of our day.

How about you? How do you start your best day?

April 7:

Keep the Plane Flying

My father often told the story about his friend Tom, an airplane pilot he had flown with many times. One day they were discussing the crises that develop in life.

"When a crisis develops with the airplane and you're thousands of feet off the ground, Tom, what do you do?" Dad asked.

"You keep the plane flying," Tom said immediately, not even pausing to ponder the question. "As a pilot, that's your purpose. Once you have stabilized the aircraft and it's flying, then you start looking around to see what caused the crisis. If you can fix it, you do. If not, you look for a place to set the plane down. But the main thing," he emphasized, "is to keep the plane flying. If you don't, nothing else you do makes any difference anyhow."

Tom's story gives us a good pattern to use in almost any crisis—which is, stick with the purpose of what you are doing. Don't let fear freeze you in the crisis; do what's necessary to stay steady and stabilize. Only then can you start looking around to find out what's causing the crisis and decide the next steps of action.

Whatever else you do, keep the plane flying.

How about you? How do you keep your plane flying when you are facing a crisis?

April 8:

Painting with a Small Brush

My mother was well-known for her unique style of story-telling. She had an exceptional knack for absorbing details and was willing to share most of them when asked.

"Big-brush it, Faye," Dad would plead when she got tangled up in the play-by-play of a story. "Put that little paint brush down and grab a big one," he'd tease. "We don't have all day."

In response, she'd flash that knowing smile of hers, clear her throat, and try to summarize. But her real gift was in the details.

I'd been attending a weekly women's meeting that always ended with people sharing updates about their personal lives. I always struggled with what to say, but one week, my heart was heavy. I thought about

Mom when it was my turn to put into words what was on my heart.

"Please remember Madison, my adult daughter with autism," I blurted out. "She's still having a hard time with her behaviors, hurting herself. I've found a program that may help. We're applying. It's a Neurobehavioral Unit."

The detail flew out of my mouth, like anyone would know what I was talking about. In the weeks I'd been researching the program, I hadn't met anyone (outside of my autism colleagues) who'd heard of the program, much less experienced it.

I swallowed hard, cringing at my oversharing. "I hope they accept her."

After a few others spoke, the meeting ended. Then one woman came back into the room, bringing with her another woman from a different group.

"Becky, I want you to talk to my daughter," the older woman said, gesturing to her younger companion. "She worked at that Neurobehavioral Unit. When you mentioned it, I knew I had to connect you two."

I was so stunned that I could barely absorb her daughter's words. She told me that she worked there for twelve years within every role imaginable. Described how the program worked to reduce self-harm. She comforted me, encouraged me, and then gave me the best thing ever: her email.

Thank goodness I chose to use Mom's small paint-brush that day. It gave me an incredible gift—companion-ship on a journey that had promised to be so lonely.

Details matter, Mom taught me. They separate the uncommon from the ordinary. They give us hooks that link us to each other's worlds.

⁓⤙⤚⤙⤚⁓

How about you? Has the detail from a small paint brush ever given you the gift of an unexpected connection?

April 9:

Regrouping

At age twenty-four, Madison was struggling. Despite multiple trips to the ER and two psychiatric hospitalizations, her self-injurious behaviors at her day and residential programs were escalating. As a result, she was admitted to a specialized in-patient hospital unit for nine months of treatment.

One month in, we learned that Madison's day and residential programs, where she'd resided for nearly ten years, were discontinuing adult services. Shocked and frantic, we started searching for other options.

We thought we'd found the perfect choice. We passed the first round of reviews and were invited to a site visit. A final evaluation team visited Madison at the in-patient unit, and indicated that admission was likely.

But at 6:15 p.m. the stunning answer came:

"No."

Apparently, they couldn't provide the support Madison needed. I pleaded for time to address their concerns. After almost three months of searching, this was the only opening we'd found. Brainstorming with professionals who'd helped me with Madison's previous transitions, I worked until one o'clock that night and was up again at four in the morning with ideas—a transition assessment consultation, recorded staff trainings, even an internship program.

At 7:00 a.m., I sent them in.

Hours later, the answer came:

"No."

What?! My head echoed with spent efforts. My heart ached for my daughter and what I could not provide her. I was mentally depleted and physically nauseous with disbelief.

It was like an emotional hangover.

Wait, had I binged on hope?

What do you do when you think you've done every-thing possible to make something happen and it doesn't?

Regroup.

I was down, but not out. Crushed, but not destroyed. I was in the pit, but I didn't plan on staying there long.

A friend came over for dinner. We popped popcorn and lost ourselves in the world of *Downton Abbey*. The next morning, I took extra time with my coffee, inhaling it deeply while watching sweet cream bring it to life. I let time, not my agenda, rule the day. I needed to get out of the driver's seat and become a passenger.

Eventually, it was time for breakfast. Then time to let the dog out. Then the sun peeked out from some clouds, reminding me that the day was moving forward, with or without me, so I might as well get on board and see where it could go.

Refreshed, I soon resumed my search, and eventually found an even better choice.

How about you? Have you ever binged on hope? What do you do to recover from an epic fail?

April 10:

Sibling Day Lessons

National Siblings Day is April 10. As writer Alexandra Strickler points out:

> "Your siblings literally shape who you are."

Her words made me stop and consider the many roles our siblings play:

Siblings define our place in the family. As the oldest, I became the mother hen of the bunch once my siblings were old enough to take direction. Rachel, the youngest, always seemed to know how to get attention—first with her early morning wakeups, then with her non-stop chatter (Dad used to call her "Miss Walkie-Talkie"). And Forest, the only boy, took a special pride in that role, often signing his notes to Mom, "Your only begotten son."

Our siblings' interests also become part of our life. I watched Forest's football, baseball, and basketball games. I survived Rachel's short-lived (thank goodness) effort at playing the trumpet and her obsession (still alive and well) with kittens and cats. They both tolerated my brief but recital-filled pursuit of tap, jazz, and ballet, my cartwheels and handstand practices, and my even briefer stint as a cheerleader.

We may not always love what our siblings do, but what we experience with them shapes us, often leaving deep imprints.

We get to watch our siblings cope. Whether they are the star or the bench-warmer, we have the chance to observe the outside and inside of the experience. How do they express their disappointments? Their joys?

Their successes and failures affect us too. Their battles become ours as we learn firsthand the value of support and encouragement.

Our siblings guide us, like our parents, but at a more practical level. They show us (sometimes helpfully, sometimes teasingly) what to say, what not to say, and how to fit in. Their friends often become our friends.

Siblings give us the chance to compare notes when recalling memories. We often learn different things from the same experience. Sometimes we realize we were parented differently. (And after we have our own children, some of us begin to understand why.)

National Siblings Day is a day of gratitude for me. I'm thankful to have a sister, Rachel, who shares her life with me daily, even though we live eight hundred miles apart.

I'm also grateful I had a brother, Forest, who was with me only seventeen years. Even though those precious years with him led into over four decades without him, I appreciate his role in my life even more now that I am an adult.

How about you? Has your life been shaped by a sibling? Or maybe a close friend who was like a sibling to you?

April 11:

Practicing Gratitude

Shifting into a gratitude gear is the quickest way I know to nip a pity party in the bud. When I'm feeling down, I try to think of three things I am grateful for. It can be as simple as a good night's sleep, a cloudless sky, or the fact that I got the trash out on time.

I often keep a running list of things I am grateful for on my bedside table. Sometimes I add to it in the morning and review it right before I go to bed. I've noticed that when I appreciate the small things, it helps shift my perspective on whatever negative issue I'm grappling with, making it seem much less daunting than it did before.

As Brené Brown reminds us, "I don't have to chase extraordinary moments to find happiness—it's right in front of me if I'm paying attention and practicing gratitude."

⌁

How about you? What three things are you grateful for today?

April 12:

The Fear That Inspires Me

⌁

"You cannot motivate another individual," my father often said. "You can only stimulate them."

Makes you think, right? Why do we do what we do? What sparks us to action?

I'll admit it; a big one for me is FOMO, or Fear of Missing Out. Although the term didn't come into use until the early 2000s, once I was introduced to it and began to apply it, I discovered that it'd been sparking me to action for quite a while.

I think FOMO's fireworks began when my youngest left for college and my daughter and her husband moved to the West Coast. I was afraid of becoming disconnected from one of the relationships I value most: family.

So when I discovered that my kids were in a group text that I couldn't join because of the age and type of cell phone I had, FOMO struck, and I bought and learned how to use an iPhone.

When I learned that my son's wrestling coach tweeted match scores far faster than Facebook posts, FOMO hit me again, and I got up to speed on Twitter.

And when I discovered my niece was using Snapchat to communicate daily with her friends, FOMO seeped into my thinking once more, and I dug in and learned Snapchat so I could keep up with her life.

FOMO found me, once again, in one of my online classes. Everyone was sharing introductory videos, but they had to have been uploaded to YouTube. Yep, it took some real effort on that one, but I learned how to record and upload to YouTube too.

The nagging fear grabbed me, reminding me that I was going to miss out on something that mattered to me if I didn't take action.

I don't like missing out. I don't want my knowledge to limit me. (Heaven knows my paralysis limits me enough!) So with each new challenge, I gathered my courage, opened my mind, and took the time to learn something new.

I was FOMO-inspired.

For me, FOMO is a powerful stimulant, right up there with my grande nonfat cappuccino from Starbucks.

How about you? Have you ever experienced FOMO? Does it inspire you to take action and learn?

April 13:

On Sheer Will Alone

As parents, we often find ourselves in situations where our children and their circumstances are unlike ourselves and our experiences. We find life hard as we search to meet their needs, nurture their talents, and prepare them for independence on roads we have not traveled.

"I don't get it," a child tells us when struggling with homework, and we may soon find ourselves in the world of tutors and specialized instruction.

"I'm bored," a child tells us verbally or behaviorally

in the classroom, and we may soon find ourselves in search of a more challenging environment to stimulate a gifted mind.

And then there is the child who doesn't talk at all, which leads us to the complex world of disability.

When my son Matthew developed seizures at three months of age, I had trouble giving him the prescribed phenobarbital.

"How do other parents do it?" I asked the pediatric neurologist, thinking she'd have a special technique to get the baby to swallow the bitter medicine.

"In my experience," she said as she looked intently in my eyes, "it is the sheer will of the parent."

Great, I remember thinking. *That's no help.*

I wanted instruction, and she gave me philosophy.

But she was right—and over the years, that philosophy yielded the practical instruction I needed. Our "sheer wills" can provide the engines in our lives that keep us moving beyond our comfort zone and experience. And steadfast determination can make all the difference—for our children, and also for us.

How about you? Can your "sheer will" help you persevere through a challenge today?

April 14:

A Little Bit of Mischief

My sister Rachel had flown in from Georgia to spend a few days with me over the Easter holiday. This gave us the chance to continue a special family tradition: boiling and coloring Easter eggs, then facing off in our celebrated "crack-off" challenge (one person holds an egg with one end up and tries to crack an egg held by the another; the "winner" is the one whose egg doesn't crack in the hand-to-hand contest).

Through the years, our family's competitive zeal has prompted us to play many a joke on one another. My grandfather once used a wooden egg!

This year was no exception. My sissy got me. She colored a raw egg. And yes, it splattered all over me when she "won."

After we cleaned that mess up, my dog Tripp decided to investigate this new-to-him tradition, watching us crack the remaining boiled eggs. He nuzzled in between us, watching us crack each end of the egg, up close and personal.

Way too personal, we discovered, when he lurched into the cracking area, snatched the egg, and ate it shell and all!

So much for that winning egg.

But as football legend Bum Phillips once said, "Winning is only half of it. Having fun is the other half."

How about you? Do you have competitive family traditions that invite fun and mischief?

April 15:

The Momentum of Better

Although I'd maintained a gratitude journal for a while, I needed a boost. Somehow, listing observations was not giving me the forward momentum I needed.

I needed to see movement. Progression. Encouragement. I needed to see something specific that had improved over a short period of time.

So I came up with a "better" list. Before I went to bed every night, I would think of at least one thing that was better than it had been the day before.

It wasn't good. It wasn't the best. It was simply *better*.

The weather was better—partly cloudy instead of pouring rain.

I got a phone call from a friend I hadn't talked to in years.

I was able to drink eight glasses of water instead of six that day.

I reflected on what was unique about that day, something that made it better than the day before. And when I called out the "better," named it, and let its value sink in, the momentum of it got a hold of me, encouraged me, and kept me moving forward.

Perfection is rarely possible. But *some* kind of better almost always is.

❧

How about you? What is better about today than yesterday?

April 16:

Expectancy vs. Expectations

〜〜〜

Nineteen months after my paralysis, I ventured out to a seminar designed for and by spinal cord–injured patients. First, we heard an upbeat presentation on spinal cord research. Then we learned that renal failure and disease had been greatly reduced. In fact, they were no longer the leading cause of death in spinal cord–injured patients.

"The leading cause of death"—those words froze the pen in my hand as I looked up at the speaker and tried to absorb what I had just heard.

"In general, of course," he continued, "the spinal cord–injured population has a life expectancy less than the normal population."

Boom. There it was. The whole truth was out.

I suppose the fact that I was a member of the spinal cord–injured population was obvious. It's funny, though. I'd never thought of myself that way. I always felt like I was simply Becky Galli without use of her legs. It'd never occurred to me that I'd joined a group.

But if kidney problems are no longer my new group's leading cause of death, what is? I wondered.

As if he'd heard me, the speaker announced, "The current leading causes of death in the spinal cord–injured population are: 1) respiratory or pulmonary complications, and 2) suicide/accident."

My notes stopped there. But I couldn't help wondering afterward what would be the cause of my death. Is it really more likely to happen to me solely because I sit in this ridiculous wheelchair? More importantly, am I going to let it change my expectations in life?

So, when I got home, I wrote my expectations down:

- I expect to grow as a parent, nurturing my children and creating an environment for their success.
- I expect to publish my writing.
- I expect to become as independent as I can be *from* the wheelchair. I want to vacation, to travel, to experience as much of life as possible from this contraption I must use.
- I expect to be ready for recovery, however small it may be.
- I expect to become involved in at least one major philanthropic effort that will benefit those with my disabilities or the disabilities of my children.

After listing all these out, I felt sure about one thing: my life expectancy would not change my expectations in life.

How about you? What expectations do you have in life right now?

April 17:

Rethinking Old Habits

My father once told me the story of a newlywed couple enjoying a meal together.

"Honey, why do you cut both ends of the ham off before cooking it?" he asked his bride.

"Because my mother did it that way," she replied, finishing the side dishes and sitting down at the table.

Sometime later, the husband spoke with his mother-in-law, during which conversation he dutifully raved about the ham feast her daughter had prepared. When asked the secret of cutting both ends of the ham, the mother replied, "Why, it was to make it fit into the pan!"

I had to laugh, thinking of other times in life I'd done things without really thinking about why.

We all can get stuck in our ruts for the wrong reasons. We may unknowingly inherit not only routine ways of doing things, but also routine ways of *thinking* about things. From heirloom recipes to unintended biases, we may need to poke each with a good "why?" from time to time to reevaluate for usefulness or relevance.

How about you? Do you have a legacy habit or mindset that's ripe for rethinking?

April 18:

Tag-Teaming Family

"We're not going to make it—we're absolutely not going to make it," Brittany mumbled as she tended to ten-month-old Blakely Faye.

We were supposed to arrive in Columbia, South Carolina, at three in the afternoon, but our GPS said we would get there at four thirty—for the six o'clock wedding.

"We're not going to make it," Brittany kept repeating. "We have too much to do!"

Her panic was understandable. Before going to the ceremony, we had to check in, unload, shower, get dressed, get dinner ready for Blakely, and feed her. And my niece Ashley would be babysitting Blakely for the first time that night.

"I need to show Ashley the nighttime routines, Mom," Brittany said, her eyes searching mine. "I thought we'd have more time for them to get to know one another."

Although a happy baby and good traveler, Blakely was in a separation anxiety phase. She preferred her mom to anyone else.

"Rachel's there now," I said. "She can grab some food for Blakely. What will she eat?"

I jotted down the foods and called my sister to craft our arrival plan. Rachel pre-checked our rooms to confirm that mine was accessible and adjoined to Brittany and Brian's room. Rachel's husband David and her daughter Ashley, our babysitter, picked up Blakely's food, met us in the lobby, and helped us carry the luggage to our rooms.

From my room, I could hear my daughter instructing her twenty-year-old cousin.

"Blakely can feed herself. I'll change her. Then we'll put on her pajamas. After I leave, give her a bottle. Put her down in the crib, no blankets. Leave her for a little bit, she will cry and then go to sleep. Text me if you have questions, Ash."

I closed the door to our adjoining room to finish getting ready. Minutes later, we all met up in the hall.

"Is Ashley set, Britty?" I asked.

"I think so," she said. Although Ashley was comfortable babysitting, she didn't have much experience with babies.

"She'll be fine," Brian said, taking Brittany's hand.

After the ceremony, Ashley's pictures lit up our phones.

"Looks like she's having fun, Britty!" I said.

"Wait," she said, "she's texting questions."

"Is everything alright?" Brian snuck in behind her to read the text.

They both burst out laughing.

"What's funny?" I demanded. "What happened?"

"Well, apparently Blakely fell asleep without crying. Ashley wanted to know if it was okay to skip that step!"

We all doubled over with laughter.

"Now that's a rookie question!" I said.

"Blakely doesn't usually cry," Brittany said, "but I wanted to prepare Ashley, just in case."

Little Blakely slept well that night. She and Ashley became fast friends and we all enjoyed the time together. It took a team effort to make it happen—but isn't that what family is all about?

How about you? What tag-team efforts have you experienced with your family that have made a complicated situation easier?

April 19:

Weathering Storms

Sometimes life's troubles layer their heaviness upon us like stratus clouds—uniform, wide-ranging, and grey. We aren't in a pit. Yet, we can't see clearly what's next. It's hard to find the will to weather the storm, much less press on through it.

In her book *Cherished*, Kim Crabill offers a story with a soundbite that may help:

> An elderly woman was asked to share her favorite passage in the Bible for facing tough times.
>
> "It came to pass," she said confidently.
>
> Puzzled, the group leader asked her to clarify.
>
> "Well," she explained, "It came to *pass* reminds me that it didn't come to *stay*!"

I chuckled out loud when I first read that story. But those words, "It came to pass," continue to help me, even prompting a smile, when life's storms threaten. I often go outside and look up. Both clouds and shadows move, and the rain doesn't last forever.

How about you? Could this interpretation of "it came to pass" help you through a time of trouble?

April 20:

Spring Awakening

She's teased us for weeks. But finally, she's getting serious and beginning to dominate.

Spring has flexed her muscles, pushing her way through winter's tight grasp. Granted, an occasional skirmish results in flip-flops one day and boots the next. But spring is gaining momentum. She may have passed the point of no return. Perhaps this season of growth and renewal is here to stay.

With spring's arrival, nature reawakens.

In our gardens, frozen futures thaw, releasing winter-stored energies into bushes sprouting new growth, tinged with color. Trees trimmed in the lace of spring prepare for the load of full-grown leaves and brace themselves for summer winds that will demand strength through flexibility.

With spring's arrival, human nature reawakens too.

A little boy stops by a garden wall and leans his bicycle, pausing for a few moments to contemplate the tulips and stealing a smell. Joggers strip to shorts, hanging up winter warm-ups, basking in the freedom of lighter loads and longer days. Park benches sport more clientele as people-watching resumes in the warmth of the gentle spring sun. Even the voices of people strolling down the sidewalk seem more vibrant, with an energized cadence and pitch fueled by the newness in the air.

Our molecules seem to move faster as spring invites us to participate in her rebirth.

Yet spring's fickle nature reminds us that daily life, like the weather, is constantly changing. There are ups and downs, joys and sorrows, successes and failures. No two days are alike in this transitional season; no two days are the same in the arena of life.

Nevertheless, as we witness spring's steadfast progress we can be inspired to keep pressing forward as well, toward the good that we know is ahead.

I love how writer Susan J. Bissonett describes it:

"An optimist is the human personification of spring."

Yes! Now's the time to let spring's optimistic nature inspire ours.

How about you? How will you let spring enhance your optimism?

April 21:

The Courage to Trust

I had a migraine, but I kept my commitment to tape an interview with writer and podcast host Kim Acedo. The next day, I was concerned that I hadn't been at my best, so I asked if we should re-tape. Kim assured me the interview was fine and even offered to have me on her show again.

Without listening to it, I let her publish it.

Why?

I trusted her.

Brené Brown, research professor and best-selling author, would say that this was the beginning of a courageous moment. In her Netflix talk *The Call to Courage*, she suggested there is no courage without vulnerability.

But to be vulnerable, we need to trust.

"Trust comes before vulnerability," Brown emphasized.

Why did I trust Kim?

In the months prior to our interview, I'd joined her email list and listened to her podcasts. We'd exchanged information about writing disciplines and technical support for our online platforms. We'd come to value each other's opinions, and I knew we shared mutual goals.

I trusted that she would not want me to fail.

Courage does require vulnerability; I can see that. We put ourselves at risk when we "walk into the arena" of uncontrolled outcomes. Like my migraine moment with Kim, trust was essential for my willingness to be vulnerable, my willingness to get in that arena and risk failure.

The challenge becomes how to create enough trust to risk failure. With Kim, I managed to get there.

And guess what? The interview turned out to be just fine.

How about you? How do you build trust? When is the last time trust enabled you to have a courageous action?

April 22:

Once Only Hoped For

It'd been one of those mornings. I'd stayed up way too late the night before. Squirrels had run around in my head for most of the time I was supposed to be sleeping. I'd woken up groggy and tired and was having a hard time getting it into gear.

I was stuck in neutral, idling.

Then I read this quote from Epicurus: "Do not spoil what you have by desiring what you have not; remember that what you now have was once among the things you only hoped for."

Hmm.

. . . what you now have was once among the things you only hoped for.

That was a new thought for me, perfect for my neutral gear. As I mulled it over, I started looking around the room at the ordinary things that I had that I had once only hoped for.

The blooming flowers on my deck. Weeks ago, the planters had sat empty, begging for spring temperatures to make them safe for planting. I now enjoyed those flowers, once only hoped for, every morning.

The polished black boots perched on my footplates. Six months before, I'd needed to find boots that were easy for me to put on but were tight enough to keep my ankles from swelling. I'd searched online and in stores for months—leather, mid-calf with a zipper, extra wide but fitted through the ankle—and I'd finally found a pair (of course I bought two!). I now wore those boots, once only hoped for, every day at home.

My dog resting peacefully beside me. In their teenage years, my kids wanted a dog. After they pleaded, researched, and even wrote a proposal for me, we visited a pet shop and Tripp became our family dog. Fifteen years later, that dog, once only very much hoped for, was my beloved companion.

As I observed what I had and then considered its history, a fresh perspective lifted my spirits. I was so lucky! It was time to start appreciating it.

How about you? What do you have now that was once only hoped for?

April 23:

Guarding Serenity

"God grant me the serenity to accept the things I cannot change; courage to change the things I can; and wisdom to know the difference."

This prayer from Reinhold Niebuhr is revered in my family; we've come to protect it quite fiercely, albeit playfully.

Serenity is a named priority, guarded by accepting what we can't change.

But we also work hard to keep it and not letting others take it. We've become mindful of who or what situation is trying to take our serenity from us as well as our role in giving it away.

"You're not taking my serenity," I've heard more than once in our household during a disagreement that was becoming heated.

"I was upset, Ma, but they didn't get my serenity," one of my children reported after a challenging conversation with a colleague.

Treating serenity as a prized possession has helped me keep silent when my opinion hasn't been asked for and to stay in my lane when I've been tempted to meddle in others' business.

We may not be able to control how we feel about a situation, but weighing its impact on our serenity can give us the time needed to consider a more thoughtful response.

How about you? How do you guard your serenity?

April 24:

Suffering Is Optional

The parallel-paths concept that my therapist had introduced to me came to the rescue again when I was first paralyzed and needed to pursue two outcomes at once:

Would I walk again—or not?

The facts didn't help. One third of those affected by transverse myelitis recover fully. One third recover partially. One third have no recovery at all.

Which third would I be a part of? When would I know?

To help me cope and stay "in gear," I defined my parallel paths. On the path of no recovery at all, I took driving lessons, learned how to swim, joined two advisory boards for the disabled, and researched permanent modifications to my home to make it more accessible.

On the path of full recovery, I bought a power stander machine to help lift me to practice standing, a workout table so I could continue the exercises I'd learned in rehab to avoid further muscle atrophy, and started dietary supplements to address bone-loss issues that could complicate any future hope for walking. I also heavily researched nerve regeneration progress and subscribed to Internet lists to keep current on all spinal cord–recovery research.

As I journeyed on both paths, two things happened. First, I became more engaged in the present—a present where there were unfortunately no signs of recovery. Then I gradually began to let go of the past and the life I wanted back so badly. This process brought with it its own pain. Letting go of dreams was loss, just as real as the loss of the use of my legs.

A new motto helped:

"Pain is inevitable; suffering is optional."

It became my mission not to suffer. I found that parallel paths kept suffering in check. Pursuing two paths required a vigilance that left little time for suffering.

In time, the path of no recovery became my reality. In the meantime, parallel paths helped keep me moving forward, easing me into the new reality while minimizing suffering.

How about you? How could you use parallel paths to help you through a painful situation?

April 25:

Going On

It's a favorite phrase I like to use when I'm wrapping up a conversation or signing off from a column: "And on we go . . ."

But after six weeks of isolation during the COVID-19 pandemic, the idea of "going on" eluded me. Life had lost its punctuation. It felt like one giant run-on sentence, with no commas, semicolons, or colons to segment it in clarifying ways. There wasn't a period in sight.

But there were plenty of questions marks:

- *How long will this go on?*
- *Will I get the virus? If I do, can I survive it?*
- *When will it be safe to resume the life I knew?*
- *How can I possibly know how to "go on" when I'm not sure exactly where I am?*

The unanswered questions closed in. The uncertainty of not knowing what was next sent me into that place I fight so hard to avoid—the pity pool.

After a while, though, I grew frustrated with my meltdown. I know how to get through tough times. My life is riddled with no cause/no cure experiences; one child's autism, another child's epilepsy, and my own paralysis. I'm a veteran of dealing with unexplained adversity.

Why couldn't I use what I'd learned and get on with life?

Because, my tears reminded me, you can't deny the pain of loss, or skip over its steadfast companion—grief.

Grief. Was that what was I was experiencing?

Then the words of Robert Frost guided me yet again:

"The best way out is always through."

Of course! There are no shortcuts around the valley of pain and loss and its sidekick, grief. I needed to treat this unpunctuated life as what it was: one more journey through grief.

When grief had disoriented me in the past, I'd learned to focus on the present and what I needed to do right then to care for myself: Sleep. Nutrition. Exercise. Connection to others.

But I also considered what I allowed to take up space in my mind. Although I wanted to be informed, I limited my news consumption while increasing time spent with nature. I sought out messages of patience and hope, and I slowed down my routines so I could sense the slightest progression.

After a while, I felt the momentum of forward motion once again and could say with newfound conviction and great relief:

"And on we go . . ."

❧

How about you? Have you ever experienced a hard time and realized you were grieving? What helped you keep going?

April 26:

Energy-Zapping Tolerations

For seven years, I overlooked it.

Literally.

When I wheeled up and down my driveway to walk the dog or grab the morning paper, it glared at me:

Bermuda grass.

It didn't bother me as much during the summer, when it blended in with the fescue grass that was supposed to rule my lawn. But when it refused to grow as quickly in the spring or die as slowly in the fall as the rest of its neighboring grass, the lazy brown patches annoyed me.

The words of my father, who practically manicured his lawn year-round, kept playing in my mind. "That's Bermuda grass," he'd often said when we passed lawns peppered with burnt-looking spots. "It can take over your lawn. Fast-growing. You can't crowd it out, either. You have to kill the roots."

Each spring and fall I'd remember, sigh, and then naively hope it would go away.

But it didn't.

The grass wasn't to blame, though. In the right environment—golf courses, Florida lawns, and croquet fields—it was fabulous. But in my area, it was a pest, an eyesore that intruded on the part of my day where I sought nature's inspiration, not relentless problems.

My lawn care company said to seed it with fescue and fertilize heavily. We tried for two years. The patch got larger. Another company offered to dig it up, replacing it with sod. That price tag didn't fit my budget. So I tolerated it, and over the years watched a small patch become a twenty-yards-long-and-almost-as-wide menace.

Finally, I found a company who specialized in eliminating Bermuda grass. They would kill it, aerate the ground, and replant plugs of fescue.

"Your lawn won't be pretty for a while," they warned. "But we have to make sure the roots are dead before replanting."

Their plan worked. And I couldn't believe the relief I felt when I got rid of that toleration. I'd never realized how much mental space that unresolved issue was stealing from me.

Perhaps tolerations are energy zaps, like the unused windows on my desktop or apps on my iPhone. Too many open ones take up space, slowing response times and even the ability to open new windows or applications.

What once annoyed me now energizes me. Those sprouting fescue plugs work just as well as my Starbucks cappuccino.

Well, almost.

How about you? Are there any energy-zappers in your life that you've shut down lately, or need to work on shutting down?

April 27:

Unseen Processes

Beyond the steadfastness of sunrises, spring has much to teach us. Nature, in all her glory, demonstrates the courage to relax in the mystery of what we cannot see.

Mark Nepo calls this "The Courage of the Seed." In *The Book of Awakening*, he writes, "All around us, everything small and buried surrenders to a process that none of the buried parts can see."

How true! Oh, to be like the seed—to rely on unseen forces that will nurture us, sustain us, and foster a growth we cannot imagine.

As my father often reminded me, especially when struggling through a difficult time with unclear choices, "BB, honey, sometimes we have to trust the process."

I smile at those words. I remember challenging them a few times. It seemed so passive to release control of a situation to the unknown when I was sure there must be something I could do to fix it.

"But Dad," I protested once, "I thought you taught us, 'What's planned is possible.'"

And he had. He walked that talk in every stage of his life.

"Still true, BB," he said with a nod. "But sometimes we don't know all the possibilities. We do what we can and then we have to trust."

And so spring reminds us to have the courage to surrender, to trust, and to be confident in the processes we cannot see.

❧

How about you? Do you have trouble trusting processes outside your control?

April 28:

No, I Love You

The story is a family classic. I was seven years old. My sister Rachel was three.

The rain was coming down in torrents, one of those gully-washing, gutter-bending downpours. Rachel stood in the den looking intently through the window at the rain.

Our father walked into the room.

She turned and fixed her mischievous green eyes on him. "Diddy," she said, using her pet name for Dad, "can I go out and play?"

Dad glanced outside. It was still raining.

"Sure," he said, masking his tease. "You can go out."

"But it's raining out there," she reminded him, pointing outside.

"I know."

"But I'll get wet."

"Yep, you probably will."

"If I get wet, I might get sick too!" she exclaimed, raising her voice.

"That could happen," he said seriously.

And then, with a real trace of hurt in her voice, she said, "Diddy, you don't love me?!"

I smile at my sister's unvarnished honesty in this moment. Rarely do children explain their sometimes-outlandish requests and actions with such transparency. They're usually more subtle and veiled in conveying their feelings.

But the motivation is the same. They want to know, "Am I loved?"

Rebellion, defiance, antagonism—all are often nothing more than attempts for children to learn if they are loved. Sometimes they test parents just to see how far they are allowed to go before they hear a good, solid, no. Because that no says, "I love you."

Oh, they will fume, fuss, and want to fight about it. But down deep inside, they know they have heard what they wanted to hear.

Restrictions and rules are the backboard against which a child can rebound while they are growing their own set of self-restraints. Over-permissiveness is not necessarily an expression of love; it may be the opposite. Sometimes it is easier to say yes and keep the smiles coming. No nagging. No arguing. Household peace reigns.

On the other hand, being overly strict or coercive doesn't automatically demonstrate love either. It may be spawned by a parent's inner fears, frustrations, or insecurities, stifling the necessary growth that only measured freedoms can bring.

The balance can be tricky.

And yet firm boundaries show we care. And thoughtful consequences show how deeply.

How about you? What boundaries have you set or faced that showed love?

April 29:

Whys and Hows

Albert Einstein's quote wouldn't leave me alone:

> "The important thing is to not stop questioning."

Is it? I questioned.

Ha.

I was still recovering from a seventeen-day hospital stay for post-procedure sepsis, and I had a lot of questions:

> *Why did this happen? How did this happen? What can I do to prevent it from ever happening again?*

It was exhausting—and yet Einstein encourages it. Is it really healthy to keep questioning, especially when there are no clear answers?

Then I considered the value of questions—both the ones we ask ourselves and the ones posed by others. Questions can convey care, concern, and curiosity. But asking questions can also be a risky business. They can reveal our ignorance, the limits of our understanding, and even our lack of sensitivity.

We are vulnerable to the indignant *You-don't-know-that? Haven't-you-paid-attention?* response as well as the puzzling look of annoyance that says, *You-are-asking-me-that? Can't-you-see-the-hurt-it-may-cause?*

It's a wonder we dare ask anything!

Yet we persist.

We are curious beings, relentless in our pursuit to understand, to grow, and to relate. At some point, however, despite our best research and investigations, we will fail to find satisfying answers to our questions.

What do we do then?

It's been a lifelong battle for me. Why my brother's death at age seventeen? Why my son's degenerative disease? Why my daughter's autism? Why my paralysis?

The more useful question, I've learned, is not why, but *how. How can I live fully within these questions?* Perhaps that is the real value of continuing to question, as Einstein suggests.

Questions open our minds to new information that can revitalize our thinking, enable our empathy, and expand our knowledge. If unanswered, they still have value, reminding us to respect and revere the mysteries of life, even as we let them rest gently.

Questions, answerable or not, kick us into gear, whether it's to learn and grow or absorb and accept. And, most important, they keep us moving forward, engaging with others along the way.

⚜

How about you? Do you have a why in your life that needs to pivot to a how?

April 30:

Letting Laughter Overcome

After three years of paralysis, I'd finally purchased a customized minivan. With the flick of a switch, the floor lowered six inches and a ramp unfolded to the ground. Hand controls gave the driver the option of using hands or feet to drive. Although not a driver yet, I was transported in the van routinely.

During a visit from my parents, we braved a trip to the mall. I entered the van, parked my wheelchair, and buckled the shoulder strap. I didn't bother with the straps that anchored my wheels to the floor since they were cumbersome and difficult to maneuver. Instead, I opted to use the handle on the back of the passenger seat to stabilize myself. This was no different, I reasoned, than bus passengers hanging on to the rails.

As Mom and I chatted and I put lotion on my chapped hands, Dad climbed into the driver seat.

"Are we ready?" he asked.

Before we could answer, the van lurched forward, jolting everyone backwards. I lunged for the seat handle, but my lotioned hands slipped. I flipped on my back. My lifeless legs sprawled above me, leaving me staring at the ceiling, turtle-style.

Mom gasped. "Oh, Becky, are you alright?"

"You okay, honey?" Dad exclaimed, turning around to look.

"Yes," I sighed. "I'm okay."

As Mom looked at me, she began to shake. She quickly turned away, but the shaking continued.

"Mom?"

She couldn't answer.

"Mom!"

Finally, she turned to look at me.

"Mom, you're laughing!"

"BB," Dad said with a chuckle, "your mom is tickled. You know how she gets when she gets tickled."

I looked at Dad through my airborne legs and the hilarity of the situation struck me too. I laughed, watching Mom's bout of tickle-box turnover escalate. She was already at the nonverbal stage, and tears soon followed.

"What did you do to make the van start off like that, Dad?"

"Well, I thought I'd check out these hand-controls," he replied. "I'd say they're a tad sensitive."

Laughing through the process, I was upright and operational within twenty minutes.

Thankfully, I've inherited that tickle-box from Mom and am forever grateful for it. Humor is a wonderful life-long companion. It can give perspective, twist reality into amusement, and lighten heavy discussions with a shift of wit.

Too often, we let grief, pain, and fear overcome us. What a beautiful change of pace it can be to let humor overcome us.

⟿⟆⟿

How about you? Do you ever let laughter overcome you?

MAY

May 1:

Embracing Susceptibility

It was hard to admit, but I fit all the criteria—medical history, age, and underlying health conditions. All of those annoying challenges from life as a paraplegic, the limitations I try so hard to discount, were highlighted regularly in the early stages of the pandemic. Daily, if not hourly, I was reminded:

I was susceptible to COVID-19.

Like most of life's hard times, this one required me to accept what I couldn't change so that I could get on with living in and through a new reality.

The most important thing I could do was to put my health first so I didn't require medical attention. Like many others, I self-quarantined and stocked up on food, medications, and medical supplies. I developed systems and protocols for accepting meals, packages, and the mail.

For my mental health, I chatted regularly with friends, family, caregivers, and my team of medical professionals.

Thankfully, I stayed healthy and safe.

That word, *susceptible*, still stung from time to time, however. When it began to darken my mood, drain my energy, or create a defensive posture that started to shrink my view of the world, I reminded myself of my mom's sage advice: "BB, honey, you need a change of scenery."

So I'd take my faithful companion, Tripp, and we'd go outside.

Nature has a way of infusing her confidence into mine. She never disappoints. In fact, when I'm open to her influence, she energizes me, even encourages me with her unspoken messages. As I moseyed up and down the driveway, the steadfastness of spring's debut prompted me to look at susceptibility in a different way.

Perhaps it could be a gift.

Maybe I could allow susceptibility to enlarge my world instead of limiting it. Perhaps I could open my mind and be susceptible to the positive influences around me—the kindness and generosity of others, friends' creative expressions of love and concern, and the novel ways we were all inventing to spend time with one another in that unprecedented time of isolation.

My body may have made me susceptible to COVID-19, but I was determined to keep my mind in learning mode, susceptible to all the positive gifts I could find.

How about you? What unexpected gifts could you discover if you embraced susceptibility?

May 2:

Funk-Busters

I couldn't get in gear. My list stared back at me, unchecked and glaring. I felt inertia begin to creep in. Was it the beginning of a funk?

Then I remembered an acronym my sister Rachel had introduced me to years earlier. "When you can't focus and think you may be sinking into a funk, remember to HALT," she said. "Ask yourself if you are: Hungry, Angry, Lonely, or Tired."

Sure enough, I was tired that day. I hadn't been sleeping well for the last two nights. So I rearranged my plans to allow for an earlier bedtime and even snuck in a quick nap.

It helped!

Rachel's checklist continues to be my first step when I feel a funk coming on.

- If I'm hungry, I grab a healthy snack.
- If I'm angry, I try to resolve it or at least journal or talk through it with a friend or professional.
- If I'm lonely, I call a friend or family member, especially my sweet sissy.
- If I'm tired, I make time for extra rest.

How about you? Could this checklist help you bust a funk?

May 3:

Dreams in Action

My good friend Beth was climbing Mount Everest. She wasn't a hiker, runner, or rock climber. She was a carpooling mother of four with a huge heart and, apparently, an even bigger sense of adventure.

Although she'd traveled in an organized group with itineraries and professional guides, she'd gone on the three-week trek alone, inviting no family or friends to join her. She'd begun the journey in Kathmandu, Nepal. Her destination: Mount Everest Base Camp, more than 18,000 feet above sea level.

When she'd first told me of her plans, I couldn't decide if she were brave or stupid. Who invites such adversity into their life? Some of us have had quite enough, thank you very much.

Granted, she was not attempting to summit this beast of a mountain. Nevertheless, this trek was incredibly arduous, especially the adjustments to the terrain, weather, and altitude. Some do not finish. One fellow trekker, an avid hiker and rock climber, fell prey to altitude sickness mid-journey and had to be evacuated.

But Beth was going strong. And some of us were "virtually" tagging along. Through the wonders of a specialized GPS tracking-and-messaging device, Beth's husband Tom faithfully updated 114 admirers throughout the trek. We could click on a link and see a satellite picture of her progress online, updated every fifteen minutes.

But Beth's detailed notes were what made it real for me. Wild dogs followed the group for a while. In one village they needed the protection of a red ribbon around their neck to avoid an army's guns. Dinner one evening included a special treat—fried Spam. She had no shower for thirteen days and slept in the same clothes for two days since it was "too cold to take them off."

Tom sprinkled his updates with quotes sent to Beth for encouragement.

"Not all those who wander are lost," her mother (and Tolkien) advised.

"You miss 100 percent of the shots you do not take," husband Tom (and Wayne Gretzky) offered.

Watching Beth put her dreams into action, I thought about all the dreams some of us have left lying listless on the table.

As we turn the corner of spring to face the new pace of summer, perhaps we need permission to wander a bit too. And to take one of those "shots" off the table . . . and put it into action.

⁓⧢⤳

How about you? What dreams do you have lying on the table, ready for action?

May 4:

Something New

"What did you learn in school today?" my father was asked by his grandfather every time they saw each other when my father was a boy.

And "nothing" was not an acceptable answer. Dad's grandfather expected him to both learn and talk about his learning, to share his knowledge with the world.

These conversations connected my father to his grandfather in a special way. It also affirmed for him the importance of learning something every day.

Learning makes us better people. So does trying new things.

It's okay to occasionally do something new and announce, "Never again!" That shows you have pushed yourself out of your comfort zone. Foie gras? Never again for me. I liked it—but my body didn't. It really didn't. So, never again, but I learned something new.

For my closure party after my divorce, I designed hot pink T-shirts that said, "When's the last time you did something for the first time?"

Love that. Still do.

Learning keeps us growing. And growing helps us stay positive.

How about you? When's the last time you did something for the first time? Did you like it? Or was it a "never again" for you? Either way, are you glad you did it?

May 5:

The Black Chair

When I was twelve, Forest ten, and Rachel nine, we decided to address an equity issue that had been brewing for some time. We filed silently into our parents' bedroom.

Dad sat in his black leather chair while Mom stretched out on the bed, both reading the newspaper. With my siblings flanking me, I boldly addressed our father.

"Dad, who do we tell off when we get mad?"

He put down the paper and studied our faces. "What do you mean?"

"When you and Mom get mad, you tell us off. So, who do we tell off when we get mad?"

"Me . . . your mother . . . both of us."

"No way," I shot back, but then added, "sir."

Rachel and Forest nodded appropriately. Gladys Knight may have had the Pips, but I had my brother and sister for backup.

"We don't dare tell you off when we get mad," I said. "You'd punish us!"

The Pips uttered affirmations.

Dad sat up and pressed his fingertips together, his signature gesture for deep thought. "Okay," he began. "Anytime I'm sitting in this black chair, you can tell me off. You can say anything that's on your mind."

Mom raised both eyebrows and then nodded in agreement.

"But you'll get mad and punish us," I protested.

Dad paused, then leaned forward, elbows on knees. "So, I can't promise I will not get mad—but I do promise I will not punish you for what you say."

Wide-eyed and open-mouthed, we froze . . . but rallied quickly.

"When can we get started?" I asked.

"Now."

And we were off. For over an hour, we unloaded every injustice we could remember, naming date and time, chapter and verse. It was great! We could tell them anything, unafraid of punishment.

In time, the Black Chair became our code name for a safe place to talk. The kitchen table chair was the Black Chair when one of us shared about having our first beer. The living room lounger became the Black Chair when another shared the confession of a sleepover at a friend's house—that wasn't. And the back-porch rocker became the Black Chair when a heartbroken sixteen-year-old wondered aloud if she would ever be asked out on that first date.

The Black Chair fostered openness—a safe place to be truthful without fear of consequence.

How about you? Have you ever provided a safe place to talk or been given one?

May 6:

What Counts

The jogger's T-shirt made me smile:

Nothing Behind You Counts.

Maybe. Maybe not.

I considered that point as I watched the symbolic tassel move at my nephew's high school graduation.

For those heading to college, a new year and new school is a fresh start—a unique opportunity to reinvent themselves. They can leave their reputations in the past and discard their high school roles with one swipe of that tassel.

Yet only a few months earlier, everything behind them counted. Those college applications demanded to know who they were, complete with supporting evidence to prove it. Grades, test scores, class rank, teacher recommendations, and essays short and long were required, based on the premise that *everything* behind them counted.

What a mixed message!

As I mulled all this over, the high school principal offered a more elegant view: "The moving of the tassel," he told the crowd, "represents the opening of a curtain and is symbolic of the opening of one's mind to the next act of life. It moves from right to left, coming to rest over the heart."

And maybe that's the real message of "nothing behind you counts": keep opening new curtains to the next acts of life.

"Past is prologue," Shakespeare reminds us. We can't discount it altogether. But if we allow the negatives of the past to count more than the positives in the present it can become a burden, narrowing that open mind we need for the next act of life.

So we must put the past in its place—even as we strive to keep our minds open to the future.

How about you? How do you stay open to the future without discounting what's come before?

May 7:

Exhaustion's Respite

Sometimes we should welcome exhaustion. It simplifies life.

We're too tired to get into mischief. Too tired to worry or obsess. Too tired to care about anything except for the basic necessities in life.

It may be the good kind of exhaustion, the kind we feel when we've given a project everything we've got to achieve a goal.

Or it may be the unexpected exhaustion, the kind we feel when something beyond our control has sucked up our energy without our permission.

Regardless, exhaustion often clarifies what's important. We get back to the skeleton of our basic needs, the necessities that the rhythm of daily life requires.

Good sleep. Good food. Good plans, structure, and support for how to replenish what's been depleted.

Exhaustion gives us what our minds and bodies require: respite for recovery.

❧

How about you? When has exhaustion provided a needed respite for you?

May 8:

Seasonal Mindsets

I was in a quandary about canceling plans because my body, once again, was misbehaving. Although I was recovering from a recent hospital stay, I was eager to resume my usual activities.

"I feel like a wimp," I lamented to my friend Cheryl.

"With all you've been through," she responded, "'wimp' has no place in the realm of wise choices. Whatever your body tells you is what will keep you at your best."

Relieved, I thanked her—but added, "For the record, sometimes I hate being so 'wise.' I miss being a risk-taker—and succeeding."

She gave me pause with her next comment: "Risk-taking has its seasons. It's okay to be in the season of wisdom now."

Wow.

The season of wisdom. I wasn't sure how I felt about that promotion. What did it mean? Would I always be limited? Could I ever take a risk again?

Perhaps the challenge in the season of wisdom is to hold new limitations lightly, letting them move through us much like we navigate each year's seasons, adapting as necessary. Then wisdom is less about "giving in" to the limitations and more about "accepting for now" the choices that are in our best interests.

How about you? Can a seasonal mindset help you make choices that are in your best interests today?

May 9:

Doing the Work

Madison had been denied admittance to a residential program that I thought was the perfect fit for her. Would she have to go out of state to get the services she needed?

"You must first exhaust all the possibilities within the state of Maryland," I was told. "Here is the link to the website."

I pulled up the page, a sea of blue lines that linked to over 200 agencies. There wasn't a way to sort for openings. But most listed an email contact.

As I thought about these email addresses, the holders of the future of my daughter's next home, I tried to envision their decision-making process and crafted this subject line:

Subject: URGENT: Opening for adult female for residential and day program? Y or N.

Then I briefly listed Madison's needs in the email.

For ten hours one Saturday and Sunday, I copied, pasted, and emailed 229 providers and updated my tracking spreadsheet. My goal was to send all requests by Sunday evening and wait for replies to trickle in.

Wrong! Sunday afternoon, yes *Sunday* afternoon, I started getting responses. At 2:38 p.m. I sent one email; at 2:47 p.m. I had my first positive response! Many came with encouraging notes:

- "We don't have an opening, but wish you the very best in your search for the perfect housing for Madison!"
- "I know this process can be very frustrating for families and wish you the best."
- "We don't have an opening but are willing to look at the possibility of renting a house to accommodate your daughter."

By Sunday evening, I had fourteen responses. By the end of the week, I had twenty-seven positive responses. I was impressed—not only by the responsiveness, but also by the heartfelt good wishes.

Maybe I shouldn't have been surprised. After all, these people were in the business of caring, a fact easily forgotten when it's hidden behind that sea of blue lines.

Perhaps I should even be grateful that Madison *wasn't* accepted into the first program. I would never have guessed there were so many possibilities for her.

I guess sometimes you have to ditch the drama of trying to understand why something happened and simply *do the work*.

The results can be surprising.

How about you? Have you recovered from a setback by doing the work? Were the results surprising?

May 10:

Mama Attacks

She was a good family friend. In her early forties, with almost-grown children of her own, she'd flown in to visit her mother. My father spotted her in the congregation one Sunday morning and made his way over to chat.

"How long are you here?" he asked her.

"I flew in late Friday night and I am leaving today on the 1:50 p.m. plane," she said.

"What did you come for, a match?" my father joked. Our relatives from the hills of North Carolina used that comment when our visits were brief, harking back to colonial days when matches were scarce and people traveled long distances just for a match and then hurried home to start their fires.

"No," she said. "I just had a 'Mama Attack' and had to see my mother."

A Mama Attack. I knew that feeling. I'd had many through the years. Those times when sharp pangs of nostalgia sent me in search of the comforts of home, where responsibilities were small and the "buck" didn't stop with me. Where there were others there for me—older, wiser—who'd known and cared about me from birth on and could buffer the weight of whatever pressures were overwhelming me.

Those returns home provided a safe haven from whatever life storm was brewing. Perhaps it provided comfort to my parents too.

I remember my father calling my siblings and me to the family room for no apparent reason on various occasions throughout our childhood.

"What do you want, Dad?" we'd ask.

"Oh, nothing. I wanted to be around you—just to smell you," he'd say with that teasing grin of his.

And we'd shake our heads, smile, and bring whatever we were doing into the room.

Maybe he was having a "Children Attack."

I now know that feeling too. Before each of my children's visits home, no matter how brief, I dive deep into my memory bank to recall the details of what made our family time special. Was it the recipes? The conversations? Or was it just being together, smelling each other, and letting the time in each other's midst knit us closer?

Most often, the answer is a simple one: a good meal with lots of time for talking—but mostly listening.

How about you? How to you make the most of your visits with family—even brief ones?

May 11:

Bloom Where You're Planted

The plaque still sits on my kitchen shelf. It reads:

BLOOM WHERE YOU ARE PLANTED.

My mother embodied those words.

As a minister's wife, she moved six times in twenty-five years. I never saw her struggle with the transitions—yet she was there for me as I struggled with each of mine. I went to elementary school in one city, middle school in another, attended high school in yet one more, and was a freshman in college during the last move. Every step of the way, she not only guided me but also showed me how to "bloom" where I was planted.

Here's what I learned:

Get involved. Mom found opportunities to plug in, learn, and contribute. From Sunday School teacher to Den Mother to Grade Parent to "hostess with the mostest" for Garden Club, she knew the importance not just of participating but *engaging*, no matter what her experience level. She wasn't afraid to be a rookie or a leader and was always willing to grow or give.

Nurture relationships. Friendships matter. Mom knew that and lived it. "To have a friend, you need to be a friend," she often said. She kept a calendar by her kitchen chair with hearts and stars marking her friends' and family's birthdays, anniversaries, and other special days. Although she shunned the computer, she was a gifted and vigilant note writer. Mom cared for people in a real way, remembering their special days and rejoicing and crying with them as they moved through the celebrations and sorrows of their lives. She was a great listener.

Stay patient and receptive. This one is sometimes hard for me, but I still strive for it. Mom eased into new situations slowly, observantly. She was gracious, never demanding. She never rushed. In fact, she didn't like for us to even use the term "hurry up." Instead, she encouraged, "Take your time." She didn't mind waiting, always finding something to do in the meantime, whether crocheting, reading, or chatting with a stranger to make a new friend.

Mom taught me so much, but how to flourish anywhere may be her most enduring gift.

⤜⧟⤏

How about you? What helps you "bloom where you're planted"?

May 12:

The Power of Awe

For four days, I'd worked nonstop to meet a deadline. The morning after I finished, I woke up with what felt like a hangover, even though there had been no alcohol involved—at least not on that day.

My head hurt. But it wasn't a pounding or piercing pain. My thoughts meandered—heavy, slow, and laboriously inert. My mind felt empty, not of information but of motivation.

I think I had a "Deadline Hangover."

With no schedule or plans to structure the day, I wandered outside and was drawn to my peony garden, blooming mightily in the mid-afternoon sun. I plucked three pastel pink beauties, plopped them into a sparkling crystal vase, and let myself get lost in the wonder of their creation.

Somehow, I felt better.

Why?

Writer Polly Campbell would say that I was experiencing the power of awe. "Awe has the power to enrich our lives," she writes, citing the work of Stanford PhD candidate Melanie Rudd, who led a study on how awe expands our perception of time.

According to Rudd, awe is triggered when we perceive something to be vast—physically or metaphorically bigger than ourselves or our experience. But vast can be "as big as the night sky, or complex like quantum theory, or even small, intricate, or mysterious such as a spider's web, or the shimmer of a hummingbird's breast, or cells under a microscope." The awareness of vastness changes how we experience a given moment in time.

"With awe, your brain can't immediately comprehend what it's seeing or how it works," Rudd contends. Awe helps bring us to the present moment as we slow down to absorb the experience and try to make sense of it.

And so it was with the precious peonies. As I studied the intricacies of each flower, the stages of growth and hues of each bloom, I marveled at their grace, their steadfast pursuit of becoming.

I was in awe. And my "hangover" haze began to clear.

Rudd's studies found that nature, art and music, and other people's accomplishments are three of the big things that often encourage awe.

How about you? Where have you experienced the power of awe?

May 13:

Food Love

"I can't believe we're here!" I whispered as we settled into the studio audience. My friend had invited me to a live taping of the *Rachael Ray Show.*

Rachael Ray's style and cooking skills had changed my life.

"She never cooked before paralysis," one family member joked about me when my adaptive kitchen lessons began. "I don't know why she'd start now."

But I did. In rehab after paralysis, I learned not only how to care for my changed body but also how to adjust my daily practices to accommodate my wheelchair.

It wasn't an easy skill to pick up. Even with modifications, my kitchen wasn't wheelchair friendly—stovetop buttons too high, oven door too low, sink too deep, refrigerator difficult to open.

A decade and a remodeled home later, my daughter introduced me to the Food Network. Its stars—especially

Ray—made cooking look easy and fun. Her casual, simple style invited me to do more in the kitchen; her passion for the home-cooked meal was contagious.

No recipe was too simple to break down or too complicated to repeat; she faithfully recited every ingredient after each commercial break, and patiently showed how to dice an onion and wash a mushroom. Even with five pots working, she still made it look effortless.

Or at least doable.

Armed with a laptop cutting board and RR's orange-handled knives and cookware, I tackled her recipes with surprising success. Inspired, I created my own specialized Venn-diagram cooking style, preparing meals that intersected my family's food preferences.

One loved Whole30 recipes; another preferred keto. My athletes required extra protein and complex carbs. Another was a vegetarian. I wouldn't say cooking to please was easy, but it *was* rewarding.

"Hey guys," Ray said after the show one day. "Any questions for me?"

"What's your favorite meal to prepare?" someone asked.

"Depends on who is eating with me," she replied without hesitation. "I like to make what pleases my guests."

No wonder I liked this woman so much. Granted, her 30-Minute Meals took me at least an hour to make. And the ingredients she recited from memory sent me into note-taking mode.

But what required neither time nor pen to track was her passion for cooking—that relentless enthusiasm for sharing meals as a way of showing she cared.

How about you? Does meal preparation offer you the chance to show you care?

May 14:

In Full Bloom

Today's inspiration comes from an event I attended in support of Pathfinders for Autism. The event, HeART for Autism, showcased beautiful paintings by artist Mary Beth Marsden, a former Baltimore broadcast journalist and news anchor whose sixteen-year-old daughter has autism.

It's not often I meet a fellow mom who is parenting a daughter challenged by autism, since at this time autism affects males five times more than females.

My daughter Madison is ten years older than Mary Beth's daughter. As I strolled through the art gallery, I thought about Madison at age sixteen and how the services and opportunities for children with autism have changed and expanded since that time.

Then I thought about what the next ten years could hold for our girls.

I was drawn to Mary Beth's bold yet gentle renderings of flowers, especially one beautiful pink bouquet. The vibrant shades of each blossom in all stages of bloom seemed to stretch up and out with a relaxed grace: content, at peace, yet still full of promise.

So often I let the fear and worries of tomorrow rob me of the full beauty of the present. As I considered the future for our girls, somehow those blooms in their various stages comforted me.

Of course, I'll still wonder about the next ten years for my Madison; the "planner Becky" part of me will always have multiple options swirling around in my mind. But I've decided to let Mary Beth's beautiful artwork remind me to look for and enjoy more the fullness of each stage as she grows.

How about you? What image, art, or experience brings you back to the fullness of the present?

May 15:

Advice and Good-Byes

I'd called my son-in-law to check in and see how he was doing. Although we don't speak regularly, when we do catch up, it's thorough—and lively. He's always got a lot going on with my daughter and their three active kids.

"So, are you calling to tell me good-bye?" he asked.

"What do you mean?"

"Well, you said your father rarely offered unsolicited advice. But he said if he ever saw someone going over a cliff, he'd at least tell them good-bye!"

I laughed hard, impressed he remembered that story *and* that he seemed to want my opinion. But I wasn't calling to offer advice, only to catch up. "No, I don't see you going over a cliff at all, Brian. From what you've told me, you've carefully thought through each of your decisions."

And they'd made a lot of them in a short amount of time. In the last three months, they'd launched two new careers with new companies, sold one house, bought another and moved their family eight hundred miles.

Their life was nuts, but well-grounded—at least in my opinion.

Advice-giving is a tricky business, especially when children become adults, I've learned. I've tried to adopt my father's approach and advise only when asked—or when I see a cliff ahead.

How about you? How do you decide when to offer your opinion or give advice?

May 16:

Putting Entitlement
in Its Place

In early spring, I noticed a young man working on the fence across the street from my home. Each day he would strip two sections of the fence. The next day he would paint those two sections.

As he neared my property, I wheeled across the road to introduce myself and offer him water. I learned he worked for the nearby school and would be stripping and painting the entire fence. I told him how grateful I was for his hard work and how exciting it was to see the difference a coat of paint was making for our neighborhood.

He toiled for a few weeks. Then he stopped. When he resumed, he started a different method, only stripping the fence. Not painting it.

Unfortunately, he stopped right in front of my driveway.

For a while, gratitude and patience prevailed. Each day Tripp and I made our morning jaunt to the end of the driveway, I was hopeful that day would be the day I would find my section had been painted.

But after a few weeks, annoyance started to set in.

Why was it taking so long? Why did he change his technique? Why did he have to stop in front of my driveway? Isn't my home deserving of a painted section too?

I'm not sure what it was—maybe the glare of unfinished business, or the uncontrollable nature of the pace, or the uncertainty of the plan—but I began to notice that the status of the fence was starting to set the tone for the rest of my day.

Had my gratitude turned into entitlement?

Yikes!

As I considered the facts, I realized the situation had not changed. What *had* changed was my attitude about it.

I could do something about that. So, I decided to reset my thinking to gratitude.

I swapped out my demanding thoughts, reminding myself to be grateful for the generosity of the school, for the efforts of the young man, and for the return of pleasant weather, which was surely making his work more comfortable.

Then I ran across this quote from La Rochefoucauld:

"Happiness and misery depend as much on temperament as on fortune."

Within a week, a fully painted fence greeted me. When I saw the young man, I thanked him for the fine work he'd done to beautify our neighborhood.

What about you? Has an unexpected gift become an entitlement? How did you change your attitude about it?

May 17:

Misplaced Optimism

I can't remember the topic, but I remember the feeling all too well.

It was a time when my firstborn, now an adult with children of her own, courageously, but gently, let me know that something I'd said wasn't helpful. At the time, my heart sank, spinning on its descent.

We had been having a catch-up call, a rare lengthy one, the kind that goes beyond factual updates to the core of real conversation—feelings. She was sharing about one frustrating incident, giving details that explained her annoyance.

Hoping to broaden her perspective and lessen her angst, I offered alternative interpretations. After our third exchange—my attempt to point out the sunny side and her corresponding rebuttal—she paused and said, "Mom, can't you just see my side? Can't you admit I have a point here?"

Silence filled the phone connection as I replayed each of my efforts at optimism. Then it clicked.

"Oh my," I said. "I'm sorry, honey. I was just trying to help you get through it. I do very much see your point."

"I know you didn't mean it," her voice quivered back, "but it feels like you don't get what I am saying."

"You're right. I'm so very sorry. I should have just listened and supported you."

We talked on and ended on a good note. I was grateful for her honesty and told her so.

Days later, I ran across this statement from author Gretchen Rubin that crystallized the experience for me:

> "Denying others' bad feelings intensifies
> them; acknowledging their bad feelings
> allows their good feelings to return."

Unintentionally, I had discounted my daughter's feelings, pushing her to justify feelings she probably wished she didn't have. Since then, I've tried hard to listen and support first, then consider if optimism has a place in the conversation.

How about you? Have you ever experienced misplaced optimism?

May 18:

The One Question

‿〜‿

During my separation, I read one book that still has a prominent place in my library. Its title alone provokes a quick grab off the shelf to search for its answer.

The book—*One Question That Can Save Your Marriage*, by Harry P. Dunne Jr.—promises "a powerful way to save relationships."

And the question he asks is a jarring one:

"What's it like to be married to me?"

It's a truth bomb that disarms the blame game, neutralizes the fix-them fetish, and invites self-reflection.

Although answering this question didn't "save" my marriage, I've taken that question with me through the years, modifying it along the way.

"What's it like to have a daughter like me?"

"What's it like to have a friend like me?"

And yes, "What's it like to be divorced from me?"

In the midst of counseling, I told my therapist that if my husband and I could not create a good marriage, then I was determined we would have a good divorce. I've never regretted the efforts I made to ensure that would come to pass.

Granted, in the early days of divorce, it's difficult for some of us to let go of shared dreams and watch the uneven pace of starting over. Anger can seep in, even on the high road.

Children often get caught in the crossfire when parents divorce. Even though we are adults, our most childish behaviors can emerge when we are hurt, betrayed, or unjustly treated. Some are so hurt they make it their mission to create misery for the ex-spouse and use the children as pawns, moving them in and out of adult games that can leave a lifetime of scars from youth.

However, watching divorced parents wage mental warfare only confuses children. They want to love both parents. We need to give the children permission and opportunities to continue that love. We may not be married anymore, but we are still parents and must be mindful of what we are teaching by how we treat one another.

Perhaps we may benefit from asking ourselves, "What's it like to have a parent like me?"

How about you? How can you use the phrase "what's it like" to give insight into a current relationship?

May 19:

Cutting Back

My shrubs were out of control. I don't know if the cause was the new fertilizer or the cool, rainy spring weather, but my azaleas had gone nuts, ruining the shape of the beds I'd worked so hard to maintain.

"Can we level them off?" I asked Tim, the lawn expert helping me with my dilemma.

"No, not really," he told me. "We have to be careful not to cut too severely or we'll lose the blooms. But we can try another method. It will take some time, though," he warned.

He described a technique that involved hand-cutting areas down to the center of the bush, allowing sunlight to get to any new growth. Once the new growth became healthy and stable, we could cut away the over-growth and recover the old shape.

I must admit that those deeply dimpled shrubs looked odd for a few weeks as they waited for the sun to do its work. After a while, though, I could see bright green leaves when I peered into the dimples. It was strangely exciting to see those small possibilities emerge.

Yet they could only flourish if the overgrowth was cut back, then removed.

Hmm.

I wonder what possibilities exist for our own personal growth if we dare to cut away some overgrown parts of our lives.

Too much TV? Too much social media?

Or maybe it's more personal:
Too much talking? Not enough listening?

Or even:
Too much criticizing? Not enough encouraging? Too much judging? Not enough compassion?

Yikes!

It may take some time, as Tim cautioned me, but sometimes our best chance at flourishing requires some cutting back—and some awkward growth stages.

How about you? What personal growth could happen if you trimmed back some overgrown areas in your life?

May 20:

Mowing vs. Cutting

There's a difference between mowing the lawn and cutting the grass, my father often said each spring.

Mowing the lawn sounds soft, almost French if you say it fast. "Mow de lawn," Dad would whisper with his Southern charm. The genteel flavor in the phrase kicked up an aroma of freshly harvested grass, complete with a professional and astute operator behind that powerful whirring machine.

"Cutting the grass," in contrast, sounded harsh, like an execution carried out by high-powered motors and blades functioning as mini-guillotines. It evoked images of robotic operators attacking the terrain as if it were an enemy standing between them and their free time—a race to the finish.

The machine that one person uses to mow the lawn can be the same machine another person uses to cut the grass. The applicable verb depends not upon the vehicle but upon the operator's approach.

Before paralysis, I, too, enjoyed mowing the lawn. With my firstborn in my backpack carrier, I'd push our mower across our yard. The sound put my child to sleep, giving me time to connect my scattered thoughts as I let the uniform mowed tracks bring beauty, order, and something uncommon in those early days of parenting—visible results.

Perhaps the same two approaches exist in the business of life.

Some mow the lawn of life with respect and reverence, seeking to honor and preserve beauty by constantly doing those things that enrich relationships and improve the quality of living. They take time to trim, edge, and consider the nature of each person.

The grass cutters, however, have one aim: to get through life. Their mission-driven mindsets focus on making things happen, and they run their machine over anyone unfortunate enough to get in the way. The complexities of human nature are but weeds to be cut, void of unique purpose or talents. Efficiency rules, leaving little time for reflection.

Truthfully, I've done both. Although I'd like to say

I've "mowed" more than I've "cut," there have been times when life has been so thick with complexity that all I've been able to do is cut my way through and try to make it to the next day.

⁓§§⁓→

How about you? Do you mow the lawn or cut the grass? Will you choose to mow or cut your way through the events of today?

May 21:

The Law of Averages

One summer, as a college student in the 1950s, Dad sold books door-to-door. One day he and a fellow salesman were sitting on the side of a rural road trying to deal with their lack of sales and growing homesickness.

As they talked, they absentmindedly picked up small rocks, flipping them across the road at a barbed wire fence, attempting to hit one of the wire strands. At twenty feet, the percentage of success was limited. And their lack of sales was depressing, almost enough to push them to turn in their sample cases and head home for more secure and regular-paying summer jobs.

As their level of anxiety rose, their aim at the barbed wire fence declined. Finally, in utter frustration, my father picked up a handful of small rocks and threw them hard at the fence—and the spray of pebbles hit several strands of wire.

"That's it!" yelled his companion.

"What's it?" my father replied, scooping up another handful of rocks, hoping to vent more anger against the fence.

"Throw those rocks again!"

My father did. Again, several rocks hit the target.

And with that, the realization hit my father too. The young men began to recall what their sales manager had told them in the weeklong sales school at the beginning of the summer.

"The more calls you make, the more presentations you can make, and the more sales—and money," he'd counseled them. "Don't let non-sales bother you. Non-sales are not failures, they're teachers. Learn from them."

But he wasn't done yet: "Remember," he said, "beyond failure lies success. So go out and make a lot of failures every day, and in the process, you will find success. You have to trust the law of averages. If you make enough calls, the old law of averages will rescue you."

Recalling this advice, homesickness waned, and a new spirit rose within the two young men. Energized by their new discovery, they picked up their sample cases and got back to work.

And as their efforts increased, so did their success.

Fifty-five years later, I passed this story on to my daughter Brittany upon her college graduation. With limited job prospects that year, I suggested she grab a large handful of dreams and throw them at as many opportunities as she could find.

Failures were ahead, I told her. And each one would be laced with learning.

But as long as she showed diligence and persistence, the law of averages would be ever ready to usher in success.

How about you? Have you experienced the law of averages in your pursuit of success?

May 22:

A Life Uncaged

"If you look at the people in your circle and don't get inspired," says Nipsey Hussle, "you don't have a circle. You have a cage."

Yikes!

It's a fascinating exercise to consider the people "in your circle" and their effect on you. Some, like friends, you choose; others, like family or colleagues, you don't.

Each is a personal influencer.

Some enrich. Some restrict.

The word "inspiration" comes from the Latin word *inspirare*, meaning "to breathe into." We experience it when we feel mentally stimulated to act, especially to create.

When we are inspired, we feel filled with ideas and fueled to try new things. Without it, our lives can become stale and limited.

And yes (gulp), even caged.

How about you? Do you feel inspired by the people in your circle—or caged? Who inspires you?

May 23:

Laundry Nostalgia

We did laundry for two days.

My daughter Brittany warned me about her pile of dirty clothes. But we hadn't counted on the Gatorade explosion in the car-top carrier. The lemon-lime powder nestled in deep, then baked during the seven-hour journey to make a messy, if fragrant, arrival.

But I didn't care. I was so happy to see my daughter. She'd just finished that treacherous, unpredictable, emotionally charged transition year: the freshman year of college.

I welcomed every bit of her that came back—her boyfriend, her eight pairs of jeans, her eleven pairs of flip-flops, and even that mound of laundry. I wanted to hug her world.

They say that by the time your child finishes high school, you're ready for them to leave. Nerves fray during college visits, the application process, and endless graduation celebrations. You become impatient with each other.

The calendar becomes the heartbeat of your days. You meet deadlines, print checklists, and wonder if that tiny subset of eighteen years of living will fit into your car.

It does. Then the adventure begins for both parent and child.

They create their own new world, filled with all the drama of high school and none of the house rules. They meet a stranger and live with them, unchaperoned. They eat, sleep, wash, and brush to their own rhythm.

Sometimes they do laundry. Sometimes they do not.

You wince when you return home to that empty room, praying you've prepared them for this journey. You struggle with how much to be in touch—enough to show you care but not so much that you send them into a homesick tailspin.

You do your laundry—and miss theirs.

Meanwhile, roller-coaster phone calls electrify the connection between your worlds:

"I want to come home." Oh, no.
"I really like my roommate." Oh, yes.
"He broke up with me!' Oh, no.
"I got an A on my paper!" Oh, yes.
"I dropped a class." Oh, no.
"I met a cute boy." Oh, yes.

"I am in the infirmary." Oh, no.

"I finished my exams." Oh, yes.

"Can I throw away what won't fit in the car?"
Oh, no.

"Cute boy and laundry are coming home with
me." Oh, my. Oh, yes!

They reenter your world.

They are the same, and yet so very different. And
your heart smiles at their growth—and your growth too.

And, together, you do laundry.

*How about you? Has doing laundry ever been a special
memory for you?*

May 24:

The Ground Before Us

"Excuse me. Wheelchair coming through, excuse me."

The sea of Tar Heel blue parted as 3,371 future
University of North Carolina graduates, including my
daughter Brittany, allowed me to wheel through.

"It's the only way I know for me to get in the
stadium," I told Cindy, Brittany's stepmom, who was
pushing my wheelchair. The rocky, unpaved terrain to
the parent entrance had proved too treacherous for my
wheelchair, so we'd been left with Plan B: using the only
paved path available, which meant maneuvering through
a beehive of excited graduates.

As Cindy dodged robes and tassels, I focused on
the ground before us. My goal was to avoid rolling over
sandaled feet and manicured toes and make sure no one
landed in my lap. (More than once since my paralysis,

I've surprised a poor soul who's backed up to find a set of immobile knees behind theirs.)

"I'm sorry," I kept repeating to the graduates' feet. "It's the only way I know. So sorry."

They kindly moved—for all of us.

Because Cindy and I were leading a conga line; behind us were Brittany's father, then her brother, and finally her boyfriend, who was balancing her six-year-old half-brother on his shoulders.

If only we'd had an aerial view.

Eventually, we made our way through the madness and to our seats.

"We made it," I said to Cindy with a grin.

And so had those graduates.

During the ceremony, I spied several fellow alums searching for their graduating children. There's a special bond when you travel the same path—even after thirty years. The same buildings and dorms, and even some of the same professors, have become part of your children's history too.

Even so, Brittany's college path differed vastly from mine. During her tenure, she both experienced the tragic murder of UNC's student body president and, through her boyfriend's eyes, witnessed the Virginia Tech shootings. The shock of these events ushered in a new culture of caution to the carefree college life.

Yet they moved through that challenging terrain the only way they knew. One step at a time, they adjusted. They took self-defense classes, adopted new security measures, and refused to give in to fear. Volunteerism soared, with mottos like, *Celebrate. Remember. And Fight Back.*

Life's paths are rarely smooth. When we find ourselves on the treacherous ones, sometimes all we can do is focus on the next step of the ground before us and keep moving forward.

⚬⚭⚭⚬

How about you? Has focusing on the next step in a difficult situation helped keep you moving forward and adapting?

May 25:

Our Superpower

The ability to change your mind is a superpower.
—Shane Parrish

It should be easy to use a superpower, right? And yet it's hard to change our minds. It takes effort, thought, comparison of old to new, a willingness to learn, and even a touch of humility.

Yet if we've been given a superpower, we probably should use it.

How to go about doing that? It can begin with a simple shift in perspective.

During a renovation project in my home, my friend Leslie asked me to follow her to a table in my sunroom.

"Tell me what you see," she said.

"The kitchen and the family room."

"Now let's move over here," she directed.

I followed her three feet to the left of the table.

"Now what do you see?"

"The kitchen, the family room, the front door, the stairway, and the hall to my bedroom—that's amazing!" I said.

"Exactly," she said. "When considering a renovation or redesign, you need to see the project from the fullest perspective, considering its impact on other rooms. When you see a room from another perspective you can then allow that view to inform the choices you make."

In her own gentle but definitive way, Leslie (who happens to be a respected designer) helped me "change my mind" many times. I found that if she could help me "see" it, then I could better understand her opinions, even the ones I didn't like—which made me consider the value of perspective.

Perhaps Leslie prompted what Duke University researcher Mark Leary terms "intellectual humility," when we admit we may be wrong—or at least in need of further education—and "consider the perspectives of other informed people (including those whose viewpoints differ from theirs), and revise [our] views when evidence warrants."

Humility, defined as "remaining teachable" (my favorite), is a choice. We choose to learn from others' perspectives—or not.

The ability to change our minds is indeed a superpower. We've been gifted with cognitive capabilities that allow us to learn, grow, adapt, and change. We alone, though, determine if we use that superpower and are open to what other perspectives can teach.

How about you? How have you used your superpower today?

May 26:

Owning the Wait

From time to time, the gameboard of my Words with Friends app would freeze and then darken for no apparent reason. Immediately, the following message would appear:

"Repairing. Do not close the app. Your games are being repaired. This will take several minutes."

Although the interruption was annoying, I was patient with the process—a trait I rarely display with misbehaving electronics.

One night as I stared at the message for the third time that day, I wondered why I was so tolerant of the game's disruptive downtime. Perhaps it was the message: sixteen words clearly defined what was happening and why, and even gave me a timeframe for when all would be well again.

My game had set clear expectations for me.

If only all waiting was this easy.

Days later, as I tried to sit patiently in my doctor's waiting room, I wondered what other clear messages could improve my tolerance. Would it always help if I knew what was happening and why there was a delay? Would a time frame always help reorient my expectations?

My father had a unique perspective on patience—a characteristic he admittedly lacked.

"I have plenty of patience," he would claim when challenged. "I've just run out of the allotment I had for you!"

Waiting can feel like a waste of time. But is it? How often do we long for a few more minutes to read, rest, relax, or just have a little "me" time with no immediate demands?

Perhaps the key is "owning" the wait, reclaiming that time blocked out for someone else when it is unexpectedly returned to us.

Maybe we need to reassess that allotment of patience, informing it with our own messages of how best to use this newfound time.

⤙⧸⧸⤚

How about you? What helps you get through unexpected wait times?

May 27:

Pulling Out the Pin

"Anger is like gunpowder. It's what you do with it that makes it explosive."

I'm not sure who said it, but in my experience it's true.

Before my paralysis, I discovered a set of tapes from self-help author Earnie Larsen titled *Unresolved Anger* that helped me deal with my anger about my brother's death, my children's special needs, and my divorce. The tapes rescued me again when my anger flared at each missed milestone in my effort to recover the use of my legs.

Larsen contended that anger is always "justice related."

I'd never thought of anger in that way, but when I took stock of each incident, I discovered that my "it's not fair" button had been pushed (if not smashed) each time, priming me to lash out at whoever or whatever had caused the injustice.

People. Circumstances. God. Even myself.

I wanted to hold someone accountable for the injustice I felt.

Then Larsen took it a step further with the alarming thought that unresolved anger had an even more adverse effect, stating: "Unresolved anger fixates us in our point of pain."

He used an analogy of a science project in which pins are stuck into insects to mount them onto a Styrofoam board. Just as the pin affixes the insect to the board, so our anger fixates us to our pain. We must remove the pin in order to be free to move on, he advised.

And that takes effort.

We have to manage anger it so it doesn't manage us.

Whether it's talking it out, writing it out, or working it out physically, anger needs to be processed, not denied or discounted.

Until we name it, we cannot tame it.

How about you? When was the last time you experienced justice-related anger? Are you moving through it or are you still stuck in it?

May 28:

Sticks and Stones

Today's inspiration comes from a story illustration my father used to describe negative communication:

> The captain entered the following information in the ship's log:
> "The first mate was drunk today."

> A few days later the first mate read the log and found the statement written by the captain. He then entered the following in the ship's log:
> "The captain was sober today."

Although the first mate's words were true, what he communicated was false; he was pointing out the captain's sobriety as if it were noteworthy—setting forth a negative representation of his superior. This, Dad said, was "negative communication."

Words are powerful tools that we can use or misuse. That classic statement, "Sticks and stones may break my bones but words will never hurt me," couldn't be farther from the truth.

Wars are started with words; families are divided by words; careers are derailed by words; relationships are torpedoed with words; and people are killed because of the use, misuse, and power of words.

We hurt people in two ways with words.

First, we say negative things—"Did you hear what so-and-so did?" Then we proceed to tell what we've heard, often adding opinion to the story.

Everything we say about the situation may be true. But do we need to tell it?

Some folks like to pass on tidbits because they feel exclusive knowledge is power. If they know something you don't know, they have the upper hand. Telling it puts them front and center in a conversation, in the power place.

The second way we hurt others with words is by asking questions. "Is so-and-so about to be fired?" "Are the Browns having marital issues?" No facts are needed to raise the question. And you haven't *said* anything negative. You've just innocently asked a question.

Yet those words are steeped in innuendo, ripe for unhealthy replication. After two or three mouth-to-ear recitations, the question mark is often dropped and the rumors begin.

Sticks and stones may indeed break our bones. With a good doctor and a few weeks of healing, though, broken bones can be as good as new.

But words? Sometimes the damage they wreak is permanent, beyond the reach of the power of healing.

So how do we prevent negative communication?

Dad ended his story by suggesting three questions to ask before passing along information about another person: "Is it true? Is it kind? Is it needed?"

When I'm at my best, I remember those questions and that indicting story of the captain and the first mate.

❧

How about you? Have you experienced (or used!) negative communication?

May 29:

Jell-O Salad Resilience

As kids, we often had prominent guest ministers in our home for Sunday dinner. On one occasion, Mom made her famous Jell-O salad, a congealed fruit cocktail salad gussied up with fresh strawberries and pecans. She'd made it the night before and refrigerated it so it could set up in its festive decorative mold.

While Dad was chatting with our guest in the living room, we helped Mom with final preparations. As instructed, Forest, then eight, took the mold out of the refrigerator and brought it to the kitchen sink. Mom placed it in warm water so the salad could release from the mold. Rachel, age seven, brought Mom the serving plate while I, age eleven, shredded lettuce for garnish.

And then we watched Mom perform the magic we'd seen her do many times over the years, although none of us had ever been brave enough to try it. She placed the plate on top of the mold and quickly flipped it so the mold was now on top. We held our breath as she lifted the mold, hoping the salad released completely.

It did and we quietly cheered, fist-pumping our mom.

But then her elbow slipped. The perfectly shaped gelatin lurched, slid off the plate, and dropped into the sink, where it promptly slithered down the disposal.

"Mom!" we whispered. "What happened?"

She was silent, staring deep into the abyss of the sink. The only thing left of the salad was an errant grape that was rolling around like a golf ball trying to find the hole.

She sighed and said softly, "Oh my."

"Mommy, it's okay," Rachel said. "We don't like that salad anyway."

"Shh!" Forest practically spat, nudging his elbow into her tummy. "Don't hurt her feelings, Rae," he whispered.

I stepped in front of both of them, grateful Mom didn't seem to have heard them as she kept staring down into the empty sink.

After a moment more, she gathered herself, threw her shoulders back to her usual erect posture, and reached for a towel to wipe the plate. "It's okay, kids. Accidents happen." She turned around and flashed a warm smile to us. "Let's shred some carrots and cut up a green pepper for the salad Becky's started."

In less than five minutes, we'd watched our mother move from elation to disbelief to acceptance without blame to recovery with a smile.

A lesson in resilience.

How about you? What lessons in resilience have you observed or experienced from kitchen mishaps?

May 30:

The Confidence of Others

"If you're too sedated for the procedure to be effective, we may have to wake you," the anesthesiologist warned me with his George Clooney eyes.

I watched my doctor and team prepare the equipment. Then room began to blur. I was out, ready for my cardiac ablation.

For years, I'd had heart palpitations, or PSVT—paroxysmal supraventricular tachycardia.

My heart's abnormal electrical circuitry allowed a loop of high-speed beating. A rush of adrenaline from excitement, physical movement, or a seemingly unrelated event could trigger it. Although my normal heart rate was 60 beats per minute, during palpitations it reached 200. Although the condition wasn't life-threatening, it was life-altering. "Paroxysmal" (meaning from time to time) was the operative word for me, since my episodes were absolutely unpredictable.

In high school sports, my heart pounded so forcefully you could see it pulse through my jersey. But it only lasted a few minutes. Medications helped, but as I grew older the episodes grew in frequency and duration. In one hourlong episode, my heart rate reached 285 (my personal best).

This ablation would destroy the faulty electrical pathways creating these episodes. A probe at the tip of a catheter would be inserted into my heart, trigger a palpitation, and then ablate, or remove, the abnormal tissue.

A beeping sound awakened me from my induced sleep.

"Oh, hi," I mumbled to the anesthesiologist, partially hidden behind a machine.

Then I heard my doctor call out a number. I felt a sharp tingle in my heart—a zap of sorts, like a bump to the funny bone.

"Wow, I felt that."

"Yes," the anesthesiologist replied, moving toward me. "Remember, I said we may have to wake you if we had trouble getting your heart to palpitate?"

I nodded.

Another number was called. Another zap.

"I can't stay by your side right now," he said. "Got to get back here."

I didn't comment this time. I realized I better let him go do his job.

More numbers. More zaps. Finally, my heart began to race.

"You got it!" I attempted shouting. "Bingo!"

But no one acknowledged me. They were all busy doing their jobs.

"All done," my doctor announced.

I smiled back, thankful that bingo game was over.

It could have been a scary situation, but the truth is I was never afraid. Because these folks were professionals, prepared for every possibility and determined not to be distracted from their work. Their confidence fueled mine.

Preparation, focus, and confidence—a great combination for facing any scary challenge.

How about you? When has the confidence and pre-
paredness of another eased your fears?

May 31:

The Weight of Words

Children almost always hang on to things tighter
than their parents think they will.
—E. B. White

This statement affirms and encourages me, both as a daughter and as a mother.

As a daughter, I doubt Mom and Dad knew how much I treasured their words. They knew of my love for them—I told them nearly every time we spoke. But did they really know how much I relied on their wisdom to guide me?

Even now, years after their deaths, I hear their words differently as I grow and my perspective changes. From being in an active household with four kids to an empty nest to grandkids and living solo with a dog, I have found that life moves on, but my parents' words are often a timeless anchor.

As a mother, I've noticed that it isn't always evident my kids are listening. But they probably are—and maybe more closely than I realize. It's worth it to keep the channels of communication open and positive, to speak thoughtfully and lovingly, and to keep my mouth shut on things that don't really matter. A good friend of mine once noted to me that our words "gain weight" as our children move into their own adult journeys. That reminder has helped me consider even more carefully what I say and how I say it.

How about you? What have you held on to from your
parents? If you have adult children, have you consid-
ered the increased "weight" of your words?

JUNE

June 1:

Permeable Borders

It's that time of year again, when family reconfigures itself.

Final exams send our college kids homeward while end-of-the-year celebrations launch our younger children into the unstructured days of summer. Clockwork routines relax into summer camps, part-time jobs, and family vacations.

We welcome the new rhythm but also feel the bumps of recalibration. Multiple agendas sometimes conflict as new opportunities interfere with family traditions.

Do last-minute reunions trump a scheduled family gathering? Do summer jobs preempt family vacations? And what about the cooking, the cleanups, the laundry, and the ubiquitous "put things back where you found them" lament?

Our finely tuned patterns of living can short-circuit quickly if unchecked change blasts too rapidly into our homes.

What boundaries are worth holding on to?

During one college visit years ago, a parent asked the admissions speaker about their freshman honors program. Although the program was designed for two hundred top students, the speaker said, anyone could take an honors course if the class had room. He deemed the program "highly selective, with permeable borders."

Sounds like a good definition of family to me.

Yes, there are borders in the family unit, the highly selective kind that keep us connected and focused on the values we share. Regular time together cements lifelong bonds.

Yet if permeable, these borders allow the free flow of new people and plans. There's a special joy in getting to know the friends of our family members. These additions give us a window into each other's lives like no other, enriching both the individual and the family unit.

Family is a living, breathing entity that has room for both old traditions and new adventures. When we open ourselves to reconfiguration, we foster an unlimited capacity for growth and enrichment.

᭯᭯᭯

How about you? Do you experience benefits of perme-able borders in your family?

June 2:

A Friendly Face

Madison was happy on the drive there, but when we pulled into the respite camp drop-off, the tears began. She might as well have reached in and ripped out my heart.

There is nothing more agonizing than seeing the eyes of your sixteen-year-old daughter fill with tears, especially when she can't tell you what's wrong. Words elude my Madison. Although scripted phrases convey many needs and wants, her feelings aren't easily expressed.

Autism has robbed her of the full language that others enjoy. Each utterance is a struggle. Yet for me, every sound, smile, or tear is a precious puzzle piece—a clue to the mystery of what's going on in her mind.

"What's wrong, Madison?" I asked her.

More crying . . . then sobs.

"Madison," I prompted. "Say, 'I want . . .'"

"I want," she repeated back with a blank stare. She couldn't find her words.

"Madison," I redirected. "What's your schedule?"

"First, Mommy's van," she began, still sobbing.

"Then?"

"Then"—she paused to form her words—"camp and friends." She again dissolved into tears.

"That's right, Madison," I affirmed, rubbing the back of her neck.

She leaned forward, pressing her chest into her lap for pressure that always seems to comfort her—but this time didn't.

Her tears perplexed me. She loved camp; she had friends there.

She let me lead her from the van to the check-in room. As we entered, she held my hand quietly, tears running down both cheeks.

Then a camp counselor walked in. As soon as she did, Madison released my hand, reached out to this young woman, and looked directly into her eyes.

The crying stopped.

"Do you know Madison?" I asked the counselor, now a certified angel in my mind.

"Yes," she said, smiling. "I'm Emily."

"Madison, it's your friend Emily," I repeated.

Madison stood up, grabbed Emily's hand, and practically skipped away to the waiting area.

"Bye, Madison," I called after her.

"Bye-bye, Mommy—see you later!" she boomed in her best Barney-of-purple-dinosaur-fame voice.

What?! Emily had prompted Madison's famous Barney voice, the deep musical voice she used when life is good and she's happy?

Relieved and grateful for counselors like Emily, I knew Madison was in the right place.

What a difference a friendly face makes!

⁓⧓⤳

How about you? Have you ever had a special person—a camp counselor, a teacher, a babysitter—help you or your child through a difficult transition?

June 3:

Snap! Where Are You?

School had just been dismissed for the summer. My twelve-year-old brother, Forest, dashed into the den and flung his books to the room's corner, where they would rest for the next three months. He barely said hello to me before hollering down the hall, "Dad, could you please take me to the swimming pool?"

"Sure, buddy," Dad called back. "Give me five minutes."

"Alright!" Forest fist-pumped, flashing a smile at me. He bounced down the steps to his room to get changed and was back up in less than five.

As he headed out the door he stopped abruptly, opened his arms wide as if to embrace the whole world, and said, "Now, for the good old days!"

I smile at my little brother's words, dripping with an enthusiasm and insight. As he inhaled the fresh summer breeze that launched his new days of freedom, he looked forward to finding the good old days—the ones just ahead of him.

Most people look back on their lives and say, "Those were the good old days." But not my brother. He was looking neither back nor ahead, but only at the present—the moment of *now*.

And he was right. The present—the now moment—is all we actually have. These are the "good old days" because they are here, now, in this present moment.

Forest's appreciation of the present prompted our family to adopt the catch phrase, "Where are you?"

during our family summer vacations. If one of us slipped into reminiscing mode with, "Remember when . . . We used to . . . It's not the same anymore . . ." another family member would interrupt with, "Where are you?" and punctuate the jolt back to reality with snapping fingers.

Snap! "Are you stuck in the past?"

Snap! "Are you worrying about the future?"

We'd smile, adjust our thought process, and reorient to the moment at hand.

As Anne Morrow Lindbergh says, "If you surrender completely to the moments as they pass, you live more richly those moments."

How about you? Snap! Where are you? Are you present to all this moment has to offer?

June 4:

Commit to It

My father often spoke about the work ethic of fellow Wake Forest University attendee Arnold Palmer, a man he admired greatly.

"Arnie was a good golfer at WFU, but not the best," he'd tell me, setting up his favorite story. "In fact, did you know there was only a one-stroke difference in our scores?"

"Really?" I'd reply.

"*On each hole!*" he'd quip, breaking into gentle laughter. "Got you, didn't I, BB?" he'd say, using his pet name for me.

Eighteen strokes is a far cry from the one-stroke score difference he'd implied. Although he joked about his classmate and their golf game scores, Dad had

222 | Morning Fuel

tremendous respect for Arnold Palmer and his "no off-season" work ethic.

But Palmer didn't start out as a legend.

"He was not Wake Forest's number one golfer," Dad said. "He became the number one golfer by not indulging in the off-season."

Palmer practiced golf on the little nine-hole college course day in and day out, rain or shine. He'd play his long shots until dusk, chip until darkness fell, and then go to the number seven green, turn on his car lights, and putt until his car's battery nearly depleted itself.

Dad's point, however, was not to encourage work-aholism, or even recreation-aholism.

"The challenge," he concluded, "is to live life consistent with one's gifts, cultivating those gifts to their fullest potential."

There is no such thing as an off-season for life, either, Dad contended. Life is daily—lived day in and day out, rain or shine. Time moves on, either with us, actively engaged, or through us, passively detached.

What makes life unequal is found not so much in differing gifts as in the level to which we choose to nurture those gifts. Whatever our venture—personal growth, marriage, family, job, profession, or athletics—the key that unlocks potential is found through one word: commitment.

Not much ever happens without commitment.

Arnold Palmer knew that and lived it.

Life must certainly include respites—vacations where we can hit our reset button to gain perspective and restore our weary wills.

But success is not a switch we can flip. Rather, it is a steady current of committed effort, sustained over time.

⊱⧓⊰

How about you? Have you experienced the benefit of sustained commitment?

June 5:

Pause for Happiness

"Now and then it's good to pause in our pursuit of happiness and just be happy."

What a great reminder from Guillaume Apollinaire to pause *in* happiness and let our pursuits rest.

Enjoy yourself!

Take a minute to appreciate where you are and who you're with. For the moment, let go of plans and planning.

Absorb the fullness of the moment and claim the joy it can bring.

How about you? Can you pause to be happy right now?

June 6:

Sound Checks

It was one of my father's more unusual habits, one I witnessed many times during my youth: he would call his own office but use a phone line the secretaries would not recognize.

"Why do you do that, Dad?" I once asked.

"I want to see how they answer the phone when they don't know that I'm the one calling. Their voices are often the first contact people have with our church, and I want that to be a positive experience. I want to hear firsthand how we are represented."

As senior minister of the church, he wanted a warm, welcoming voice to greet each caller, no matter who they were. I'll never forgot his conclusion. "Your voice is your image, BB. Take care in how you use it."

I've thought about that advice, often wishing other businesses would conduct the same exercise. I wonder what they would learn about how they are represented.

Then I thought about my own voice, especially when answering the third or fourth telemarketer call of the day. My exasperation often grows with each interruption until I became gruff, even rude. Once I even barked, *"Hel-looo!"* only to discover the caller was a physician returning my call. Embarrassed, I apologized. But I wonder what lasting image of me he recorded.

Since then, I've tried to give myself a sound check before answering the phone. Before I pick up, I ask myself, *What will my voice represent about me?*

A little care can go a long way.

How about you? What image do you want your voice to convey in your next phone call?

June 7:

Two Sisters, Two Memories

"Hurry," my brother Forest, then ten years old, called out to us as he ran back from his walk on the beach. "I found something!"

Mom and Dad hopped up from their chairs. Rachel and I abandoned our sandcastle to follow Forest.

Skipping ahead of us, he pointed out his find: sticking out of the sand was a half-sunken steering wheel.

We dashed to the house, gathered shovels and hoes. Hours later, we uncovered a dashboard, two seats, and the revelation that we'd found a jeep.

Our imaginations kicked in hard. We could drive home in a jeep!

Then turf battles began. Whose jeep was it?

"Finders keepers," Forest proposed.

At age twelve, I'd get my license first, I asserted, so I should probably own it.

I can't recall Rachel's exact angle, but as usual, she was the most vocal, even at age eight.

We dug and debated—but mostly had fun pondering the jeep's new place within our family. The day ended with high hopes to finish the job the next day.

Up at dawn, the whole family raced to the beach.

But the jeep had disappeared. The tide had erased every trace of the vehicle—which, we later learned, had broken loose from a string of abandoned World War II military vehicles placed offshore years ago to prevent beach erosion.

Although devastated by the loss, through the years, our family discovered the true value of that experience. "Remember Forest's jeep?" someone would say, time-warping us back to that special family feeling before we lost Forest at age seventeen.

The snapshot vignette still warms my heart—the excitement, the debate, and the disappointment that somehow bonded us to the moment.

I called Rachel one day a while back to reminisce.

"Sure," she said, "I remember that jeep."

"What kind of memories, Sissy?" I asked, imaginary Hallmark music playing in my mind.

"Well, about how stupid we were to think we could dig up a jeep and drive it home the next day," she shot back.

Stunned and speechless, the Hallmark record screeched to a stop in my mind. My mouth dropped open. Then laughter set in.

"What?" she asked between my gasps. "What's so funny?"

"Oh Sissy," I said, finally catching my breath. "That's it? No warm and fuzzy nostalgia?"

She paused for a minute. "Nope, that's all I've got."

We each had memories, alright. But how could the same experience evoke such different feelings?

Then it hit me. That's what makes family life so rich! Multifaceted memories rooted in the same experience.

Let the memory-making season begin.

How about you? Have you experienced differing family memories of the same vacation? Might be fun to compare notes!

June 8:

Toggling Through

At age sixteen, my daughter Brittany had just made her first flight to Europe, solo. She'd also just experienced her first traveling adventure. A passenger on her flight had become sick, delaying the US departure, so Brittany had missed her connection in London. Her rebooked flight had put her in Paris two hours later than originally scheduled.

At 8:25 a.m. I got her call. No one was at the airport to meet her. She'd dutifully called all the contact numbers she'd been given but couldn't get through.

"Have you asked anyone to help you?" I asked.

"No one speaks English where I am now, Mom. I don't want to leave my bags."

"You're right. Stay put." I winced at the thought of my stranded child but refused to let the worry show in my voice. I pulled out my itinerary copy and called the same numbers she'd called. She was right. None of them worked.

At that moment, her father called from his out-of-town business trip. He knew the host family, so he began making calls as Brittany waited for instructions.

I toggled between the two calls. Brittany was calm. Her father was no-nonsense in his mission-driven search. Deep breaths between toggles helped me hide my angst.

We learned the host family had decided to pick up Brittany, hoping to surprise her. But they had arrived for the original arrival time. We hoped they were still were there, but Brittany saw no one she recognized.

During one toggle, I lost her call.

Then I lost her dad's.

I sat perched by the phone, waiting to find help for my child stuck in Paris at Baggage Claim Number 6. I lost the battle with the tears and prayed for her safety.

Suddenly, the phone rang, making me jump. Brittany's pitch was an octave higher. The host family had found her! A bright smile beamed through her voice.

We exchanged "I love you"s and she hung up. Her father called again and I relayed the good news.

Relieved and grateful, I was still shaken, perhaps by the sheer fragility of life.

So often reality intrudes into our best-laid plans and we're stuck toggling between what is and what should be. When this happens, all we can do is exchange "I love you's often, celebrate smiles in voices, and pray we're equipped to handle life's inevitable adventures.

How about you? What helps you "toggle through" life's adventures?

June 9:

Kid-Friendly by Design

It was the thank-you note to die for:

"I have such fond memories of the time that I spent at your house," my daughter's friend Lauren wrote when she acknowledged her graduation gift. "Thank you for always making us feel welcome. I will never forget all the fun times and memories."

"Yes!" I shouted to myself, fist-pumping my success. "I did it!"

Years before my eldest's thirteenth birthday, I'd set a goal of creating a comfortable environment to encourage my children's friends to spend time in my home.

A well-stocked refrigerator and pantry framed an eat-in kitchen with easily accessible barstools. A finished basement included areas for music and movies. And our family room's coffee table provided ample space for puzzles and games.

Although I wanted my home to make the kids comfortable, I also strived to protect the parental prerogative by allowing plenty of room for "parenting by wandering around."

Granted, I don't know every single thing that happened in my home during this teenage reign. However, I do know the kids were comfortable enough to open the fridge, grab some taco dip, and heat it in the microwave. And I was comfortable enough to ask them to rinse off their plates, put them in the dishwasher, and wipe off the counter.

Perhaps it's worth the trouble to create a comfortable place where kids can "hang out" and develop friendships. Building safe and trusting relationships may improve, enrich, and even extend their lives.

And if we're lucky, we may be thanked for our efforts.

How about you? Have you experienced benefits of creating a kid-friendly environment in your home?

June 10:

Plus or Minus?

My mother said there were two kinds of people in this world—plus people and minus people.

I have to agree: when you think about it, most folks do either give you energy or take your energy away.

Mom taught me to put myself in the midst of people that are positive, who create energy. But she also taught me that if I had to be around a person who is negative, I should find the positive within them. Because rarely is anyone 100 percent negative.

My pastor father could find something positive to say about anyone, even the devil. "He's active," he'd say with his playful smile and a wink.

Look for the positives. Make it a habit.

How about you? Who is a plus person in your life? Are you a plus person?

June 11:

The Prepared Loser

One of my family's favorite actors was Don Knotts, whose antics as Barney Fife helped make a success of the 1960s sitcom *The Andy Griffith Show.*

In 1961, Knotts was awarded the first of what would become five consecutive Emmys. Standing before the microphone with that first Emmy in hand, he said, "I don't know what to say about winning this. All my life I've been a prepared loser."

Knotts summed up what many people feel about themselves. As "prepared losers," many of us have been told what we *can't* do more than once.

Parents may unintentionally program their children with statements like, "Johnny can't do this; Jane is not good at that." Some teachers, coaches, and mentors pick up where parents have left off, focusing on weaknesses rather than strengths.

Research tells us that praise and positive reinforcement are generally more effective than rebuke and criticism. Parents today are encouraged to balance feedback to their children by "catching them being good" instead of only correcting errors. We are coached to foster high self-esteem and to help our children feel good about themselves.

Some of us may have overachieved.

Self-esteem can morph into a surge of self-importance when everyone gets a trophy regardless of performance. Participation can be confused with excellence, discounting hard work and talent.

We may need to acknowledge that indeed, "Johnny can't do this," and "Jane may not be good at that." The important lesson to learn and to teach is not that everyone is good at everything, but rather that it's okay to *not* be good at some things. We can't excel at everything or win everything.

Although we don't need to criticize every part of our children's characters or point out each negative tendency until it becomes a self-fulfilling prophecy, it may be worthwhile to help them create realistic expectations.

Perhaps being a "prepared loser" is part of the process.

Often, we learn the most about ourselves when we don't succeed. We may discover a limit, yet we can prevent it from being limiting by learning from it and moving in another direction.

"Move to your strengths," my father often counseled.

Learning through losing can guide us in assessing our strengths.

Perhaps there are benefits in preparing to win *and* to lose—because life has an abundance of both.

How about you? What lessons have you learned from losing that may have prepared you to move to your strengths?

June 12:

The Value of Price Tags

People are funny when it comes to yard sale shopping. There are the "priced *only if* marked" folks who ignore price labels on groupings and ask the price for each item in the group. There are the diggers who mine to the bottom of every box or plunder the unmarked territory of the far corners of the garage, seeking a hidden treasure. Most, as expected, are the dealmakers, who group items for a discount.

And then there are those who *must* have a deal, no matter what. One dear lady at my last yard sale inspected jewelry, clothing, and housewares for almost an hour before selecting one Capiz shell angel ornament, marked at 25 cents, and asking, "Would you take a dime for it?"

I smiled, swallowed my weary, you've-got-to-be-kidding-me retort, and agreed to the price.

But the most interesting phenomenon was the "price tag effect." On the second day, I put a sticker on every single object. It streamlined the checkout process and reduced the brain strain of remembering prices.

It also increased my sales—amongst my family and visiting friends. My sister bought $20 worth of office supplies. My nephew bought Yugio cards and Pokémon books. Even the painter staining my deck found a bucket of toy airplanes for his son.

Price tags make a clear statement: This item is worth a specific amount to its owner. It is for sale. If you want it, this is what it will cost—at least at the beginning.

My therapist once pointed out that relationships have price tags too. A relationship functions best when two people are clear about their expectations. Compromise works only when you realize the value of what you are negotiating for.

Price tags help.

What is the value of a family dinner, a night out with the girls, an uninterrupted conversation with a friend, a leisurely workout, a Sunday in church, or a vacation for just the two of you?

Because we often forget to state clearly what is important in our lives, those in our lives often find themselves dealing with items whose worth is concealed.

Price tags create a starting point. I've discovered it's worth putting some time into pasting those labels onto the things that matter most to me so my loved ones get a clear picture of my value system. How else can they honor it?

How about you? What price tags can you use to communicate what is of value to you?

June 13:

Maturing

Midway through his round of eighteen, my father stopped at the golf course clubhouse where he met a golfer who was eighty years old.

"He shot his age the other day," my father's golfing partner told him.

"An eighty on *this* course?" my father replied, stunned because the course was considered difficult on anyone's score card.

"Yep."

"Well," my father joked, "maybe when I'm eighty, I'll shoot eighty!"

His friend laughed. "Not unless you start shooting eighty right now or real soon."

Although I'm not sure my father ever shot his age—he died at seventy-two—I know he had fun trying. And what he learned from the encounter lives on.

"Age has a way of maturing our talents," he wrote, "but it seldom makes us better at what we were never good at."

Perhaps the reality is that age matures who we are and where we've devoted time and energy in our lives.

How about you? What talents and interests do you have now that could grow with you in the coming years?

June 14:

Denial and Resilience

It was the summer of 2020, mid–pandemic and just after the horrific televised death of George Floyd. We were a nation reeling from multiple health, economic, political, and social reckonings.

I was in the middle of that tired debate with myself: *Do I watch the news, or not?*

Listening to the news had become more than a current-event update. It had become the hard-to-answer question of: *How much more can I take?*

I wanted to be informed. But did I have the energy to witness the raw footage of the worst of our humanity? The mental acuity to crack open and understand more varnished sound-bites? The courage to examine my own biases and patterns of understanding?

Where was the narrative in this chaos, the unvarnished truth? Was there one?

The words of psychologist Nick Wignall jolted me back to reality: "You can't be emotionally resilient if you are living in denial."

Was that what I was preparing to do? Skip the news and live in denial, a state that could prevent resilience?

Resilience, at least for me, is the ability to keep going, no matter what. It requires persistence, determination, curiosity, and a lot of hard work. It's not fun, enjoyable, or a favorite pastime of mine by any means. But, boy, can it give life depth, meaning, and, most importantly, the ability to live fully even in the worst of circumstances. In my life, it's a requirement.

So, if denial was going to prevent my resilience, I had to ask: *What reality am I denying?*

After pondering this question, I wrote down what I knew from experience.

Life is not fair, never has been, but a long look back into our exclusionary ways and pervasive attitudes is particularly difficult to absorb and admit.

Life is hard, filled with mistakes, wrong turns, and flawed thinking. Our ability to communicate has been our friend and our foe when it comes to examining truth, making wise choices, and behaving well.

Life is uncertain, frequently darkened by unthinkable acts and unpredictable responses that are shaped by skilled and unskilled editors of word and film.

Somehow, writing all those realities down, so timely and timeless, strengthened me.

Wignall was right. I needed to first accept reality before I could keep going. With affirmed insight, I began managing my news consumption by choosing and recording credible news sources and watching them only when I was ready. Over time, with greater patience with my pace and my progress, I found ways to examine and accept some hard truths and made my way back to resilient living.

How about you? Have you discovered renewed resilience after accepting a difficult reality?

June 15:

Just Enjoy It

My pastor father was often sought out for his words of wisdom. He had this way of listening with his heart and always seemed to know just the right thing to say.

I remember hearing him speak about the ups and downs of parenting in the family life programs at church. But after two years of parenting my own firstborn, a willful but loving child who kept me on guard and challenged me ninety percent of the time, I asked for some personal instruction.

"What's the most important thing in parenting, Dad? Out of all the tips and techniques you've used and experienced, what's your best advice?"

The simplicity of his answer surprised me.

"Enjoy them, BB," he said. "Always remember to enjoy your children."

Through the years, I've tried to remember that guidance. From toddler time-outs to my kids' many teenager shenanigans—complete with prom dramas and the highs and lows of competitive sports—to that tricky period where you watch your child date the wrong one while keeping your mouth shut and praying the right one is just around the corner, I've tried to find the moments of enjoyment and cherish them.

And I've never been disappointed by the results.

How about you? What relationships (with children, pets, or even plants) can you choose to enjoy today?

June 16:

The Joy Within

Joy. That word had been flying around a lot.

I'd just finished another tidying-up frenzy, this time using the method that Japanese home organization guru Marie Kondo promoted in her book *The Life-Changing Magic of Tidying Up.* Keep only the things that "spark joy," she demanded.

But what is joy?

Joy is not the same thing as happiness. Joy is an inside job, based on what we feel and our internal experience, according to *Until Today* author Iyanla Vanzant. Happiness, on the other hand, is based on the way we think and our responses to external events.

Joy comes through you. Happiness comes to you. We should pursue joy, Vanzant contends.

Why?

If you seek joy within, you will be happy no matter what is going on around you.

No wonder sparking joy is such a successful way to tidy up!

How about you? What can fill your heart with joy and strengthen you today?

June 17:

Obstacles and Purpose

During a Tony Awards ceremony, Ari'el Stachel from the musical *The Band's Visit* directed his closing remark to "any kid that was watching," and said: ". . . know that your biggest obstacle may turn into your purpose."

Wow. I hit the pause button on my DVR and rewound it three times.

What a bold way to look at adversity!

So many of the obstacles we face in life feel like anything but our purpose. From annoying to unjust to unexplainable, life's challenges are often the enemy—to be dealt with and destroyed so we can get on with the life we want, the one we've planned. And even when we fail in that effort, we may find peace once we accept the reality. We may even make the best of the situation and strive to live fully despite the unwanted circumstances.

But what if we looked at the obstacle as a discovery zone for our purpose?

To be honest, I'm not sure I'm that highly evolved yet. To think my purpose could come from my paralysis or my daughter's autism or my son's young death is a stretch for me. However, I must admit that journeying through each one has connected me with others who are doing the same and as a result has both enlarged and enriched my life in unexpected, if not stunning, ways.

With that in mind, Stachel's comment—". . . your biggest obstacle may turn into your purpose"—lingers.

And inspires.

How about you? Have you experienced an obstacle that could reveal your purpose?

June 18:

Back to Me

We were waiting to board the plane to Orlando for our first-ever seven-day cruise. I listened intently as daughter Brittany, then fourteen, described all the items she had packed for the vacation.

In response, I told her about one special outfit I'd packed, apparently offering too much detail.

She looked me straight in the eyes and said with a slight smile, "That's enough about you; now back to me!" and dramatically fanned her hand to her chest.

My mouth dropped open. "What did you say?"

"You know," she said with a shrug, "I just said, 'Back to me.'"

My eyes widened, as did hers. Then we both burst into laughter.

"Where did you ever get such a comment?" I gasped.

"Jamie." She grinned.

I should have known. After my paralysis, college students helped me with the kids from time to time. This latest crop included a bubbly and energetic Towson University junior, Jamie, with a Julia Roberts smile and who used word choice like the secret chili-pepper ingredient in a favorite chocolate recipe. I was always on guard around her, never knowing when a new term or comment would come flying my way.

This one had staying power.

There was an unusual, almost ironic, honesty nested in my daughter's retort, especially coming from a teenager. So much of the teenage world centers on self.

Maybe, I thought, I could use it to my benefit too.

I began to look for opportunities to say "back to me" when we were talking, just to make her aware of the shift in focus in the conversation.

One evening, during dinner with a friend, I told

the "Back to Me" story. She practically suffocated with laughter. For the remainder of the dinner, we used that comment as a transitional phrase to steer our conversation. I'd ask a question about her, let her respond, and then say, "Back to me." She did the same.

I must admit it was a jarring experience when I'd be telling what I considered a most fascinating story, riding high in the saddle, and then she'd quip, "Back to me," ripping the reins right out of my hands.

Yet as the conversation progressed and we refined the timing of the selfish request, we noticed that one person's story combined with a "back to me" comment created a rich conversation, bound with the give and take of self-disclosure. As we swapped "war stories," we discovered that—as long as we were mindful of connecting the conversation—a "back to me" could weave others to self and self to others.

"Back to me" says with brutal candor, "I matter."

However, a *creative* "back to me" transition says, "Your thoughts matter enough that I want to connect my experience with your experience."

It adds, "Back to me—as it relates to you."

How about you? Want to liven up your conversation with your teenager or a friend? Ask for their opinion or thought on a topic, then inject, "Now back to me!" Trust me, the reaction will be priceless.

June 19:

Make It a Good Day

It was his favorite departing line for years. "Make it a good day," my father would say, clicking his heels and waving his hand in farewell.

And folks would smile back—twice. Once with polite acknowledgment. And then again, after absorbing his unexpected meaning.

I recently discovered the story that shaped his signature greeting.

While pastor for a week at the famed Chautauqua Institute, Dad had coffee with Dr. Karl Menninger, the noted author and psychiatrist who founded, along his father and brother, the Menninger Clinic.

Menninger was ninety years old when my father met him. While his physical body had some limitations, his mind did not. Between ages eighty and ninety, he'd written ten books and was at Chautauqua to lecture that week.

During their coffee time, a conference attendee came over to speak with "Dr. Karl," as he was frequently called. Upon departure she said, "Have a good day, Dr. Karl."

He nodded politely. But when she was out of hearing distance, he told my father, "I hate that statement."

And he launched into the issue, for which he had a burning passion.

"How do they know I want to have a good day?" he asked my father. "I may want a bad day." He smiled as he started stirring up all the angles. "Pastor Smith," he said, "there's a problem with that whole concept of 'have a good day.' It sounds like all you have to do is drop by some market somewhere, pick a Good Day off the counter, and wear it out of the store."

He paused to ask the waiter for another round of coffee, and then he got to his point.

"You don't 'have a good day.' You *make* it a good day."

And he paused again.

"Don't ever say, 'Have a good day,'" he concluded. "Say, 'make it a good day.' We do have that privilege and responsibility. Every morning before I get out of bed, I pray, 'God, help me make this a good day.' The responsibility for the day is ours."

Makes sense to me. No wonder Dad took his advice.

With that shift in perspective, we can look beyond each day that we have and see it as the day that we have been given.

How good will it be? Depends on what we make of it.

❧

How about you? What will you make of this day?

June 20:

The View From

Arthur W. Hewitt was a pastor in rural Vermont. One Sunday after worship, he and his wife drove a teenage girl home. The road skirted along a beautiful lake. He was alternately looking at the lake and the road when the young girl said, "Stop! We're here."

Pastor Hewitt looked at the house—little more than a shack on the hillside.

The young girl saw his shock and surprise. "Oh sir," she said as if to apologize, "it's not much to look at, but it is a wonderful place to see *from*."

What a statement. Home—a wonderful place to see from.

It's what we all strive to give our children—a creative, healthy, and wonderful place to see from. A place that instills security and trust. A place where love's warmth and depth accept the uniqueness of each person.

A wonderful place to see from.

Home is a place that brings children into the world and then brings the world to the children. It's their first school, helping them discover their talents and develop skills, giving them both a sense of wonder and a sense of yonder.

For many years, a cherished cross-stitched quote hung on the den wall in our family home. Given to Mom and Dad by my sister Rachel, who labored long hours with a needle and thread to make it, it read:

ALL THE LOVE WE COME TO KNOW IN LIFE SPRINGS FROM THE LOVE WE KNEW AS CHILDREN.

Of course, every parent hopes that the child will develop far beyond what is received in the home. But if children are to see farther and do more, we must make sure that home is a wonderful place to see from.

As I look at my own home now, its nest empty, I wonder what view of life I gave my children—what I taught them, what they learned. It would be nice if those were the same things! Whatever the truth, I hope I at least gave them a wonderful place to see from.

How about you? What view of life did you receive from your family home? What view of life are you giving your family now?

June 21:

On Bending Nails

My grandfather was a craftsman. He operated a lumberyard by day and pursued his woodworking passion in his spare time, building unique pieces of furniture that found their way into exalted positions in my childhood homes.

As a boy, my father would often help him. Once they built a new set of steps for a family friend. Per his father's instruction, Dad drove big nails down through the boards to hold the thick lumber in place. But when his father told him to crawl under the steps and bend the nails up against the lumber, my father challenged him.

"Nobody will ever see those nails," Dad argued, not wanting to crawl in the dirt and waste energy on something that did not show.

"Maybe," his father replied. "But I'll know they are there."

Dad never forgot that experience, and when my siblings and I were children he regularly reminded us of its message. Every time something needed doing that did not "show" and we could "get by" without doing it, he would recall the "bending nails" story.

"I have not always bent all the nails," he once wrote, "but I've never escaped hearing that tape start playing when I ignored responsibility."

Upon my father's death, one column reader emailed me about a chance encounter with my father. She had witnessed Dad leaving the supermarket with a few bags of groceries. Someone had left a cart in the middle of the parking lot. It wasn't in my father's way—but it wasn't where it should be, either. So, after tucking his groceries in his car, he fetched the errant cart and patiently guided it back to its proper place.

No one asked him to do it. No one was watching him, so he thought. He just saw a job that needed to be finished and completed it.

I wonder if he was thinking about bending nails.

I still do.

❧

What about you? What do you do when no one is looking? Do you bend the nails?

June 22:

COVID Chronicles

During the pandemic, COVID living ushered in a twilight zone of the real and the imagined, distorting our perspectives. Although its ripples affected each of us differently, we had to accept what we couldn't control and we had to adapt.

Each day required reassessment: What was possible to do that day? Were there new ways to do old things? Was it safe? Was it worth the risk?

Sure, I'd written a book entitled *Rethinking Possible*, but this was ridiculous! Continually "rethinking what's possible" was one grueling, energy-zapping effort. This repetitive rethinking often made us brittle, impatient, and even unkind. It was hard to be generous when we felt so much had been taken from us.

The antidote?

Gratitude. It's always gratitude. It works every time!

But you can't get from acceptance to gratitude without rethinking your situation in the most positive light. Sometimes we have to revisit our resources and re-anchor.

Although I'd faithfully continued my morning readings, I started relying on a daily thirty-second video update from my son-in-law Brian. He called them "COVID Chronicles." For months, his smiling face popped in daily to remind me of one positive thing—a positive infinity of sorts.

I'm not sure if it was his smile, his comforting voice, the assurance that he and his family were okay, or the fact that I could count on his reminder of what day it was, but I so looked forward to those little snippets. In a strange way, they grounded me, reminding me of the many things I could be grateful for.

The clouds of uncertainty that hung over us all during COVID living were bearable as long as the sun poked through from time to time. I learned to savor every ray of gratitude and connection that reached me—and even now, with life mostly back to normal, I continue to try to do so.

How about you? What re-anchored you to gratitude during COVID or has done so in another challenging time?

June 23:

One Key to Living Well

In her talk on *Life Reimagined*, author Barbara Bradley Hagerty, former National Public Radio correspondent, offered her insights about living well, especially when struggling with life's inevitable challenges. One of her key messages: "Choose purpose over happiness."

She introduced me to a new word: *eudaemonia*, from one of my favorite Greek thinkers, Aristotle. Eudaemonia is the idea of living a good life by pursuing goals that give meaning to life. It is striving toward goals, large or small, that give us an abiding satisfaction. If we pursue long-term meaning rather than short-term happiness, we will likely find both.

So, if we're smart, we'll choose purpose over happiness.

When you think about it, some of the most meaningful endeavors we pursue in life don't yield instant happiness—raising children, beginning a new career, or choosing a pursuit that requires sustained effort.

Like, for example, my Mount Everest–climbing friend Beth, whose most recent adventure was a fifty-day, 2,500-mile, Route 66 bike ride from Los Angeles to Chicago. Or my son's commitment to wrestle at the collegiate level, the culmination of training and practices that began at age six. Or even my decision to publish a memoir that took me twenty years to write!

These pursuits didn't make us "happy" every day, that's for sure. But did they have the potential to yield fulfillment and give our lives meaning?

Absolutely.

And there's an unexpected bonus, Hagerty says. Eudaemonia can make us robust—can energize us. And when we "find a reason to get up in the morning," she reminded us, the research confirms that we will live longer, enjoy a happier old age, and better retain our memory. We will be more likely to not only survive the setbacks we meet along the way but also thrive through them.

How about you? What goals are you pursuing that have a deeper purpose?

June 24:

Listen Up

The participants in a seminar on effective communications were asked to complete this questionnaire:

> Which of the following do you feel represents your biggest problem in communications?
> Select only one.

1. Making yourself understood.
2. Writing an effective letter.
3. Telling a funny story well.
4. Presenting your ideas in a clear, forceful manner.
5. Making a good speech before people.

6. Listening.
7. Making snappy comebacks or witty remarks.

When finished, the attendees were asked how many of them had selected number 6—listening. Few had done so. But as the facilitator informed them, listening is the number one problem encountered in communication.

Usually, we think the ability to express ourselves to another person is the greatest need in communications. But effective *listening* towers above all the rest.

In my IBM sales training years ago, I learned the value of listening from our classes on customer-oriented selling. To discover a customer's business needs, we were trained to listen to the customer first and then repeat back what we'd heard, this time in our own words, to check for understanding.

"If I understand you correctly, your concern is . . ."

"So, what I hear you saying is . . ."

"So, in other words, you feel . . ."

This rephrasing element was difficult, demanding attentiveness to not only what was said but also what was left *un*said. The results were remarkable. Customers were much more receptive to presentations that were rooted in their restated business needs.

Yet the power of listening extends beyond the business setting. Think of a person you know who is a good listener. Chances are that you like—really like—this person. You feel good when you are with them. Something about them draws you in—there's a magnetism. They make you feel good about yourself.

In fact, a person's ability and willingness to listen to you can improve how you feel and think about yourself. When people listen to you, they are saying, "You are important." When silently attentive, they are loudly communicating that you are valuable and what you have to say is worth their time.

In truth, we may have a greater effect on people through the way we listen than through the way we talk.

Or as the caption on an image of a long-eared puppy at my veterinarian's office reads, "You can make more friends with your ears than your mouth."

How about you? What benefits have you experienced when you've listened closely to a family member, friend, or colleague? Have you noticed you feel better after they have listened to you?

June 25:

Letting Life Unravel

I'm not sure who said it first, but I know my father said it often—especially when I became impatient and pressed him for his opinion about a situation to give me *the* answer or requested affirmation on a decision I was anxious to make.

He would take that massive hand of his, gently lay it on top of mine, and say to me: "Don't cut what you can unravel, BB."

And his blue eyes, clear and steady, would calm me down, at least long enough for me to regroup and consider his advice.

Oddly, patience was never a particular strength of my father's—and he knew it. Mom would often point it out. "Now R. F., honey, you were awfully short with that person," she'd say in her soft Southern drawl. "I believe you lost your patience."

"No, I didn't," he'd reply, his eyes twinkling at the love of his life. "I have *plenty* of patience. I've just used up my allotment for that person."

I still smile and shake my head at his antics and his trademark verbal mischief. Yet there was deep wisdom in those words. Unraveling isn't only about patience, I've learned. It is also about perspective.

Often we may think we're done, finished—that we have "had it." Sometimes we feel pressure from others to cut the yarn and make a decision. But in truth, we may not have enough information. We may need to wait for life to unfold a bit more, for time to pass, or for space to come into the process so the next step is a little clearer.

From confronting someone about a needling concern to dealing with life's major decisions about career and family, sometimes we need things to unravel at a slower pace.

Unraveling has served me well. It may take me forever to make a decision, but when I do, I generally have no regrets. It took me two years after my paralysis before I was willing to consider learning to drive with hand controls or putting a lift in my home to get to the second floor. I had to be patient with myself—let myself adjust to my new reality—before making such big changes.

Unraveling gives us time to consider and learn—to make peace with the process.

How about you? What decisions have you made that have benefited from the patience for life's unraveling?

June 26:

Rocking the Boat

A troublemaker is a person who rocks the boat then persuades everyone else there is a storm at sea.
—Unknown

Ever met a troublemaker as in the above quote? They're unpredictable, even scary. You tiptoe around them because you aren't sure what mood will prevail or what situation will erupt.

Will they support an issue or criticize it? Be an ally or enemy? Help solve a problem or create a larger one?

These folks come in all sizes and shapes. Little ones start boat-rocking about age three. At thirty, some have perfected their wave-making styles. And others consider themselves pros in retirement years.

Why do they do it?

Perhaps it's the desire to control.

If they cause a crisis or discover one in progress, they can leverage the urgency of the situation to control the household or organization or community.

They control by alarm. Using the old shock method, they keep people off balance, taking the best of news and making the worst of headlines out of it.

They control by manipulating information. They seek information not for knowledge, but for personal advantage. "If I have information that you don't," they reason, "then I'm in control."

Often smart and articulate, these folks sometimes see themselves as "devil's advocates," keeping everyone honest and on their toes. Yet their meddlesome ways often distract, and sometimes destroy relationships.

If we're honest, we've all done it. We've all rocked the boat with an issue we thought was storm-worthy only to realize later that perhaps we overreacted.

Maybe we were seeking control. Maybe we wanted attention. Or maybe we were having a bad day and let our emotions churn unchecked, creating a horrific storm that should have been nothing more than a short sail though some rough waters.

Life has enough of its own stormy seas. Let's make sure the waves we make are appropriate—and needed.

❧

How about you? When have you experienced a trouble-maker's unnecessary storm? Have you ever created one?

June 27:

To Fake or Not to Fake

During a particularly hard day, I realized I have four "members" living under my roof: my dog, my house, my paralyzed parts, and my non-paralyzed parts. When they all misbehave at the same time, it's a disaster.

After one such day, the experience settled in deeply and I began to feel like I was losing my mojo. Thankfully, just as I began to succumb to my gloom, my father's words came to mind:

> "Sometimes we have to act our way into the new way of thinking."

I didn't feel like "acting"—not one bit. I didn't feel like getting out of bed. I didn't feel like having coffee. I didn't feel like getting dressed. I didn't feel like being with people.

But I had commitments.

So, despite my feelings, I got up. Had my coffee and quiet time. Got dressed, did my hair, put on makeup and jewelry. It was a fight, but I pressed on.

Then I called my sister and told her, "I'm gonna fake it till I make it, Sissy!" And sent a text with a selfie to prove it.

It worked! I kept my commitment for lunch and deepened a new friendship. It felt strangely refreshing to be out and focusing on something besides my homelife challenges.

"Great lunch!" I reported back to my sister.

A few days later, I found this quote from happiness expert Gretchen Rubin: "To change your feelings, change your actions. A 'fake it till you feel it' strategy may sound hokey, but it is extremely effective."

I see the wisdom in these words—but I wonder, is it healthy to fake how we feel? To pretend life is good when underneath it all we are struggling?

Honesty is important, I've learned, both with ourselves and with others we trust. Traveling through uncertain times is difficult; traveling through them alone can be disastrous.

So fake it sometimes, if you need to. But not every time. Both struggles and successes are better when shared.

How about you? Who can support you if you decide to "fake it till you make it"?

June 28:

Backing into Life

The plan was simple: Put Cookie, my black-and-white cat, with Domino, another black-and-white cat, and have a litter of feline Dalmatians.

I grew up with cats. I'll never forget watching one calico give birth to seven kittens in my bottom dresser drawer. I hoped my children could witness a birth too.

After checking with our vet, we arranged for Domino to have a sleepover with Cookie. Since both were indoor cats, we gave them their own private room overnight.

Sixty-eight days later, Cookie gave birth. I'd told the children that Cookie would probably disappear one day to find a safe place to deliver.

Wrong.

At three o'clock one Saturday afternoon, my sister Rachel and I were chatting in my bedroom. She glanced out the door and stopped mid-sentence.

"Becky, Cookie is labor!" she whispered.

My eyes widened. "Where?"

"In the hall. Right now!" she gasped.

I heard a pained meow and wheeled in just in time to see Cookie stretch out and contract. Within seconds, a kitten was born.

Sprawled out on the hardwood floor, she labored—birthing, cleaning, nursing, and birthing some more. The kids perched quietly around as Rachel knelt beside Cookie, stroking her head. Cookie began to purr.

Then the rhythmic contractions stopped. Cookie wailed in pain. With a fierce meow and gigantic spasm, the final kitten bolted out.

"Mom, he's breech!" Brittany, my fourteen-year-old, cried during the birth.

And he was. White feet first, this little guy had just backed his way into life, traumatizing his mom and the natural order of things.

Cookie took a moment to recover from the pain, but finally resumed her duties to stimulate his life, nurturing that little fella just like the rest of the litter.

As I watched Cookie tend to those precious balls of fur, I wondered about the lessons of her last kitten's birth. Literally and figuratively, children often "back their way into life," turning their parents' world upside down.

With strong-willed kids, special needs children, and those who thrive on testing limits (I have all of the above—and love them dearly), we often parent a child very unlike ourselves in circumstances much different from our experience and expectation.

And yet we recover from each challenge. We find our footing in the new territory and focus on the task at hand, resuming our duty to stimulate their life—just as Cookie did.

How about you? Have you parented a child very unlike yourself? Or were you a child who was very different from your parent?

June 29:

Plant Where You Are Blooming

One of the most valuable lessons I learned from my mother was, "Bloom where you are planted."

"We need to plug in, kids," she said each time we moved. "It's important to find a way to plug in, grow, and flourish in the community where we live."

Dad, too, believed we should bloom where we are planted. But he also believed we should plant where we are blooming.

"If you find yourself in uncharted territory, you might as well dig in, learn, and give back to the community, who could benefit from what you're learning," he counseled us. "Share what you've learned. Plant where you are blooming."

Maybe that explains my passion for Pathfinders with Autism. Sharing with other parents what I continue to learn from parenting a child with autism and learning from those parents in turn continues to be both exciting and rewarding.

Our struggles gain value when we use what we've learned to help others.

Our success nurtures theirs.

How about you? What can you plant where you are blooming?

June 30:

Let Love Be Larger

~⚬~

While they were on their honeymoon, I wrote a letter to my daughter and her husband. They'd recently bought a puppy, Dudley—a puggle like my dog Tripp—who seemed to be more mischievous than most pups. He tested their patience often and intensely, beyond anything than they had imagined.

> *Brittany and Brian,*
>
> *From this moment on, you will face life together as you have never faced it before. You are a couple, committed to one another for life. It is a special, sacred commitment. I hope you can find guidance from this one simple thought:*
>
> *Let your love be larger.*
>
> *Let your love be larger than adversity, than issues, than people or circumstances that threaten to pull you apart. Let it prevail, triumph, overcome.*
>
> *Release the urge to be right, the urge to win, the urge to remember each time you have been right and won. And let your love be larger.*
>
> *Love is all the things the Good Book tells us—patient, kind, understanding—but it is also the most powerful force we have. Use it wisely. Cherish it. Sustain it and nurture it.*
>
> *Before you act, ask: Is it kind? Is it necessary? Is it loving? And let your love be larger.*
>
> *And as your circle of friends and family expand, let love teach you that it has more than one way to be expressed. That judging others' loving ways is a useless exercise. A more important action is to let your love*

be larger—and learn from it. What can a different expression of love teach you about others? Respect it, honor it, and open your heart a little wider to include it, even though it may be so foreign to you.

And with your children, remember that they are a result of your love for one another. Your love came first, then your shared love for them.

Let love overshadow the small stuff, embellish the large stuff, and wrap a layer of warmth around the cold realities that you may face.

Love is what we're meant to do, you know. Share our lives with another. Love can't fix all of life's hard times, but it sure can make whatever journey you are on, richer, fuller, and most importantly, shared.

And just like your precious care for Dudley, love despite—because you can.

Love (each other) despite—because you can.

And always let your love be larger.

How about you? How can you let your love be larger today?

JULY

July 1:

Summer's Pace

⌒

Summer, with its change of pace, has blown in with heated breath, disrupting schedules, demanding change, and maybe—just maybe—renewing our energies with a new perspective. The corner of summer is a good time to make extra space for the special people in our lives.

The longer days invite the leisure of potluck dinners and cookouts—the perfect place to reconnect. Technology is a newfound helper. Emailing invitations streamlines the party preparation process, often prompting conversations beyond the RSVP. And with all the social media how-tos, nonstop cooking shows, and online party ideas available to us, it's easier than ever to be inspired to try something new.

But first, it takes a plan. As one of my Southern girlfriends likes to say, "Dinner doesn't just fall on the table."

And neither do friendships.

Although we may start friendships in spontaneous ways, sustaining friendships takes effort. Often, it takes both creative thinking and planning to keep a relationship alive.

Friendships are easier to maintain than to restore. The busier we become, however, the easier it is to let our friendships fade. But, as Gandhi reminds us: "There is more to life than increasing its speed."

Summer can be the perfect time to slow down and recalibrate our focus. Faded friendships are easily renewed with one phone call, a thoughtful email, or an invitation for a cup of coffee. And both old and new friendships await that quick invite to a potluck or cookout.

Good times are only one invitation away.

How about you? How can you use this corner of summer to enrich your friendships?

July 2:

Halfway Through

We've just crossed the halfway point of the year. Although the summer months give us permission to relax the structure of our lives, they also give us time to review what habits are working and which ones may need an update. After all, as Aristotle reminds us:

"We are what we repeatedly do."

Maintaining good health is a priority for most of us. In order to achieve this goal, we first need to decide what is important to our long-term health; then, we need to create a sustainable routine to address it. I know that in order to be on my game, I need good sleep, a balanced diet, plenty of water, attentive self-care and maintenance to prevent paralysis issues, and my daily reading and reflection time. These days, I start each morning with a glass of water with a generous squeeze of fresh lemon (this helps kickstart the body in a positive way by boosting metabolism and flushing out toxins). After tending to my dog, I make a cup of coffee with a splash of almond creamer, wheel into my sunroom, and park myself at the end of my breakfast table so I can look out into the backyard for nature's inspiration. That time for reading and thinking allows me to get centered—to be alone, absorb a few new thoughts, and take stock of what is doable in the next twenty-four hours—before continuing my day.

As you know, I believe that how you start your day sets the tone for how you get through the rest of it. And early July—smack dab in the middle of the year—is a good time to check in and check up on your daily habits.

How about you? Which of your habits are working, and which ones need an update?

July 3:

Easily Pleased

The holiday weekend was coming. Friends and families would soon be gathering on the Fourth of July for picnics or neighborhood cookouts. Some were traveling to the beach or mountains or had booked a special getaway weekend.

Not me. My far-flung family would not be celebrating with me on the Fourth. But I was okay with that.

Why?

I'd decided to conduct an experiment to embrace a new mindset and mantra based on this thought from Mark Nepo:

"One key to knowing joy is being easily pleased."

So often, high expectations and exacting preferences are thought of as sophisticated or worldly. It's easy to be critical and to form an opinion. I wondered if would it be as easy to simply be pleased?

That weekend, I gave it a shot. With #Easily-Pleased as my mantra, I tried to find joy right under my nose, taking extra time to look for it.

For inspiration, I observed my dog Tripp, who is always so easily pleased. His life is simple. If he likes something, he wags his tail. And he wags his tail—*a lot*. Sunshine, a comfy bed, a pat on the head, or a rawhide bone dipped in smidgen of peanut butter—these are the things that please him. He even takes extra time to smell the flowers during our walks up and down the driveway.

For the entire long weekend, I focused on being easily pleased. I slowed my pace, lowered my expectations, and let life touch me in the simplest ways. From the rich fullness of a fresh tomato sandwich to the gift of low humidity and a gentle breeze that invited me to enjoy my morning coffee on the deck to the darting hummingbird's visit to my geranium's glorious blooms, I was easily pleased.

And, yes, joyful.

How about you? Do you find it to be hard to be easily pleased? Do you find joy when you are?

July 4:

The Freedom Not-To

Everyone has an opinion, a fact that proves we have the capacity to think. An unexpressed opinion can be a virtue, however—especially at a flashpoint in an explosive situation.

We can't help how we feel. Feelings are neither right nor wrong; they just are. When someone hits us with a fist or with hurtful words, we feel the impact. No amount of positive thinking can make us not feel the punch and pain. And so often we cannot control what brings us that pain in any aspect of our lives—home, love, or professional. But we can control how we respond.

When something or someone hits us, we can hit back with fists or slap back with words. We have that freedom.

But we also have the freedom "not-to" do something if we know that action will have a negative impact on other people. We may possess knowledge we need not impart, an opinion we need not voice, an observation we need not reveal, feelings we need not express. In these cases, freedom not-to is freedom practiced with responsibility.

We can choose when to respond, how to respond, and even if to respond. Our best thinking may at times guide us to wait and reflect before choosing an action.

Action by action, our behaviors reflect who we are. What we say and do—and the way in which we do it—reveals our character.

So when we respond too quickly, too fully, or too dramatically—even though we have the freedom to do so—our character is right out there with it. We can't rewind and delete or even modify what's been said, much less control its impact on our reputation.

Warren Buffett states it clearly: "It takes twenty years to build a reputation and five minutes to ruin it. If you think about that, you'll do things differently."

We all have the freedom not-to. This may well be our greatest possession, and our best exercise of real freedom and responsible living.

Restraint is the freedom we all-too-often forget.

How about you? When is the last time you exercised your freedom not-to? Are you glad you did?

July 5:

Don't Learn That!

It was an awkward moment. At my son's fourth birthday party, five of his buddies gathered around the kitchen table to sing "Happy Birthday."

"Hey, Pete," one friend shouted, interrupting our song. "Listen to this!" And the child promptly began to burp each letter of the entire alphabet.

Mortified, I tried to redirect, distract, and otherwise get the child to stop. But he persisted, boldly belching all the way to Z.

The table erupted, hysterical with laughter. I couldn't get back in charge and I didn't like it. Pete began to burp the alphabet, as did all his friends.

We survived the incident, even laughed about it later. But that hand-wringing, helpless feeling stayed with me, challenging my parenting skills.

What can you do to shape new, freshly implanted information? What's a good parental response to an experience like this one?

A few years later, I overheard a sitter telling Pete about skipping a class and not studying for a test.

"Hey, Pete," I interrupted them both. "Don't learn that!"

And there it was, in all of its honesty. I did not want my child to learn what he was hearing. I flashed a knowing smile to soften the remark, playfully winking at the surprised sitter. But the message was clear—to both of them.

And the phrase stuck.

I began to say it—and say it often. Anytime I didn't want my kids to learn something we'd both just heard or experienced, I'd inject, "Don't learn that."

And they would smile back, darn sure of how I felt.

I then began to use the flip side of the remark. As my daughter Brittany's boyfriend (now husband) helped me unload the car and put the groceries away, I called out to my son, "Hey, Pete, learn that!"

And maybe he will. But even if he doesn't, he knows that I think it is worth learning.

We can't control what our kids hear or experience—but we can at least offer commentary on how we feel about it, right?

How about you? How do you guide your kids or others in your circle of influence through teachable moments?

July 6:

Moment by Moment

As a senior whose college wrestling career included an additional redshirt year, my son Peter was being interviewed about his chosen sport.

"It's hard—that grind is hard," he told the interviewer. "Everything about what we do every day is hard. That's just part of it. For me, this is my last go-round. In March, I'm done. That makes it a little bit easier. But five years of it is a long time."

"Was it worth it?" the interviewer asked.

"Yes," Pete said. "Even if it's just moments. It's not like I've had five years of a being a very successful wrestler. I'll be very honest. I've had good matches, bad matches, injuries, and disappointments. But I've had moments. And those moments are the ones that I look back on that I love and that I'm am very grateful that I got the chance to have."

Pete wasn't the only one to be shaped by the sport. I learned some things too.

For nearly eighteen years, I was one of those "wrestling moms." My life was a roller-coaster adventure of training and competitions and wins and losses and good refs and bad calls and 6:00 a.m. lifting and three-a-day practices and reading labels and measuring food to the ounce and injuries and casts and splints and bandages and trophies and medals and awards and a room wallpapered with brackets and oh my goodness the smelly laundry.

Yet I grew as parent and person as I watched my son navigate through some hard lessons and tough seasons.

What's special, even inspiring, about the grind of struggle is each moment we've loved, Pete reminded me.

So often I get caught up in the grind and struggles of daily life that I forget to be grateful for the moments I've loved. But when I stop to consider them, I know they are worth remembering, reliving, even retelling.

We can't be successful our entire careers or our entire life. But we can look for those special moments that we've loved, and we can let them inspire us.

How about you? Are there moments of success or joy you can relive now that can help fuel you through a current struggle?

July 7:

Telling All You Know

When I was six years old, my parents wanted to teach me the mannerly way to answer the house telephone, a staple in homes in the mid-1960s.

If they were unavailable—in the shower or bathroom or otherwise indisposed—they instructed me to say, "He/She is busy, tied up, or unavailable right now. May I take a message, please?"

Evidently, I had problems with those lines.

I remember thinking that it wasn't exactly honest to say they were "tied up." They certainly weren't bound up in ropes. And often, they *were* technically available—they just didn't want to stop what they were doing to talk on the phone. Plus, I didn't like saying they were too busy to talk to someone. It might hurt their feelings.

Given all this, I felt the need to explain more about their indisposed circumstance. I distinctly remember one conversation.

"Hello . . . Yes, he's here . . . No, he can't come to the phone. He's on the potty right now, and it may be a while."

I also distinctly remember Dad's response upon hearing me say this: "Becky, you don't have to tell all you know!"

I thought about that incident during some tests at the Johns Hopkins Transverse Myelopathy Center. Al, a family friend, waited with me.

"You're having an EMG today," the receptionist said, raising her eyebrows. "You know, that's the most painful test we have here. Glad you have someone to hold your hand. Honey, you're gonna need it!"

I looked at Al and shook my head. "You don't have to tell all you know!" I wanted to shout at the receptionist.

The test involved inserting needle electrodes into my muscles, applying an electrical stimulus to nerve points, and following the impulse to the spinal cord and brain. At least I wouldn't feel the ones in my legs.

As the technician began attaching the electrodes, he described one energetic twelve-year-old patient who had also been paralyzed by transverse myelitis. "She was spunky, incredibly upbeat for such a young person," he told me. "But she cried through the entire test."

"You don't have to tell all you know!" I wanted to shout again. But instead, I went to the beach in my mind where I did not shed one tear.

Indeed, those tests hurt. But I wonder if they hurt more because of my dread, amped up by stories that didn't need to be told.

How about you? Have you ever had someone tell you more than you wanted (or needed) to know?

July 8:

Grabbing Life by the Lapels

Life loves to be taken by the lapel and told: "I'm with you kid. Let's go!"
—Maya Angelou

Engaging in the life you have isn't easy sometimes. We can sit on the sidelines with those "what if" and "why" questions and become a spectator in our own lives if we choose to.

Or, we can step into the fray of chaos and embrace it, determined to participate in a life we would have never planned.

Denial is often the obstacle. You can't embrace what you refuse to accept, I've learned.

Each hardship I've faced has brought with it the opportunity to engage with life differently but still fully. The key, I've learned, was acceptance. It helps to say to life, "I'm with you, let's go," even if the adventure I find myself on doesn't resemble anything I wanted.

It's never easy to jump in a game you don't know how to play and don't have a desire to learn. But it beats hanging out on the sidelines of life, watching and waiting instead of learning and living.

How about you? Have you grabbed life by the lapels, or are you sitting on the sidelines in some areas of your life?

July 9:

Vacation Preparation

Perched on the outer edge of a vacant picnic table bench, the white-haired woman propped her back against the table and peered out onto the sandy beach. The hubbub of the festive pavilion cookout behind her offered no distraction.

She was oblivious, lost in the magic of the shoreline.

I wondered what she was thinking—but I was fascinated by what she was wearing.

A pleasingly plump grandmotherly type, she wore a bright aqua straw hat adorned with fuchsia and purple silk flowers artfully wrapped around the hatband. Her white, freshly permed hair puffed out like soft cotton balls under the brim.

Citrus greens and more purple joined the aqua theme on her loud Hawaiian-print blouse. Complementary capri pants finished the look, but not before her white sneakers revealed perky aqua socks, the exact color of her flowered hat.

This woman had come prepared to vacation. Her outfit and her steadfast focus on the shoreline told me she was worthy of imitation.

I'm convinced successful vacations just don't happen. We need to prepare, as my aqua-clad friend did, both inside and out. On the outside, beyond the travel and accommodation logistics, the more time we spend planning our adventures, the more satisfied we may be.

My mystery friend dressed for her success. She prepared to vacation and had the coordinated outfit to prove it.

Yet, successful vacations go beyond our luggage contents. We need to prepare ourselves on the inside, too, to receive our vacation. We need to relax. More importantly, we need to know *how* we relax. Whether our happy place is high-intensity workouts, spa treatments, shopping, sleeping in, sunning, detaching from anything electronic, or simply staring at a distant shoreline, everyone needs to discover how they relax and strive to include it in their vacation.

As a manicurist once instructed me, "You must be prepared to receive the hand massage." Only when the hands are relaxed, can the massage be effective.

How about you? How do you prepare to relax on your vacations?

July 10:

Resetting vs. Stretching

I'm always amazed at how pulling the plug on my phone, computer, or television can magically "fix" whatever is wrong. Interrupting the current resets each device in a way that restores it fully.

We, too, need those breaks in our routines. Truly "unplugging" can provide that mental disconnect from daily responsibilities we need to reset and even recalibrate our lives.

Sometimes, though, we get more than we've bargained for.

When I made my first-ever solo trip to the beach to visit a good friend and her family, everything about that trip was new to me—driving multiple hours, alone, on an unfamiliar route, to an unvisited town, to a new home with accommodations I'd never tested for accessibility.

Every part of that vacation challenged me, forcing the familiar to the backseat while adapting and adjusting joined me in the front seat of my adventure. When I got back, I was unexpectedly energized, both physically and mentally. Large issues seemed smaller, urgency was redefined, and tolerations increased.

By engaging in something new, I'd also stretched my mental comfort zone—my capacity for living. Perhaps it was the energy of mastery or the sense of well-being from accomplishment or the confidence from success that fueled my shift in perspective. I now understand a bit more why "extreme vacations" have such popularity. In those extremes, participants are forced to learn and to try new things—to grow.

Vacation reset or stretch? Each one offers a way to unplug with differing results. I'm grateful for the chance to have experienced both.

How about you? What vacations have reset you? Stretched you? Did you feel differently after each one?

July 11:

Diligence

The things that come easily for us usually don't require much effort. But our struggles—our areas of life where we fall short or where we seek a change that may be in our best interests—often require a sustained persistence over time.

Diligence helps.

"What we hope ever to do with ease, we must first learn to do with diligence," Samuel Johnson reminds us.

Whether it's increasing our circle of friends, adopting a new eating lifestyle, or simply getting more sleep, steadfast diligence can be your most valuable ally.

How about you? What do you need to do with diligence today?

July 12:

Present Over Perfect

Over a period of seven days, twelve loved ones from four different states would be gathering for my first-ever staycation celebration in my home. True to form, Planner Becky started thinking through each day and everyone's preferences:

- What foods they liked.
- What activities they enjoyed.
- What pace they liked to keep.

As my anxiety began to build, I stopped my list-making to consider the message of Shauna Niequist's book, *Present Over Perfect*, in which she invites readers to leave behind the pressure to be perfect and embrace the practice of simply being present.

So, I asked myself: *What's the most important thing? What matters most to me about this gathering?*

When I thought about it, what I really wanted was for everyone to get to know one other a little better. I wanted to learn what was on everyone's radars—both the joys and the struggles. After all, how can we support one another if we don't know what matters most in each other's lives?

And, of course, I wanted everyone to have fun and make some great memories.

But how to let go of the planner/perfectionist in me so I could be fully present and absorb all I wanted to learn?

Then I remembered my "easily pleased" mindset that had helped me stay present to small wonders and enjoy my July Fourth weekend, even though I was alone. That's the attitude I needed, once again.

But my family needed to know that, especially since I'm usually the "hostess with the mostest" with daily menus, schedules, and pre-planned activities. So I emailed the group about my goals and new "present over perfect" mindset, then added, "Our mode for traveling? Let's try to be 'easily pleased' and stay present, focusing on the now instead of the next."

They obliged—and that week turned out to be one of our best family vacations ever.

How about you? How can being "present over perfect" help you prepare for (or enjoy more fully) gatherings of family or friends?

July 13:

Strength in Limitation

They were alone, the story goes, playing in the grassy area on the far edge of the golf course. One little fellow, about eight, was playing with another boy, about six. When a foursome approached, one of them engaged the older boy in conversation.

"What's your name?" asked the golfer.

"Tom," said the boy.

"What's your last name?"

"White."

"And what's your dad's name?"

"John," the little fellow told him.

"Do you have an older brother?" the golfer asked, intrigued by the youngster.

"No," he answered. "But he does"—he pointed to the younger boy—"and I'm him!"

I love that story. I admire the young confidence of the little fellow who refused to be defined by who he wasn't—and instead stated clearly who he was.

He may not have had an older brother, but he *was* one; he reframed his negative to a positive, refusing to let his circumstance dictate his self-worth.

So often we judge our lives by our circumstances—who we aren't and what we don't have.

I remember in my early teens being mesmerized by the voice of a family friend who was competing in a statewide talent search. One day I asked her exactly when her voice had become so strong and beautiful, secretly wishing she would respond, "About your age," so that I, too, could have a chance for such a beautiful voice.

"I can't remember not singing," she said matter-f-factly.

After a few more months of trying to belt out her songs in the shower, I realized what I was not: a singer. I didn't have that talent, and I finally accepted that I could not manufacture it.

We can't grow older brothers, either, if we don't have them.

But knowing our limits is helpful, even fortifying, as it allows us to remember who we are and what we *are* gifted to do.

How about you? Has acknowledging a limitation helped you discover a strength?

July 14:

Life in Context

It was the kind of juicy tidbit you like to share with a good friend, one who has known you for most of your life and will fully appreciate how out of character the news will be.

I folded my hands together, scooted my wheelchair closer to the table, and leaned forward toward my friend. "Bing," I whispered, raising both eyebrows. "I've had work done." I paused for more drama, and then blurted it out: "Botox."

"What?" she replied, squinting to inspect my candlelit face over our half-eaten desserts. "Where?"

"You'll never guess," I teased, sweeping back my bangs so she could get a good look at my untouched frown and laugh lines.

"Where?" she asked again.

I paused for a beat, enjoying her shocked response, before whispering, "My left big toe." I chuckled. "It calms my spasms. My paralyzed parts sometimes have these involuntary muscle movements, or spasms. My left toe started to spasm straight up, hitting the top of my shoe and damaging my toe. Botox stops the nerve impulse to the muscle and the spasms."

"Amazing." She sighed and rolled those big brown eyes, just the way she did in our college days.

Nothing beats sharing improbable news with a treasured friend.

I'd reconnected with Bing during a trip back to UNC-Chapel Hill for an alumni meeting. She'd left her ten-year-old twins to travel ninety miles to meet me for dinner.

The next day I caught up with Joy, my potluck freshman roommate, at a football game. The following morning, I had breakfast with Debra, a sorority sister I hadn't seen in twelve years.

Revisiting my alma mater with the same friends who'd helped create those life-defining college moments released a flood of memories. Conversations flowed as they did when we were eighteen. Unscreened. Honest. Their responses and reactions were grounded in a unique perspective:

They gave my life context.

On the flight home, I marveled at those preserved friendships. Underneath the years, the core of each of our relationships was solid. We may have skipped a few chapters and changed settings, but the characters were the same.

Old friends are treasures, grounding us with a rich history that gives special meaning to our present circumstances. Common experiences equip them to fully appreciate the latest out-of-character adventure.

Even a sheepish Botox confession.

❧

How about you? What treasured friendships give your life context?

July 15:

Yellow Flyer Boldness

In 1997, autism resources were scarce, and pre-Google, research was difficult. Madison had an early diagnosis and interventions—so rare in those days—but the therapy recommendation that worked for her did not come from her physician or her teacher, even though she was getting excellent care from both. I learned about it through a scrunched-up yellow flyer I found in the bottom of Madison's Barney backpack, sent into school by another parent who was willing to share her discovery.

"Why did you do it, Polly?" I asked her years later. "You sent a flyer into an entire classroom of kids with autism, inviting their parents into your home!"

"Well, I finally found something that worked," she said simply. "So I had to share it."

Polly's bold and generous gesture not only touched my family life, it became the genesis of Pathfinders for Autism, the organization we, along with other parents, founded three years later. Our mission was simple: we wanted to help parents learn what other parents had discovered.

For over twenty years, Pathfinders has continued to provide resources, trainings, and family activities free of charge, serving 20,000 individuals annually.

And it all began with a scrunched-up flyer in the bottom of a five-year-old's backpack.

How about you? Do you have a "yellow flyer" discovery that could benefit others if shared?

July 16:

Winning Against Whining

Midway into our seven-day, seven-person, multiple-family vacation, my six-year-old niece Ashley found my last nerve and stepped on it.

The year before, I'd teased her about her high-pitched voice: "Ashley, you sound like you took a big gulp of helium."

A year of maturity hadn't lowered her pitch. And on day four of our vacation, an ungranted request led to an even shriller sound—the ubiquitous, universal, no-family-is-complete-without-it *whine*.

Adorable with her crystalline baby blues and her sunny blond hair, Ashley began pleading her case to her mom for something—who knows what. She was at the tiptoe, prayerful-hands-begging stage when she moved to the two-toned "puh-lease" escalation, the one that starts with "please," progresses to "pretty please," and climaxes with "pretty please with sugar on top."

About the time she reached the second verse of the same song, I snapped.

"Ashley, honey," I said, "can you whine an octave lower?"

She stopped abruptly, turned to me, and said in her normally heliumed voice, "What's an octave?"

I smiled, grateful for the interlude in the chorus, and replied, "It's a different level of pitch for the same note." And I demonstrated with a high "la" and a low "la."

"Oh. I get it, Aunt Becky." She attempted her refrain with a lower voice—only to crack up laughing, as we all did.

With that, we all promptly forgot whatever she was whining about and moved on to the next activity.

"Whine lower" became our new defense weapon with the war on whine. Consistently, the command elicited a laughter response, breaking the whine cycle. It even worked on the ever-present "But Mo-om" version of whine older kids chant when challenging the word all children hate to hear—"No."

Through the years, I've learned that the pitch and tone of our voices can be powerful communicators. In particular, I remember coaching folks on their phone skills in my career consulting days. "Your voice is your image," we taught our clients. "Look in the mirror while you are on the phone to see if you are smiling. People can hear a smile in your voice. Make sure what you say matches the way you say it."

Enthusiasm can be heard. Confidence can be heard. Attitude can be heard.

We may not be able to win the war on whine. And we may not be able to pick all of our battles. But we can always pick our tone and pitch, paying attention to the power of not only *what* we say but *how* we say it.

How about you? Has whining ever frayed your nerves? Could "whining lower" help?

July 17:

Today's Best

"That's not my best" is a phrase most overachievers don't like to say. We like to excel by doing our very best—*all the time.*

But everyone, even the overachiever, needs a respite from time to time. I like the way author Melanie Beattie frames it:

> "Do our best for the moment, then let it go.
> If we have to redo it, we can do our best in another moment, later."

Give a time limit to our self-assessment? What a freeing thought. We can do our best—for the moment—while giving ourselves permission and opportunity to redo things at a later time.

Sometimes I need that affirmation that today's best is good-enough-for-now, knowing that tomorrow's best may be an improvement.

How about you? What challenge are you pursuing that you could consider today's best and take a break from for now?

July 18:

Vacation Targets

We did it! All twelve of us adopted my suggested vacation mindset and chose "present over perfect" while being easily pleased.

We celebrated every milestone we could think of (graduation, new jobs, new cities, new life chapters, birthdays, and an engagement) with a "pull apart" cupcake cake that pleased everyone because it featured a variety of flavors: funfetti, strawberry, cookies and cream, and red velvet.

We also learned more about each other, my goal for our extended time together, through a few exercises.

First was the Breakout Escape Room: In this challenge, the men competed against the women in an hourlong problem-solving adventure. There's nothing like finding clues and agreeing on a course of action to give one a rare peek into how someone thinks. So fun— especially since the women won!

Next was Peaks and Pits: We borrowed another family's tradition and shared our "peak" and "pit" experiences of the day. (My favorite pit was someone regretting they fell asleep early. I was so glad they didn't want to miss anything!)

Third was Three Things: By far the most revealing activity, this exercise had each of us describe three things about ourselves—two truths and one falsehood—and then everyone else had to guess which one was false.

One of us had a tattoo. Another disliked basketball. Yet another had their front teeth knocked out in a sporting event. Oh, and one of us had their first kiss playing spin the bottle at Bible Camp. (Yep, that was me.)

My, how times change—and life goes on.

How about you? What new traditions can you add to your next family gathering that could help you get to know your family better?

July 19:

A Place Called Home

"Home is the place where," wrote poet Robert Frost, "when you have to go there, they have to take you in."

What thoughts come to mind when you consider the words, "Home is the place . . ."?

A little boy once wrote, "Home is the place where you can take a bad report card." That says something about the little fellow's home—that it was a place of acceptance, understanding, and a whole package of love.

"In my house," wrote one of Margaret Meade's oldest friends, "I was a child. In your family's house, I was a person." That says volumes about Margaret Meade's home—that it was a place filled with respect for individuals, openness to others' ideas, and a willingness to accept people as they are.

At its best, home is the place where we are accepted, warts and all.

But is home an obligation?

Frost's poetic assessment that home is the place where they "have to take you in" appears negative, at first. But his next line reveals more: "I should have called it," the poet continues, "something you somehow haven't to deserve."

That puts a whole new act on the stage. Home is not merely a place that must take you in; it's something unmerited—a gift! Home is always available to you because you are loved.

No person can ever deserve home; there is no way it can be bought. It's an experience freely given, and one that never has to be paid back. The only payment is the obligation to pass on the love and relationship experienced in your home—to share it with your own family and all the families you encounter in the world community.

Home is a gift—born of love, filled with acceptance, and eager for the opportunity to be shared.

How about you? How would you complete this sentence? "Home is the place . . ."

July 20:

I Can—But

"I can play better than I do," the golfer told my father, "but I never have."

I'm not sure if that statement was meant to comfort my father or challenge him. Either way, its layered truth stuck in my mind, reminding me of a similar confessional story.

A graduate school commencement speaker confided to a graduating senior as they marched in line to the ceremony, "I spent only two hours on this speech." He then revealed his scribbled notes, the mute evidence of his preparation deficiency, and added, "If I do well, then I'm proud of myself for being so good in such a short time. If they don't like my speech, I comfort myself in the fact I didn't spend much time on it."

Unfortunately, the latter was the case, as reported by many disappointed listeners.

I can play better (do better) than I do, but I never have.

We can apply this statement of philosophy and practice positively or negatively.

Negatively, we can use it as an excuse, always seeking to comfort ourselves with the lukewarm knowledge that "I could really do better if I put my mind to it, I just chose not to." We smugly accept our sub-potential performance and don't let it bother us.

That approach gives birth to mediocrity, where we settle for what we know is less than our best. The problem with this approach? Mediocrity does not aspire; it tires. It tires of dreaming and hoping—-but mostly it tires of working.

But on the positive side, "I can play better than I do, but never have," can move us to cope with whatever challenges we face. The knowledge of our untapped potential can fuel the drive to excel.

The difference between mediocrity and excellence may not be intelligence in itself but rather the intelligent use of time, talent, and efforts.

꘎꘎꘎

How about you? Will you choose to be moved to action or settle for being excused by your own inaction?

July 21:

Twists and Turns

"Life can be like a merry-go-round, the same view, predictable and serene," says Doug Sandler. "Or life can be like a roller coaster with twists and turns, loops and huge falls, and thrills galore. Ever wonder why the merry-go-round is two tickets and the roller coaster is twelve tickets? Because it's worth it."

Makes sense to me. Personally, I'd prefer a few more merry-go-round experiences.

But those roller coaster ones have certainly added zest and depth to my life.

How about you? What ride are you on at the moment?

July 22:

Nature's Pace

Today's inspiration comes from Henry David Thoreau:

> "Let us spend one day as deliberately as Nature, and not be thrown off the track by every nutshell and mosquito's wing that falls on the rails."

I'd just completed my morning readings and was settling in to tackle my to-do list, which was far longer than usual because my first book was going to be featured in a two-week marketing booster campaign. I was stressing over the details—the e-book pricing program, a new Book Club kit, copy for promotions, Facebook ads, and revisions on a couple of related articles.

How was I going to get it all done?

I took a deep breath, paused for a sip of coffee, looked out my sunroom window—and was greeted by a big, beautiful buck. He'd found my backyard bed, full of his favorite snacks. He raised his head, adorned by a massive set of antlers, and returned my dismayed stare, only to discount it and then return to his priorities.

He hung out for a while, nibbling here and there. He moved at his own pace, in his own time.

Deliberately. Confidently. Undistracted.

His presence helped put that to-do list in perspective. After observing the buck's unhurried movements, I was able to approach my own tasks with fresh eyes. Deliberately, confidently, I began to move through my list at my own pace.

How about you? Can time with nature help you regain your pace or perspective today?

July 23:

Stormy Lessons

"When we long for a life without difficulties," says Peter Marshall, "remind us that oaks grow strong in contrary winds and diamonds are made under pressure."

I'd never considered the value of life's storms and inevitable pressures. I was too busy preparing and protecting myself or others from its damage.

But when I look back at some of the most difficult periods in my life, I see that the hardships not only strengthened me but also revealed and crystallized core values previously hidden or discounted during times of calm or carefree living.

How about you? How have difficulties strengthened you or revealed hidden values?

July 24:

Structure's Freedom

My extended family was about to join me for our family's second annual staycation celebration.

As I was preparing for their weeklong stay, I stumbled upon a statement that stuck with me. Although I can't find its original source, its application spans much more than vacation planning: "Structure gives freedom."

Isn't that the truth?

Once we have a structure in place, an idea of how we want things to flow, then we have the freedom within that structure to experiment. Knowing a few anchor points—having a sense of what's next—takes some of the angst out of the process.

I do *love* possibilities; I must admit, however, that too many possibilities can be exhausting.

Structure helps.

So that year, we had a daily agenda with a few anchors in place: Meal menus, dinner reservations, and a long list of favorite games and activities. More importantly, there were plenty of LID (Let It Develop) chunks of time, when nothing but free time was planned.

Structured free time. Perhaps an oxymoron, but it worked.

Structure and freedom played well together. We'll be inviting both back next year.

How about you? How do you structure your family vacations? Or do you?

July 25:

Falling Upward

The title of Richard Rohr's book, *Falling Upward*, intrigued me—and his first sentences struck me hard:

> "There is much evidence on several levels that there are at least two major tasks to human life. The first task is to build a strong 'container' or identity; the second is to find the contents that the container was meant to hold."

It took me a minute to fully absorb that one.

By this stage of my life, as a sixty-something empty-nester gal, I suppose my "container" is complete. And perhaps I've even chosen the right attitude of discovery for this next task of finding its contents.

But how does that relate to idea of "falling upward"?

The message, I believe, is that our "falls," or the failings we encounter as we build our "containers" or identities, can actually be a source of strength and understanding for the next task of life. Our struggles serve to create a foundation for moving "upward," growing, and finding meaning.

I find this notion comforting and hopeful—for me, my children, and others I know who are struggling to create and fill their containers.

I envision life as more of an evolving pyramid and less of a rigid timeline. Some of us may have a larger base than others, but our experiences, great or small, can be used to enrich that second task of life. In fact, those falls and what we learn from them may equip us to handle and engage more fully in that second task of life.

And then, indeed, we can fall upward.

How about you? Where are you in accomplishing the two major tasks of life? Have your failings ever equipped you for an upcoming challenge?

July 26:

Joyfully Exhausted

I'll admit it. I was exhausted. My family's second annual staycation had been a great success, but I was bone-tired after hosting twelve loved ones in my house for seven days.

Even my paralyzed parts ached. (Yes, that is possible!)

Recovery mode was my pace, but I wouldn't have had it any other way. Every slow moment of recovery was filled with great memories.

As I recuperated, I thought often about an observation my son Peter had offered up that week: "Family and friendships are a matter of effort, not of proximity."

And yes, a *lot* of effort had gone into making that week happen, including staggered arrivals and departures from Arkansas, Wisconsin, Georgia, and New Jersey; restaurant and event reservations; daily agendas; and menu options complete with favorite and signature dishes.

But what had required the most effort and coordination was a special visit from Madison. Although she'd struggled with severe self-injurious behaviors for many years, she'd finally stabilized and was now flourishing in a new residential and day program. This meant that, for the first time in years, she was able to come spend time with some of her extended family in my home. My heart was filled with joy and gratitude for the two caregivers who helped make this special visit possible and for all the family's efforts to arrive in time to share a meal with Madison.

After everyone left, I wasn't simply exhausted—I was joyfully exhausted. Memories fueled a faster-than-normal recovery, and soon I felt ready to host again.

How about you? Have you ever been joyfully exhausted after making a significant effort to stay connected to friends or family? Was it worth it?

July 27:

Outfoxed

The fox froze, then cocked his head to study me and my nutty dog, who was barking so hard that both his front paws were lifting off the ground. When Tripp paused for a breath, the fox resumed his trot, dismissing us as if we'd interrupted his own morning ritual.

"Not again." I sighed. The previous year, that darn fox had fathered a litter of six kits in my backyard and attacked my cat. I thought he'd left.

"He's here," the professional I hired confirmed after a backyard visit. "Has a deer carcass halfway down his den."

"Great," I muttered, wondering how he'd managed that feat. Had he killed it?

I didn't want to hurt the fox, just remove him from my property. With my own backyard family event pending, I told the man I needed that uninvited guest relocated as soon as possible.

"I'll bring my dogs," he told me, and soon thereafter returned with two dogs and additional men.

One man kept wandering around.

"Everything okay?" I hollered, confused by his circling.

"I'm looking for the alternative site," he said. "Foxes have at least one back-up den."

A fox with a Plan B. Wonderful.

The dogs and men headed to the foxhole. I sat by the sliding glass door, reading, when one man tapped on the glass.

"We need to dig up some shrubs so the dogs can pass under the roots," he told me.

"Okay," I replied as a light rain began to fall.

Another tap on the glass.

"Huge roots. We need to pull them out with my truck."

"Okay."

Another tap.

"We hit rock. I need an earthmover to dig it out. I can have one here in twenty minutes."

By the time it arrived, so had a steady rain.

Four men, two dogs, and a yellow bulldozer attacked the foxhole in the downpour.

The scene reminded me of my son's early passion for mud-puddle jumping and the time he and a buddy camouflaged each other with mud from head to toe. Rain, dozers, mud, and barking dogs hunting an elusive foe must be a grown man's delight too.

One last tap.

"We got the roots and rocks out," the drenched man announced. "But no foxes."

"You're kidding," was all I could say.

"But we filled in their den," he assured me. "They won't be back."

Two weeks after my backyard family event, the furry critter was back, taunting my dog and teasing my cat.

Outfoxed again. I guess all creatures can benefit from a good Plan B.

How about you? Have you ever been outfoxed by a sly Plan B?

July 28:

Wings and Things

Two caterpillars are crawling along the ground, the story goes. They look up and spy butterflies sailing through the air. One looks at the other, shakes his head in disdain, and says, "You'll never get me up in one of those things!"

Barring an untimely death, the lowly caterpillar—regardless of his opinion or desire—will, of course, "get up in one of those things." It's the logical and biological conclusion of his creation, his purpose in life.

There are things in this world we simply can't avoid. Growth, no matter how scary it feels sometimes, is unavoidable. We're human beings, limited by time and space and confined to a physical body governed by certain laws and principles. We are here to change and expand, much like a new butterfly spreading its wings.

Children, for example, come to us as foregone conclusions. They cannot remain infants forever. For parents whose bundles of joys begin testing limits the minute they let out their first cry, that's welcome news. For those whose babies sleep well and never seem to stop smiling, it's a sad reality.

Nevertheless, growth happens.

And it's a tricky process.

At first, they need us for everything—food, clothing, guidance, love. To push them beyond age-appropriate expectations or give freedom too early can create burnout or feelings of abandonment. But to keep them dependent on us is equally risky. Finding the right pace demands the best insight parents can muster.

As children expand their circle of relationships, they join peers and invite significant others into their lives. Yet the parent who doesn't accept this "expanding life" or who stifles it risks damaging that inevitable transformation or its potential.

The parent-centered universe must shift. We have to let go.

I remember coming home from college, busting through our kitchen's back door, hugging my parents, and rattling off my plans, only to have Dad stop me with his customary request: "Now hold on, BB. Can you sit a minute, just long enough for me to smell you?"

I'd laugh at his classic line and sit with him for a hot second to summarize my latest news. But Dad knew what I learned as my own youngsters busted through my back door on their march to maturity with plans a-blazin'.

And what those caterpillars soon discovered.

They were born for those wings.

❧

How about you? What tricky stages have you experienced or witnessed on the march to maturity?

July 29:

What Envy Reveals

I saw the photo of a childhood acquaintance somewhere on social media. She and her handsome husband, along with their charming crew of children, all healthy and thriving, were traveling to an exotic place for an exotic celebration. The smiles. The clothes. The opulent setting. It was a life I'd dreamed of in my youth that could never be mine now.

And the thought, the one I fight hard to keep under control, burst through all the layers of well-adjusted thinking and blared, "Oh, how I wish my life would have turned out differently!"

Sibling loss, special needs children, divorce, and paralysis all have shaped my life in a way I could have never imagined.

But just as the green monster of envy began to move from my head into my heart, I found this statement in some of my father's writings: "Envy is but a hostile form of self-pity."

Yikes! Was that what was happening to me? Was my envy revealing a plunge into a pity pool?

Through my bouts of adversity, I've learned that wallowing in a pity pool, even when justified, can be a treacherous activity. Initially, others may be compassionate and comfort you. But eventually, self-pity exudes a bitterness that repels others, often when we need connection and community the most.

So I try hard to avoid pity pools, or at least minimize the time I spend in them. But maybe I fell into one when I saw that photo.

Maybe I needed to look at those photos through a different lens.

One that filtered out what hurt.

A polarized lens!

Not the divisive political kind but the healthy one, the one that filters out glare so that we can see more clearly.

I needed to look through a lens that didn't compare. One that sifted out self-pity and only connected to another's joy by *sharing* the excitement and perhaps even letting it fuel my own pursuit of joy and possibilities *within* the life I have.

Suddenly, connection rooted out comparison; possibilities rooted out pity.

I was envious no more. In fact, I was grateful for that photo—grateful for how it reminded me that our dreams, even if they're not the dreams of our youth, can still bring joy.

How about you? How do you keep envy out of your heart in this season of enviable tales?

July 30:

Brick by Brick

"If you have built castles in the air," writes Henry David Thoreau, "your work need not be lost; that is where they should be. Now put the foundations under them."

Today may be the perfect day to think of those dreams and consider what foundations are needed for them to become a reality. Break it down, brick by brick.

How about you? What foundations need your attention today?

July 31:

The Power of Put

⟶◦⟵

Fifteen months after my paralysis, a good friend emailed me about a tragic accident that had resulted in neurological damage and an unclear prognosis for a young teenager.

He was searching for words of comfort and wondered, "Are these pieces to a larger puzzle, or what does this all mean? I am sure you can give me some insight to the complexities of these situations."

I was flattered and honored, but in awe of the responsibility—or was it opportunity?—to learn from tragedy.

For the first time, I realized my journey could be helpful to someone else. In his questions I heard my friend asking, "How do you do it, Becky? How do you handle the pain?"

I paused as I read the email. I shut my eyes and briefly relived the hurt of my paralysis, its ongoing uncertainty. How would I give him a satisfying answer?

Surprisingly, it came quickly:

"I must place the pain to the side of my outlook on life," I wrote. "That is not to deny the hurt. That pain is real and never goes away. But I can put it in a place in my mind where I am not looking through it. Life viewed through pain can become a dismal existence. I try to put the pain to the side and prevent it from coloring the way I look at everything."

As I read my response, I was struck with my desire to "put" pain in its place. I did not ignore the pain, but accepted it.

Pain is a part of all our worlds—but we don't have to make it the center of them.

⟶◦⟵

How about you? How could you use the power of "put" to help you deal with a painful situation?

AUGUST

.

August 1:

Expanding Comfort

❧

There is comfort in routine.
—John Steinbeck

I stumbled upon the quote above after returning from a five-day vacation with family several years ago. Although I enjoyed every single minute of the trip—amazing dinners where my granddaughter had her first Maryland crab, the Iron Chef competition where the men defeated the women (sigh), family photo shoots, the grown-ups getting in on the playground fun—it took me far outside of my morning routines.

No walking the dog while chatting with my sister. No problem-solving adventures getting the newspaper out of the mulch. No brewing that special coffee blend that wakes me up so I can begin my morning readings.

I'd needed the break. And I think it's a good thing to disconnect and shake up our routines.

Still, there was something comforting, as Steinbeck suggests, about coming back to the familiar, to the little habits that help me jumpstart my body, my mind, and now, thanks to my sister, my funny bone.

Upon my return, Rachel and I added a nutty preamble to our morning chat: Snapchatting each other to wish each other a good morning.

This exchange doesn't sound terribly exciting, I know. But when you add filters, especially the voice-changing one that makes you sound like you've taken a huge gulp of helium, things start to get weird.

What a great addition to my morning routine! My dog, my coffee, and sharing a laugh with my sister. And Snapchat keeps track. As of this writing, we have a 2,673-day streak going.

Now that's a habit!

How about you? What routines bring comfort you each day? Do you miss them when they are disrupted?

August 2:

Clutter Redefined

"She may not show you her office," my friend's husband warned me before we entered their new home. "She still has some clearing out to do."

"Oh, is it a mess?" I asked. Cindi and I have been friends for over thirty years, so I'd earned the right to be direct. "I'd love to see another messy office," I teased. "Mine's always a disaster."

And we both chuckled.

"You know, it's not really her fault," her husband said. "She just has so many interests."

The good-hearted soul went on, listing his wife's hobbies, activities, and commitments—but my mind remained stuck on his perfect explanation. She wasn't messy or disorganized: she just had many interests. What a thoughtful turn of phrase. I smiled from the inside out.

And as I listened to this man defend his wife's clutter, I was struck by his love—and insight. His words revealed a tender recognition of his wife's personality: her passion for more than one interest, and her resolve to pursue them—now or in the future.

He chose to look at his wife's negative as a positive. Love doesn't come much purer than that.

Later that day, as I looked around my own office, I realized that my piles indeed represented important interests—family, hobbies, activities, and causes. Some stacks were stashed in quilted knapsacks hanging on hooks, ready to accompany me on my next outing; other, more sprawling interests (writing, photography, cooking, and crafts) were housed in large wicker bins.

I felt relieved, almost enlightened, by this new insight into my behavior, as if a shrink had helped me push through a new threshold of self-discovery. How comforting to finally have a refined diagnosis.

I am not messy. I just have many interests.

I don't have stacks of clutter. I have piles of interests.

How about you? Do you have piles of clutter at home, or do you know someone who does? What interests do they reveal?

August 3:

"Round Tuit" Boldness

Each indecision brings its own delays and
days are lost lamenting over lost days. . . .
What you can do or think you can do, begin it.
For boldness has magic, power, and genius in it.
—Johann Wolfgang von Goethe

In my teenage years, I attended a leadership conference. In one session on time management, the speaker challenged us to consider not only the items we'd checked off as "done" on our lists but also those items lingering as "undone," the ones we'd put in the "whenever I get around to it" category.

He then passed out wooden discs, about the size of a quarter, with the word TUIT imprinted on them.

"Here's your round tuit,'" he said. "You now have permission to accomplish those things you had put aside *until you got a 'round tuit*.'"

Procrastination has its costs. Delayed tasks are like too many open tabs on our computers, taking up space that affects our performance. They run in the background, hogging resources that can be best used elsewhere.

A bold decision to act, in contrast, brings with it relief, momentum, and a powerful sense of accomplishment. And we could all use more of those feelings in our lives, couldn't we?

How about you? How could you use a "round tuit" today?

August 4:

What's Behind "Whatever"

"How was the 'whatever' wedding?" I asked my friend Sarah.

"Disorganized!" she laughed. "But they were married among friends and family. So it worked out okay."

As she gave me the recap, I recalled her frustration in the early days of preparation. Her relatives' casual approach was far different than hers would have been.

"I don't want to bother her with details, but my schedule is so packed I want to make sure I can get everything done," she'd told me a couple of weeks earlier.

"Like what?"

"Like the shoes. We have bridesmaids' dresses, but I wondered what shoes we should wear."

"And?"

"She said, 'Whatever—you decide.' So I don't know whether to buy sandals or pumps, or even what color. "

"Really?"

"Yes, and when I asked about jewelry and hair, I got the same response. So I don't know whether to wear earrings, necklaces, or both, or whether to schedule an 'updo' appointment or not."

"Hmm," I said, thinking through both sides of that issue. Weddings are filled with decisions, so perhaps being casual about some details was a relief for the bride. Yet there were consequences for others involved.

"It sounds like I'm being picky," Sarah said, "but it'd be helpful to know what's expected so I can plan."

"Sounds like you might have a 'whatever' wedding in your future, Sarah." I chuckled.

And she did, as reported. But it still worked out just fine.

"Whatever," I've found, can be one of the most frustrating responses we can give or get. Although at first it gives the impression of a relaxed approach, in practice it can feel like a "Teflon" response, one that bounces the issue back into your court.

True, there are times when issues genuinely don't matter to us. But in other cases, we use "whatever" to avoid the effort of thinking it through to get to our true opinion.

Dictionary.com indicts the word more harshly, stating that "whatever" can be "used to indicate indifference to or scorn for something."

Ouch.

The next time I'm considering a "whatever" response, maybe I'll scratch beneath the surface a bit to see if I do care—even if only a little bit—about the choice. If spending just that little bit of effort will be a help to others, I'll consider it well worth it.

How about you? How do you experience the "whatever" response?

August 5:

Wonder's Promise

The new elevator in my home allowed me to return to an important nightly routine. For over three years, caregivers had "tucked" my children into bed for me. Now it was my turn.

Peter, then seven, had always had lengthy conversations prior to his nightly trips upstairs—stalling techniques, I surmised, designed to push the envelope on the bedtime curfew. However, that first tucking-in night, his ponderings were so raw, so pure, that I lost track of time.

"I'm glad you're here, Mom," he said softly. And then, after the briefest of pauses, he said, "Mom, sometimes I wonder about my life."

"Really?"

"Yes, like what my life is going to be like when I'm older. And where I am going to college."

I smiled at the detail of his wonder. Basketball season had started, and Carolina Blue had touched my downstairs life thoroughly, from light blue dishes to the UNC logo-ed blankets on our couch. But when I mentioned Chapel Hill, some seven hours away, he flinched.

"But that's too far, Mom. I don't want to be away from you."

"Honey, that's a long time from now. You'll be ready when it is time to go."

The college conversation sparked even more ponderings. "I wonder what I am going to do when I am older," he said. "What I am going to be like?"

This time I joined him with more questions:

"Do you think you will still like soccer?"

"Will you still enjoy playing with our cats?"

"Will you be in the same room with the same bed?"

"Will you have the same friends?"

When he'd answered them all, his eyes were wide and alert. "Now I can't go to sleep, Mom. I have too much stuff in my head," he whispered, snuggling into his pillow.

"Just think about one fun thing you want to do tomorrow, buddy," I said, stroking his thick brown hair. "Focus on that and you can fall asleep."

One elevator ride had linked our past with our future. The past was fixed and unchangeable. But the future was filled with possibilities. Through the eyes of a child, I, too, was reminded to wonder.

"Keep your dreams bigger than your memories," my father once said.

Wonder shows us how.

How about you? How can wonder inspire you today?

August 6:

Pivoting

It had become a closing sentiment at the end of many conversations with my adult children. After a healthy discussion on such life-changing topics as house purchases, relocations, or career opportunities, to the practical matters of menu-planning for a multigenerational gathering, post-shoulder-surgery comforts, or how to entertain my two-year-old grandson who was going to be in a cast for five weeks from a broken femur, I'd hear four words that would reset the conversation:

"We'll figure it out."

It'd become a dismissive signal to me. "We've got this," it said to me at one level.

Yet, on another level, I felt, "We don't need you."

Wincing, I couldn't help but think, *Is what I have to offer no longer of value to you?*

Ouch!

Then one child's added comment jarred me hard, pausing my pity-party spiral. After my third suggestion of what pillow to try for the spica cast on little Baxter's broken femur, I heard the familiar, "We'll figure it out." Then my thirty-five-year-old daughter, with ten years of marriage under her belt, added: "We always do."

I smiled at her confidence, then let gratitude seep in. Thank heavens—they do! I should be grateful these kids know how to figure it out. Isn't that what we want for our children, that they'll grow up to have the ability to solve their own problems?

With one quick, gratitude-powered pivot, I began to hear those four words differently. I now hear them as evidence of coping.

"We'll figure it out," is less about my loss and more about their gain.

Coping is a lifelong task. I'm grateful my kids have found the words—and the skills—to embrace it.

How about you? Has gratitude ever helped you pivot your perception from a loss into a gain?

August 7:

Becoming Acts

Every action you take is a vote for
the person you wish to become.
—James Clear

That statement will slow you down to take a beat before you act.

Singular behaviors are rehearsals for the soon-to-be patterns of performance that reveal our character—who we are becoming.

We should choose each one with care.

How about you? What do your actions today reveal about your "vote"?

August 8:

Worry vs. Concern

"There are two groups of worried people today. One group worries because of their jobs; the other worries because they have no jobs."

My father penned those words in 1989. Some things never change!

Strickland Gillilan's brief poem "On the Antiquity of Microbes" applies to worries too:

Adam
Had 'em.

But let's not confuse worry with genuine concern. There's a difference.

Worry tends to be repetitive, even circular, in that it rarely moves toward resolution. It focuses on things beyond our control.

Concern is different.

Concern is a linear thought process that moves forward in problem-solving mode. It prompts you to do something constructive about the situation, to deal with those issues that are within your control—your own behavior and emotions—and not bother with those that aren't.

Worry—thinking endlessly about a problem without positive results—weighs you down. Concern stirs you up, moving you to corrective action.

Worry incapacitates you, putting you to bed because you failed at your work. Concern gets you out of bed, putting you back to work on that failure.

Worry causes you to lament the process of growing old. Concern prompts you to schedule a medical check-up, buy insurance, and adopt a healthier lifestyle.

Worry gives you ulcers because you can't pay your bills. Concern causes you to review your finances and make a budget.

Worry makes your heart ache because you are lonely. Concern prompts you to make plans with friends or join a group.

We can get stuck in a never-ending, woe-is-me loop of worry, or we can put legs on our worries and take action.

Hard times are inevitable. But we have a choice in how we approach them. Will we be worried—or concerned?

How about you? Do you tend to ruminate on problems, or do you tend to take action?

August 9:

Precious Messages

⌒⌒☙⌒⌒

Ten weeks after my seventeen-day hospitalization for sepsis, I learned that it usually takes one week for every day spent in the hospital to recover. Although that information gave me a better perspective, it didn't do much to counteract the drudgery of my daily bouts with uncertainty.

One of the hardest parts of healing was the constant coping. The adjustment to life after such a serious disruption required a lot of extra: extra effort, extra time, extra problem-solving.

I had to REthink. RElearn. REdo. All in the hope of a full REcovery.

Many days, I felt extra tired. But my purpose was clear. I wanted to recover.

But recover to what?

What would I still be able to do? What would I need to do differently? How could I get my strength back? Was it possible to get it back, or did I have to adjust to a new normal?

A greeting card in my mailbox plucked at my tender heart:

> You are BRAVE even when
> you don't feel like it.

> You are STRONG even when
> you don't realize it.

I clutched the card and its precious message to my chest before I even opened it to see who had sent it. Deep sobs erupted, surprising me with their intensity as they called out the truth:

I didn't feel brave.
I didn't feel strong.

I felt weak, weary, and so very tired of disappointing myself and maybe even others as I found myself saying no to invitations when I really wanted to say yes.

I couldn't trust my body. I'd started new medications and stopped others, which meant I was on a roller coaster of adverse reactions and unintended bodily warfare that made my life unpredictable and limiting.

I looked again at the sweet card. Then took a deep breath, absorbed its powerful message, and renewed my commitment to pace myself and take extra time when I needed it.

Staying brave, staying strong—I could do that.

It would take a lot of extra effort and encouragement—but I would recover.

How about you? What words of encouragement have helped get though an uncertain recovery?

August 10:

Heart Memories

For eight straight years, I'd sat beside my sister Rachel on the deck of a Caribbean-bound cruise ship. During these seven-day family adventures, we'd watched our children grow—from rambunctious youngsters racing to a tunneled waterslide to nonchalant teenagers who disappeared into their no-adults-allowed clubs.

But they hadn't been the only ones to grow and change.

After finding the perfect spot to perch at the adult pool, Rachel and I observed and chatted, noting the fit and not-so-fit swimmers, the amazing range of body types, and the new, racy swimsuit styles sported by younger women. Barefaced and hatless, they basked in the heat, tans deepening by the minute.

"We're a little different now, Sissy," I said to Rachel, gesturing to our conservatively attired bodies, as we gazed from under our broad-brimmed hats and through our polarized sunglasses.

"Yes," she said, lathering on more sunscreen. "But our hearts are the same."

I smiled. There's nothing quite like a sister's on-target remark to put things in perspective.

Our hearts are indeed the same.

When we were youngsters, Rachel was the wide-open, unpredictable, blonde bombshell who never met a stranger and never doubted much. I was the blue-eyed brunette, shy in my own way, who was more reserved and prone to deep thought. We both cherished our parents and the traditions they created, and we carried them into our own homes as we became grownups with our own kids.

When we lost Dad in 2003 and then Mom in 2005, we were unwillingly promoted to leadership roles in our family. Those reconfigured roles settled awkwardly on us. Life was so different—and difficult—after losing our anchors. Yet our hearts, although deeply hurt, remained the same. And our yearly cruises and holiday visits kept us connected, even though we were 700 miles apart.

Your lost loved ones live on within you, fed by loving memories, heirloom history, and good old-fashioned storytelling. You feel their presence when you use their turn of phrase, make their signature holiday dishes, or repeat family customs passed down through each generation.

"Memory is more than a looking back to a time that is no longer," wrote Frederick Buechner. "It is looking out into another kind of time altogether where everything that ever was continues not just to be but to grow and change with the life that is in it still."

Fueled by memories and sustained by connection, our hearts can indeed remain the same.

How about you? How have you kept memories of the heart alive and connected to your loved ones?

August 11:

Truck Sign Advice

The truck was huge, the largest and longest 18-wheeler my father had ever seen. As he attempted to pass it, he noticed a sign emblazoned on its side:

Do not push or tow.

"Don't worry," my father later remarked. "There's no way I would have ever tried either!"

Parents of teens might find this advice especially useful. Parenting is often a daily exercise in switching gears; one minute you need to rein in your kid's exuberant living, and the next you need to gently nudge them to keep moving forward.

We may not be able to push or tow our teens, but we can attempt to minimize the distractions and risks with limits and boundaries. But sometimes, when we size up the situation, much like my father sized up that overgrown truck, we may realize the best move is to respect the circumstance and do nothing. Sometimes our best action is observant inaction, letting them learn at their own pace.

It's easy, however, to overstep and try to protect our kids from failure.

As I heard one teacher point out to an over-involved

parent during a conference once, "I'm not sure if your son is responsible. He hasn't had the chance to prove it."

Yikes!

If we aren't careful, we can manage too closely, creating confidence-draining, growth-stymieing dependence.

Indeed, some things will move without our intervention.

I do empathize, however, with the frustrated parent who went down to the train tracks every day to watch the trains go by. When asked why she did this, she replied, "I just like to see something moving that I don't have to push."

Don't we all!

Parenting can be exhausting—in both the doing and in the ongoing decisions of what, if anything, to do. There are many things that move without our pushing or towing them. But learning how to parent without doing either can be its own workout.

How about you? How do you resist the urge to pull or tow in your relationships?

August 12:

Error Indicators

I couldn't ignore the evidence. It wasn't even nine in the morning and I'd already wondered:

> *Did I remember to use shampoo when I washed my hair this morning? Did I throw in two Tide pods instead of one when I did the laundry? I may have even fed the dog twice— although if I did, I'm sure he didn't mind.*

I'd tried. I really had. But after two twelve-hour trips, four nights away from home, and an average of five hours of sleep per night, I couldn't rally to resume my schedule. Although I wouldn't have changed a thing about my trek to attend my nephew's wedding, I'd failed to adequately budget my energy. I'd returned joyous but depleted.

My wheelchair's battery light joined me with a sudden message:

LOW BATTERY ERROR.

Yep—when your battery is low, you are at risk for error.

So I heeded my wheelchair's warning and cleared my calendar, making time for a lengthy plug-in for my trusty companion and a power nap for me to recharge my error-prone mind.

How about you? What are your indicators that you are running low on energy? Do you become error-prone when you're in that state?

August 13:

Quiet Courage

Today's inspiration comes from a plaque hanging in my writing area:

> *Courage doesn't always roar. Sometimes courage is the quiet voice at the end of the day saying, "I will try again tomorrow."*
> —Mary Anne Rademacher

When I'm failing to make the progress that I want to make on a project, Rademacher's words encourage me, reminding me that persistence isn't just effort.

It's also courage—even when that courage doesn't roar.

How about you? Does looking at persistent effort as quiet courage inspire you?

August 14:

Taming Change

Change is hard. Sometimes it is invited or welcomed with milestone celebrations such as births, weddings, and anniversaries. Other changes, like illness or job loss, catch us off guard and create havoc.

Whether welcomed or not, change signals one thing: there's uncharted territory ahead.

In my work as a career consultant, I once worked with people facing job loss. Based on the premises of transitional consultant William Bridges, we taught workshops that described the change process as a series of "endings" and "new beginnings."

The mandatory step between the two was labeled the "chaos period."

Characteristics of the chaos period included lack of clarity, mixed messages, lack of structure, and uncertain next steps. On the more positive side, it was also a period receptive to creative ideas, new ways of doing things, and personal or professional growth. We emphasized that the path from "endings" to "new beginnings" must go through the "chaos period." The outcome might not be predictable, but the process is.

"Chaos is inevitable, so expect it," we advised. Chaos becomes part of the larger change process. We can name it, work through it, and be open to the creativeness within it.

And when change is a choice, I've since discovered, it can also become a factor in my decision-making process. I may feel like it's time for a change—new job, new home, or change in relationship. But am I ready for the chaos period that's sure to ensue if I put that change in motion?

Chosen or not, change becomes more manageable once you know there are no shortcuts. Chaos is just part of the process. To tame it, expect it with an open mind.

How about you? Would allowing—and preparing—for a "chaos period" help you manage change?

August 15:

You Matter

The thirteen-year-old was supposed to be pranking video doorbells or "ding-dong ditching" with his friends. But instead of leaving, like his friends, he left a message that made national news.

"Whoever you are, just remember you matter to someone. Just keep that in mind. Don't want you to forget that."

When his friends urged him to hurry up, he resisted, adding, "You matter, alright? There's always going to be somebody that cares about you. Just wanted to let you know you mattered, in case you needed to hear it."

Yes, that moved me to tears. That raw, insightful reminder doesn't come along very often. I needed to hear it that day.

How about you? Do you need to hear it—or do you know someone who does?

August 16:

Happy Walls

My 10:00 a.m. acupuncture treatment began with the practitioner feeling the pulses in my wrists. Tatyana, my neurologist and American-trained acupuncturist from Ukraine, carefully monitored my energy flow, locating blockages that she could release with strategically placed needles.

Suddenly, the fireplace in my living-room-turned-bedroom exploded with laughter. Tatyana's eyes widened.

"It's the workmen," I explained. "They really enjoy their work and each other's company. And they love to sing."

For five weeks, three workmen had been transforming my unfinished basement into a comfortable living area—and serenading me all the while.

As if on cue, their harmonious rendition of "Surfin' USA" filled the room. Walt, the painter, could have passed for one of the Beach Boys. That smooth buzz in his voice melted gently over a wide range of notes, blending particularly well with the high-pitched "ooowwweeeeooos."

"It's entertaining to listen to them work," I told Tatyana. "I've told them I've enjoyed their 'concerts' and they still keep singing, not embarrassed one bit."

Tatyana's soft, wise eyes returned my gaze. "It is good," she said. "People who enjoy their work and show it fill the room with positive energy."

"Really?"

"Yes, if they are happy—singing and laughing—the walls absorb their spirit."

"Wow," I mused. "So they're giving me 'happy walls'?"

She nodded in her knowing way. "It is good for you. You will feel it when you are downstairs. Their energy will be present in the work they have done."

At that time, it had been four years since the onset of transverse myelitis, and I'd finally moved forward with adapting to life with paralysis. With permanent ramps and lifts, I'd finally be able to access the basement.

And now I had an extra bonus: happy walls!

How about you? What would your walls say about you?

August 17:

One Daring Dean

The clerk highlighted the accessible route over the University of North Carolina at Chapel Hill campus, noting construction that interrupted the brick walkways. Cautiously, I cranked up the speed of my new power wheelchair and left the hotel, the historic Carolina Inn, for my adventure.

At my first turn, a professorial-looking young man asked if he could join me. "There are some troublesome spots ahead," he advised. "Maybe I'll walk with you for a while."

Surprised but grateful, I agreed. I learned the pleasant fellow was an assistant dean of student affairs.

I told him of my daughter's recent UNC tour and interest in several Southern schools. She'd traveled farther south with her father that day, giving me the day to explore my old stomping grounds where I'd attended school some twenty years prior.

Then we found the anticipated trouble. The fingers of a giant oak's roots had dug under our walkway, unearthing several bricks. Hemmed in by a wall on one side and the tree on the other, I looked down at my chair's small wheel and the hole frowning up at me.

My companion studied the predicament. "What's the best way for you to get through?"

"I could back up and gun it full blast," I replied, instantly knowing that my Evel Knievel notion was a bad one.

Ignoring my obvious mental lapse, he took his leather-bound portfolio and placed it over the missing bricks. "How about this?"

"Are you sure?" I stammered, noting the power-chair's size.

He nodded.

I inched forward, then motored easily over the makeshift bridge.

"It worked!" I exclaimed, feeling like I'd crossed the Amazon.

As our mutual path ended, I introduced myself.

"I'm Dean Bresciani," he replied.

"So"—I smiled putting the two together—"you are Dean Dean?"

He nodded, smiling back.

"Well, 'Dean Dean,' you've been my angel today. Thanks for helping me safely find my way."

He shook my hand and left, tucking his trusty notebook back under his arm.

Folks like Dean Dean impress me. Knowledgeable of the lay of the land, they anticipate possible challenges and take time to intervene. They view predicaments as problems to solve, not show-stopping roadblocks. They ignore obvious mental lapses, preferring not to judge but see possibilities. They are creative, use their resources well, and don't mind getting involved personally—and they have the tire tracks to prove it.

The world is lucky to have people like Dean Dean, who help others safely find their way—on campus and in life.

How about you? Have you ever been given unexpected, even daring, assistance? Or given it?

August 18:

Real Moments

There's an art to staying happy and content in our lives. I'm convinced that finding ways to be absorbed in the moment is one key.

In her book *Real Moments*, Barbara De Angelis says that ordinary moments are made "real" by absorbing details. "It's not what you're doing that matters—it's how you pay attention to what you are doing that makes it into a real moment," she asserts.

I read her book years ago, during my divorce. Uncertainty, turmoil, and pain plagued me during that transitional period. Yet household routines with four lively children demanded my attention. I found myself moving through the motions with a numb sense of duty. My mind was always elsewhere—figuring, worrying, wondering.

I tried her approach with Peter, then three years old. During his bedtime routine, I cleared my mind of wandering thoughts as I read to him and rocked him in my favorite cherry rocker. I noticed the smell of his freshly washed hair, the warmth of his special snuggle-hug. Minutes after carrying him to his bed, I heard the peaceful rhythm that slumber brings. I stood over him, stroked his hair, and tucked his favorite blanket around him.

I'm glad I took the time to make that moment real. A few months later, I could no longer climb the steps to his bedroom, hold him in that rocker, or stand over his bed. Paralysis robbed me of many things. But each of those real moments is untouchably secure in my heart.

When we allow ourselves to be happily absorbed, when we pay attention, we purchase our moments. And those moments remind us of what's important, renewing our perspective, energy, and delight for life.

Taking time to pay attention is worth the effort. The results can be priceless.

How about you? Are there moments today when you can be happily absorbed and bank some "real" memories?

August 19:

Misery's Antidote

Most of mankind's misery stems from feeling unloved.
—Sarah Young

So, hug the one you're with, right? If you feel it, don't be afraid to show it. And if you need it, don't be afraid to ask for it.

The thought of "preventing misery" is a powerful motivator to let our love show in caring ways.

Sending a blast of love to you—just in case you need it today.

How about you? Who can you reach out to today to show you care?

August 20:

Hanging Tough

Six months after COVID-19's invasion, life was still tough. I was hanging in there, sometimes with so much effort that I felt like my "hands had rope burns," as my dad used to say.

What helped?

Careful living—or was it carefree living? My best days were when I balanced both.

On the careful side, I was still a homebody, vigilantly attending to body, mind, and soul with structured routines. But on the carefree side, sometimes I'd pop some popcorn, lower the shades, and watch an afternoon movie.

Meanwhile, the days would come and go with very little punctuation. I was grateful for good health and the support of friends and family, but life was still so very different. I struggled daily with the question I think we all were asking:

How do we deal with life when the life we want isn't available?

It didn't help that the adverse reaction to the vaccine trials in the UK was the onset of transverse myelitis, the cause of my paralysis. After I heard that, I tucked myself even tighter into my bubble. But the truth was, I'd been living in a restricted state for so long that I was getting used to it.

The most challenging part? Pressing on without the ability to plan.

The words of author Jack London kicked me into gear with this powerful reminder: "You can't wait for inspiration—you have to go after it with a club."

Gulp.

So what could I do, where I was, with what I had?

I decided to beautify my home. Small projects that would make the place where I spent all my time even more comforting—projects that would help me feel like I had "done" something with my day.

I bedazzled an old mirror with pearls from a broken necklace; created an heirloom for my granddaughter Blakely Faye by adorning a framed photo of us with Cinderella trinkets; and spruced up my bathroom cabinets with snow-leopard shelf paper. All those projects had a beginning, middle, and end, something I longed for in that era of pandemic living.

Even when my hands were raw with rope burns, the hunt for inspiration gave me the strength to keep hanging tough.

How about you? What helped you to keep "hanging tough" during the pandemic or in other tough times?

August 21:

The Blame Game

When you blame others,
you give up your power to change.
—Robert Anthony

The quickest way for me to get out of a pity pit is to examine whom I'm blaming—and why.

Blame is other-directed. It prevents self-examination, even problem-solving. If I'm blaming someone for my situation, I can't see my role in it, much less be creative about any solutions.

Oddly, blaming others makes us victims. Relying on someone else's actions to fix things for us means we won't try to fix it ourselves.

If I can't own a problem, I lose my power to address it. And who wants to live life like that?

How about you? Has blaming others prevented your ability to address a problem?

August 22:

Beyond the Moment

I was excited but oh so weary. We—Mom, stepmom, and aunt, my daughter's trifecta of support—had already waited at the hospital seven hours, grabbed dinner, and returned to wait another seven.

Finally, after giving her mother a twenty-hour labor, my granddaughter arrived, six days late.

At two thirty in the morning, we entered the hallowed room. The sight of the three of them—Mom, Dad, and child—struck me hard, knocking off the layers of fatigue. There they were, a freshly minted family with new names and roles that would last them a lifetime.

I couldn't speak. It was as if the love and spirit of my own family of origin had joined us, filling the room to witness the birth of this family.

"The Brittany," as my father liked to call his strong-willed, uniquely spirited grandchild, had birthed a little one—his great-grandchild—whom I'm sure he would have called "The Blakely."

We'd known her first name for months. But the middle name was a secret.

"Oh my, Britty," I whispered, watching her cuddle her newborn. "So precious!"

Then the new dad pointed to the dry-eraser board, the keeper of vital information. "Did you see her name?"

I wheeled over to read the letters, hidden by the glare of the shiny board.

"Blakely Faye? Really? Faye is her middle name?" I squinted at the board, hardly believing it—my middle name, my mother's middle name, and now my granddaughter's. "Wow," I said—it was all I could manage. By that point, my fried brain and churning emotions had only one mission: get sleep so I could come back and hold her.

Twelve hours later, Blakely Faye was in my arms.

"So, you leave tomorrow, Mom?" Brittany asked.

"Supposed to, but maybe I'll stay a couple days?"

I'd never left home for more than ten days since my paralysis. Now, though already at day eleven, I couldn't imagine leaving little Blakely so soon.

Brittany shook her head. "But why, Mom? You'll have to transfer into your manual wheelchair to get up our steps at home. That's exhausting. Plus, it's a six-hour flight home. Really, Mom, we're fine. You should go home."

Again, I had no words. Who was this young woman, assessing my needs and directing me?

Had I just been parented?

I swallowed hard and looked at my daughter, who was cradling hers. Tears welled; I blinked them away.

"Okay, Britty."

And I left. In awe of my daughter. Of family. And of that circle of life that mutes us with its power of love.

How about you? Have you experienced a family moment that connected your loved ones and their roles in unexpected ways, far beyond the moment?

August 23:

A Child's View

My father's five-year-old friend Matt had a beautiful way of putting words and images together. One day, when beautiful white clouds formed all sorts of imaginable animals against a blue backdrop, Matt said to his mother, "Could we drive down the road and see if any clouds have run out of breath and fallen?"

"Have you ever seen a fallen cloud, Matt?" his mother asked.

"One time I saw a cloud caught in top of a tree, and another time I saw one floating on the river," he replied.

To be a child is to be a poet, using the sense of wonder as lyrics for the building of thoughts—thoughts that sometimes lie too deep for words but not for expression.

My eldest, Brittany, also had a unique way of expressing her wonder at age three. She'd squat down low to the ground, point that stubby finger at her discovery, and holler, "Ott!" (meaning "hot") when she'd found something new and interesting that she was not yet ready to touch.

A child's world is different. They live in a forest of legs and knees. That's all they see of adults unless they risk losing their bearings by looking far up at the tall timbers that surround them.

Some adults know the secret of entering their world. They stoop down to eye level and take interest in whatever's playing in their young minds.

Children are impressed by little things. A funny-shaped stick resembles something their minds conjure up. A sparkling rock they imagine is a precious jewel.

Their sense of adventure makes an ocean of a bathtub, a spacewalk of a pile of leaves. A mud hole can yield clay fit for a sculptor, while chairs with blankets draped over them can become a castle to be defended at any cost.

Life is simple and pretty wonder-full.

⤳⧡⤳

How about you? When is the last time you saw the world from a child's view?

August 24:

Savory Routines

⟋⟍⟋

Novelty is stimulating and valuable. However, the pleasure of doing a thing the same way, at the same time, every day, and savoring it, is worth noting.
—Gretchen Rubin

I read Rubin's advice while I was whisking my coffee with my newfangled milk frother. As I watched the bubbles whip around the edge of the mug, almost overflowing, I considered my predictable but very necessary morning routine.

Same coffee brand. Same creamer. Same time each day. And now I whip it all together with my fancy battery-operated milk frother.

Every day I do it. Every day I need it! Every day it primes me for the rest of what's next that's not a routine.

For the next few days, I took extra time with that often absent-minded routine and began to savor it, appreciate it, and delight in the pleasure of its sameness. That pause not only refreshed but enriched each morning. What was once routine became notably cherished.

⤳⧡⤳

How about you? What routine in your day could be noted and savored?

August 25:

Time for a Float

I'll never forget my first attempt to swim after paralysis. Although a good swimmer, I had no idea how to manage my paralyzed parts in the water. Midway down my abdomen, about three inches north of my belly button, both sensation and motor control were gone, dividing my body into two parts—the controllable above my waist and uncontrollable below it.

It's hard to describe paralysis, this strange, divided state where your mind commands a body part to do something and it refuses. It's a bit like when a hand or foot "falls asleep," numbed by pressure or lack of movement.

Except my limbs never woke up.

As you may recall, I like to call my lower body my "two-year-old" since it tends not to mind me, is moody, and often has tantrums (involuntary spasms) that send my knees popping up to my chest for no apparent reason.

Nevertheless, I wanted to swim again. With an instructor watching, I began my freestyle stroke, hoping my upper-body strength could drag along the two-year-old. All was well until I stopped to rest and my two-year-old decided to tantrum.

My hips spasmed up behind me, pushing my head down into the water. "Hips down, hips down!" I instructed them, but they didn't listen. I thrashed madly, choking, until the instructor pulled me to the side of the pool.

"What happened?" I said, coughing up water.

"You're fine," she said calmly.

"No, I'm not!" I wheezed. "My hips popped up, pushing my head down. I couldn't breathe!"

"Yes, that happens sometimes," she said matter-of-factly, with a hint of compassion. "Your abdominals aren't working like they used to, so you can't pull your hips underneath you." She pointed to her hips and showed me the tuck motion I could no longer do. "You can still swim, though. I'll show you."

She glided face-first into the water, using only her hands, then turned one shoulder up and out of the water and began to float on her back.

"When you need to rest, just float."

It worked! Soon I had a pattern: swim until I was weary, then float.

I think about that lesson whenever weariness starts to slow my pace. It's a helpful reminder that it's sometimes necessary to let go of the struggles beneath for a while and buoy up for a rest—to simply float.

How about you? Do you need to float today?

August 26:

The Milkshake Method

It was nine fifteen on a Saturday night. I knew if I wanted to talk to Mom and Dad I'd need to make my call right then or I would not make their bedtime curfew.

Mom answered on the first ring; Dad joined in the conversation.

They asked about my dinner party that was in progress. I'd gathered together some friends, many of whom Mom and Dad knew from earlier visits to Baltimore, for a cookout. "How's so and so?" they asked. "Tell her I said hello." They loved to plug into my world.

"And how's your ice cream?" Dad inquired next. During their last visit I had purchased an ice cream maker, and we had made some delicious ice cream together.

"Well," I began, "I don't know what I've done wrong, but it has been churning for three and a half hours and it is still soup!"

Without skipping a beat, he said, "You can always serve milkshakes!"

I had to laugh and shake my head. Milkshakes indeed.

He didn't ask if I had used enough ice.

He didn't ask if I had changed the recipe.

He didn't ask if I'd used the right rock salt.

He just made a helpful suggestion of how to use what I had to its best advantage.

That was his gift: To see the possibilities. To assess right then and there whatever was at hand—an issue, a person, a situation—and find a positive spin.

Even though a critique may be in order, moving forward with a constructive approach was always Dad's lead. It was almost an automatic response with him. If you watched him carefully you could almost see the sifting and sorting in his steady, sea-blue gaze as he allowed only the most positive of possibilities to float to the top of his mind.

Seek the possibilities within the parameters of the present, Dad taught me with his "milkshake method" of looking at life. Success and failure are no more or less than a matter of perspective.

᷂᷂᷂

How about you? Have could you use the milkshake method for dealing with a disappointing situation?

August 27:

Apology's Plea

Today's inspiration comes from my morning "Question the Day" trivia challenge about the meaning of the Maori word *aroha*. The Maori are the Polynesian people of New Zealand. This word, *aroha*, means "to have compassion."

"The word can be built on," the Alexa voice informed me, "such as in the apology '*Aroha mai*,' which translates to, 'Please show me compassion.'"

Thought-provoking, isn't it?

That's what we're asking for when we say "I'm sorry." Compassion.

How about you? Think about the last time someone told you they were sorry. Did you show them compassion?

August 28:

Rubber-Band Parenting

The seminar on family life was over. The speaker joined my father as they walked through campus, stopping occasionally to chat with students. One young man followed them and fell into step with them.

"Excuse me, sir," he began, addressing the lecturer. "Boiling down everything you said tonight, what would you say is the most difficult task in parenting teenagers?"

"Well, son," he said, "after we use all our psychological jargon about being parents to teenagers, I think the bottom line is that we must learn to live with rubber bands."

"Rubber bands?" the young man repeated.

"Yes," the lecturer said with a nod, "teenagers are really rubber bands. Take a rubber band, put it around your index finger, and stretch it a long way. When you turn it loose, it comes back to your finger. Teenagers are like that. They're only part-time adults. They must leave the nest, but they have a need to know that the nest will still be there when they want to come back to it." He slowed his pace and turned to the young man. "Learning and practicing the art of the rubber band is imperative. If stretched enough, it breaks. At some point, it *must* break. Then they're on their own—but with fond memories of what once was. And those memories move them into responsible adulthood."

Rubber-band parenting—I can think of no better description of the path to maturity for our children.

Parenting a teen is a unique experience. Sometimes our teens welcome us into their world along with their friends, classmates, or teammates. These moments allow us to see our children as others see them and to marvel at—or feel mortified by—the lessons they have learned at home or (sometimes) still need to learn. As parents, we laugh, cheer, and observe, but we also take notes on things that still need to be taught.

Meanwhile the teens stretch away again, retreating to their cars, their friends, or their bedrooms or basements for gaming, texting, and social media scrolling.

And all we can do then is wait for them to come back to the nest of security for advice and counsel—or, more realistically, money or a home-cooked meal.

❧

How about you? Have you practiced or witnessed the art of rubber-band parenting?

August 29:

The Smell of a
Banana Sandwich

The little boy was drenched as he fought the rainstorm. He could hardly see the sidewalk as he trudged along the way to his home. But through his soggy brown lunch bag, he could smell the aroma of the banana sandwich his mom had packed for his lunch.

School had been dismissed at about eleven. The teacher said a major storm was coming. It would begin as heavy rain, then sleet. She told her class to hurry home, as fast as they could. (This was back in the days of small neighborhood schools, when all the children walked to school.)

The rain was coming in torrents, and sleet was fighting for equal time. The child bent forward against the elements. Then he heard a car horn. He dared to look up, and there he saw the most beautiful sight in the world: his grandfather opening the car door and motioning for him to get in.

"I thought a boy might need a ride in this weather," the elder gent chuckled as his grandson jumped in, baptizing the front seat with rain water. "Got a banana sandwich in that little bag, don't you? I can smell it," he said. "Nothing smells quite like a soaked banana sandwich."

To this day, when I smell a banana, I remember my father's story about his soaked banana sandwich and that cold and stormy day when his grandfather sensed that his little grandson needed help.

I never knew my father's father—Papa Benfield, he was called. But I got to know him well through stories. He was a kind man. A faithful man. A man who every time he saw my father would ask him what he'd learned that day. He must have been a thoughtful man too.

We never know what memories we create for our children and grandchildren by the simple acts that cost us so little but become rich experiences for them. What stories will I give my own to tell and retell to their children? What smells will conjure up feelings of warmth and safety?

How about you? What smells evoke special childhood memories?

August 30:

Last Stoplights

Summer's edge is pushing into the promised routines of fall, reminding me of my father's tale about giving directions:

> A gentleman is sitting comfortably on a sidewalk bench in his small town. A stranger stops his car, rolls down the window, and asks for directions.
>
> "No problem," says the old fellow, pointing in the direction the car is already headed. "Just go to the last stoplight and turn left."
>
> The motorist thanks him and moves forward a few yards before hitting his brakes. Although the directions sounded simple, the question has suddenly dawned on him— *How do you know which is the last stoplight?*

This time of year is filled with "last stoplights."

"This is the last time in my bed," my niece Snapchatted me. The next day she moved into her dorm room, where more Snapchats revealed her excitement at its transformation into her new home for the next four years.

Parents may have a more nostalgic view.

Often, we don't know when we have passed "the last stoplight" in our lives. Life moves forward, and bottles, diapers, and training wheels gradually disappear. You barely sense that days are turning to months and months turning to years. The drama of life slips by softly. There's no announcement of Act I, Act II, or Act III.

And yet some decision points are clear.

An acceptance letter arrives from a college that is a five-hour plane ride away. A job offer takes nearby newlyweds to a foreign coast. A life partner is chosen; a new home is purchased.

These crossroads are choices that create last stoplights. And when we choose them, we can also celebrate the lasts in preparation for the firsts.

"They're taking a babymoon," my daughter informed me.

"A what?"

"Babymoon, Mom. Like a honeymoon, except it celebrates their last vacation together before the baby arrives."

I smiled at the thought of that last stoplight and the many firsts ahead.

"Kiss the joy as it flies," the poet William Blake suggests. Squeeze every fleeting moment, and hold every joy as close as you can.

For so many this time of year, the first of the lasts have begun.

How about you? What last stoplights could be ahead for you in the near future?

August 31:

All Fired Up

She pushed opened the door and practically lunged toward the table with an outstretched hand. As we shook hello, her alert, engaging eyes spoke louder than her words.

"I'm Maggie," she declared. "And she's wonderful," she said, referring to my fifteen-year-old daughter Brittany, one of her students.

Maggie (Ms. Springle) told me about the algebra class she taught and reviewed her teaching approach. Then she stopped abruptly. "I almost forgot. Here's my home phone number. I want you to have it. I've told the girls to call any time, up until midnight."

"Thank you," I said, "but wouldn't you prefer email?"

"No, I really want the girls to call—and for you to call, too, if you have any concerns. I don't want them to get home late from a practice, start homework, and be stressed if they have questions. I'd rather they call." She smiled confidently.

"Wow. Well, any special projects coming up?"

"No, but we have a theme-oriented snack every Friday. The girls bring a snack related to the topic of the week. They really love it."

I could see why. Actually, I could see why they really loved her.

"She's amazing," I told Brittany afterward. "One fired-up teacher. Do you like her class?"

"Yeah, we all like her," she said. "We can call her at home—until midnight," she added with those rare raised eyebrows that signal a teen's been impressed.

"She's got me fired up, too, Britty," I said. "Wish I'd had her for a teacher."

That was saying something because I always hated algebra. But I think I could have learned from Ms. Springle.

In fact, I think I did. She took a subject—perhaps the most mundane topic in high school (I know, my opinion)—and made it come to life. Her energy was contagious; her dedication obvious; and her availability unparalleled in my experience. Her mission-driven spirit permeated everything from lecture to homework to a simple snack routine.

We all need teachers in life who expect a lot but are willing to give a lot too.

How about you? Have you ever had a teacher who fired you up?

SEPTEMBER

September 1:

Work in Motion

My far-flung family gathered for a Labor Day Weekend reunion. With new jobs, new locations, career shifts, and expanding responsibilities, we had a lot to talk about.

Although grateful for the break from our labors, we soon began to talk about the challenges of too much work, not enough work, too much oversight, not enough oversight, and that age-old problem of being responsible for work outside your control.

As we shared more workplace war stories, someone asked, "Does anyone ever like their first job?"

We all laughed and nodded in acknowledgment at the nerve of truth the question struck.

Back at home, while resting up after the vacation (yes, I do that—do you?), I found this quote from Marcus Aurelius: "Labor not as one who is wretched, nor yet as one who would be pitied or admired: but direct your will to one thing only, to put yourself in motion and to check yourself at all times."

What a great reset on an appropriate approach to work!

In short: Don't gripe. Don't seek pity or admiration as you work. Focus on moving forward while staying aware of who you are as you encounter work's inevitable challenges.

Granted, we need to "feel the feeling" and vent our frustrations when we find the right time and place to do so. But we need to get it out, get over it, and get on with moving forward if we want to learn and grow.

We may not be able to control everything in our environment; however, we can always be mindful of who we are and how we affect others.

We can be encouraging of new ideas, or we can be dismissive.

We can radiate superiority, or we can show a willingness to learn.

We can discount feedback or take it to heart.

Easy to say and yet so hard to do! Then again, they call it "work" for a reason, right?

"Put yourself in motion and check yourself at all times."

This will be my motto as I strive to finish strong this year.

How about you? What renews your approach to work when you are struggling or feeling frustrated?

September 2:

Waiting Out the Fog

Today's inspiration comes from story I love to reread each fall. In "Outlasting the Fog," Mark Nepo describes a man who "built a home on a cliff by the sea, only to have a month-long fog roll in. He cursed the place and moved away. But a week after he'd gone, the fog cleared."

Indeed, fall is the time for fog—for changes, chaos, and uncertainty. Summer's sunny pace has gone, and we are waiting for the structure of fall's routines to gel, to shape us, to remind us what's important as we begin a new season.

It's a time for patience, for a little extra tolerance for

both the lack of clarity we feel and also for those we keep bumping into who may be in their own fogs.

Perhaps we just need to outlast the fog.

How about you? What fogs have rolled in for you this fall?

September 3:

Don't Tiptoe

I was a junior in college when my father's phone call reached me. My seventeen-year-old brother had hit a pier while he was waterskiing. He was in a coma. Nine days later, he would die.

Even in the best circumstances, death is difficult. But untimely death is tragic.

How do you comfort a friend who has experienced a tragic loss? Most of us can handle the initial responsibility. We go to the memorial, offer sympathy, take a dish of food, or send flowers or a donation.

But what do you do after a few days or weeks? Most of us run out of road map by then.

Here's what our family learned and experienced:

Don't try to conduct business as usual; don't ignore what's happened. The loss is real, so be real in your approach to it. Be observant as to how it's affecting your friend.

Do let them talk about the loss. They will close the subject when they're through. Don't try to close it for them.

Don't try to stop their tears. Crying does not hurt; it releases hurt and brings healing. Don't give in to the temptation and tendency to change the subject.

Do keep in touch with expressions of care, such as "Just want you to know I'm thinking about you"; "I'm hurting with you"; "I'm here for you." They will—if they need to—pick up on your offer and talk about their feelings.

Don't (unless you've been through a *very* similar experience) say, "I know just how your feel." You don't—not unless you've actually been there.

Do, however, try to communicate your struggle to understand: "I don't know how you feel, not really, but this must be so hard, so difficult." Those words encourage your friend to express to you what they feel no one truly understands.

Bottom line: Don't tiptoe around the tragedy. If you do, you become part of the problem. Be part of the solution by walking alongside the person as they face their loss.

How about you? Think about a time when you were grieving. What words helped—or didn't? How did this experience prepare you to help someone else in need?

September 4:

The Power of Observation

It was a tradition in my son's high school: On the first day of school, an English teacher would introduce himself, take off one shoe, and throw it out an open window. He would then tell the class, "Write about what you you've just seen."

I can just imagine the big eyes of the shocked students.

The antic was legendary. It made kids excited to go to school on the first day and eager to discover which English class they'd been assigned to. And no one ever forgot that lesson.

But what was the point?

My guess is the lesson was intended to teach young writers about the power of observation and point of view.

Pay attention. Think about what you saw—or *think* you saw. Know your biases and blinders.

Is there anything more important today than the power of observation? In a busy world, keeping our eyes open enables us to learn from many sources, broadening our perspective and our point of view.

How about you? What can you learn from being more observant today?

September 5:

Not Little Adults

My siblings and I, preschoolers at the time, were supposed to be asleep. But I'd slipped downstairs to hover outside the dining room where my parents were entertaining guests. I crooked my finger at my father, motioning him to come to me.

"Come in, honey," he invited. "What's going on?"

Clad in my footy pajamas, I padded in and told him that Rachel was sick.

One of the guests, a young internist physician, was urged by his wife to go upstairs with us. He acquiesced—but after examining my sister, he shook his head. "I don't know. I think you should call the child's doctor. I'm not that familiar with treating children."

Dad looked confused.

"Children are not just little adults, you know," the doctor said.

That statement stuck, often appearing in Dad's stories and sermons. And as a child, I liked it since it shifted him into a more reflective, less punitive gear, especially when he was reacting to our missteps.

Hey, we were just kids!

After parenting four children for three decades, I appreciate the sentiment even more. Children are not "just little adults"—mentally, emotionally, or spiritually.

Age-appropriate responses are a challenge.

Do we "pick our battles," letting some issues go? Or "nip it in the bud," correcting small mistakes before they become big ones?

Do we intervene through punishments or rewards? Or allow natural consequences to teach?

For some, parenting appears effortless; their children apparently need only an occasional nudge to keep moving through a life seemingly hard-wired to be goal-oriented and purpose-driven.

For others, parenting is a contact sport; every day requires shoulder pads, a helmet, a mouth guard, and a daily prayer that the right set of plays can be found for the next set of issues.

We often discover more about ourselves than our children on the battlefields of parenting, especially when we parent a child unlike ourselves. Should we expect as much from our children as was expected of us? Are we setting high expectations—or unrealistic demands?

Perhaps we should consider:

- High expectations prompt goal motivation; unrealistic demands generate fear motivation.
- High expectations create momentum; unrealistic demands destroy tender spirits.
- High expectations fuel a fire-in-the-belly drive; unrealistic demands knot stomachs, derailing focus.

Figuring out the right response at the right time isn't easy. Calling out the best that's in our children often requires us to call out the best in ourselves too.

How about you? Do you find it difficult to discern between high expectations and unrealistic demands when it comes to parenting?

September 6:

An Insight Job

You can't force insight.
—Dr. R. F. Smith Jr.

The above quote is a classic from my father, one that helps me be a little kinder, gentler, and more patient in my expectations of others.

And it reminds me of that other classic, "You can bring a horse to water, but you can't make him drink."

Insight is an inside job.

How about you? Have you ever tried to force insight for yourself or others? How did that turn out?

September 7:

Beyond the Game

Although I'd been watching games for weeks, that Friday night was the first time I could hear one.

Perched on a hillside sidewalk, I'd watched Peter's lacrosse games with binoculars. To help me find him in the sea of blue jerseys, he wore a yellow T-shirt and left the shirttail out. Once I spied the yellow-trimmed jersey, I knew I'd found my eight-year-old son.

One Friday, a friend helped me get to the field. We noticed the referee talking extensively to both teams, even after the game began. He frequently blew his whistle, after which he described the infraction and then stated the rule. In the most physical game I'd seen, the kids went down constantly from hits, trips, and, my new term for the week, "pancakes."

A "pancake," Peter taught me, is when someone is hit head-on, causing him to go flat to the ground like a pancake.

The ref seemed to be in the middle of every play, flagging and whistling errant moves, then commenting. "That's a push. I know you didn't mean it, but that's a push," he'd gently scold the offending player while helping up the pushed player.

While running beside players, he'd warn, "Don't push him if you can see his name" (on the back of the jersey, he meant).

One pancake took a blue jersey down with a thud. "That was legal," the ref allowed. "A little excessive, but legal. Are you okay?" he asked our player.

Once we lost the ref but then found him bending down to tie a player's shoe.

Another time, he ran beside a player who'd caught a ball but was jogging tentatively down the field. "Run faster," the ref encouraged.

Before Pete faced off with the opposition, the ref saw Pete's untied shoelace, tied it, and positioned both boys. Pete scooped up the ball and took it toward the goal. Defensemen swarmed around him. He spun around one guy, took aim, fired at the goal, and scored.

"Nice move!" cheered the ref.

Although we lost, Pete greeted me with a big smile at the end of the game.

"Nice game, buddy!" I congratulate him. Then I asked about the ref.

"He was cool, Mom. He learned my name. Told me I was all over the place." Pete beamed. "He talked to everyone."

What a ref! He judged clearly while instructing, making tough calls with a tender touch. He was fair but not afraid to be enthusiastic, even encouraging. A professional with a heart, he showed more than just a love of the game. He fostered a respect for the rules of the game and everyone who played it, offering not only instruction but encouragement too.

How about you? Has anyone ever guided you in a supportive and instructive way that revealed their passion for your learning? Has a special ref ever influenced your love of a sport?

September 8:

Comfort Begets Comfort

The comment fell from my lips before I realized what I'd said. I'd just introduced Cindy, my son's stepmother, to a new friend, Beth, at a back-to-school social gathering.

"Wait, you're Pete's stepmom?" Beth said to Cindy, and then stared at me.

Cindy and I watched Beth's eyes widen as she realized ex-wife was with current wife—and we were smiling.

"We share the same taste in men," I quipped.

We all paused—and then burst into laughter. Our relaxed chatter resumed. Later on, Beth took great delight in introducing us as Pete's mom and stepmom. Several folks remarked on our cordial relationship.

Our comfort seemed to breed their comfort.

But make no mistake, divorce creates uncomfortable situations and relationships. It just does.

Redefined roles ripple beyond the couple and affect family, friends, and colleagues. Children struggle to understand and adjust to all the changes. We may be divorced, but we are also still parents and must be mindful of what our children (and others) are observing and learning by how we behave toward one another.

Our willingness to adapt and adjust to new relationships will encourage theirs.

Indeed, comfort begets comfort.

For all.

How about you? Have you ever worked hard to create a good relationship for a child's benefit? Have others noticed?

September 9:

Habitual Learning

The simplest way to start something new is to start doing it alongside something you've always done.

Or, as I like to say, "Stack your habits." Pick a routine that's steadfast and simply add to it.

In my IBM days, you could set your watch by my friend Al's 3:00 p.m. coffee break. I used it as a reminder to call home to check in with the kids after school.

Daily and consistent routines like his are perfect for piggybacking a new habit.

Want to develop a new interest? Add a relevant podcast to your morning commute.

Want to try a new product that must be taken or used daily? Add it before or after your toothbrushing routine.

Want to do better about keeping in touch with friends or family? Add a phone call to your daily dog walks.

Want to increase your mindfulness? List three things you are grateful for before you get out of bed.

Our days are already bookmarked with routines. Let them help you learn and grow by developing new habits.

How about you? What's something new you can learn by stacking a habit?

September 10:

Letting Go Without Falling Apart

September seemed like a late start, but then again, that was all part of the plan. Although most college kids were already in school, those California folks have their own ideas about a lot of things—start times, grading quarters, and an odd tradition of not knowing who your roommate is until move-in day.

Regardless of the context, the reality remained—I was sending my youngest child to college. My life would soon be forever changed.

I'd been preparing for months. Traveling by wheelchair isn't easy, especially 3,000 miles away from home. But my biggest challenge was the mental preparation: trying to find that perfect zone where I could gracefully let go—without falling apart.

I sought the advice of other mothers.

Some were practical:
"Bring tissues."
"Wear dark glasses."
"Wait until you get into the car to cry."

Others laid out the unvarnished truth:
"It's awful."
"I cried every day for weeks."
"I don't know how you are going to do it.
It's so far away."

But the best advice came from a twenty-five-year-old young woman who wasn't even a mother at the time:
"You'll be fine," my wise eldest daughter texted me on move-in day. "Just think of it as so exciting!"
So I banished my stoic mantra—"He's ready; I'm ready"—for the more energized "It's so exciting!" and was surprised at the shift in my attitude. When I focused on the excitement of the unknown rather than the fear of it, the loss became filled with wonder and anticipation.
It's so exciting, I thought during our last breakfast together, letting the possibilities of the next morning's meal lighten the tone.
"It's so exciting," I repeated as we filled half the dorm room, hypothesizing about the young man who would fill the other half.
Unlike my daughter's all-day dorm move-in, unpacking went quickly. Once we finished, I was gently dismissed by my son to wander the campus until the dorm's parent-student meeting.
At the meeting, ninety-seven students and their parents crammed into the sun-filled lounge. After an

informative slideshow, hugs and tears muffled our fare-wells until only the parents remained.

"You've said good-bye, but here's one last chance to share your parting words," a voice said, breaking the quiet. "Take a marker and write a note to your child on the glass panes. It will be here all year."

"It's so exciting," I breathed out quietly, then wrote, "Deep roots. Strong wings. Big heart. Show them what you've got, Pete."

Turning from the windows, I wheeled out the door.

He belongs. He's well cared for. He's doing what we've been preparing him to do. All part of the plan.

It's so exciting.

And I made it to the car.

How about you? What words have strengthened you in the midst of a tough/bittersweet/emotional good-bye?

September 11:

The Power of RE

Summer living has come to an end, and we have some decisions to make. Whether returning, reinventing, or rediscovering, as we approach the cusp of fall—one of the year's most intense times of transition—I'm inspired by what I call the power of RE.

It's a great time to reassess what's important and what matters.

In one of my tizzies with my publisher about how to best market my book, *Rethinking Possible*, I reached out for guidance from award-winning author Heather Sellers, who graciously read and provided a blurb for my book.

"First of all," she wrote in an email to me, "*breathe*."

She followed that up with words that I've never forgotten: "I believe it is less about marketing and more about meaning."

Meaning. Of course! Focus on the pursuits that yield meaning. What a great question for reevaluating where and how to spend time—and for calming my tizzy.

That lens simplified my choices.

Although social media is a critical part of any book marketing plan, my most meaningful interactions have always been directly with readers both online and in person. A columnist for over twenty years, I cherished every response and comment, especially when my life stories intersected theirs and we exchanged insights.

So, we reprioritized our marketing to support that goal. We spent extra time creating a media kit and a book club kit and then reached out to libraries, book clubs, bookstores, and other small gathering venues and shared those materials.

Activities that were less transactional and more relational energized me.

I welcomed interviews, podcasts, and panel discussions. I also recommitted to write weekly to my Thoughtful Thursday email subscribers, some of whom had followed my life's journey since 1997—the year that I began writing about my escapades with paralysis.

The search for meaning helped harness that power of RE.

⁓§§⁓

How about you? What gives your life meaning? How can you use it strengthen the power of RE this fall?

September 12:

More Life

Dad's handwritten words snagged my skimming eyes, forcing me to re-read what he'd written three times.

"May the questions of life never stop you from seeking the answers, and even if you can't find the answers, just remember that 'knowing the real questions of life' is often more important than easy answers. The harder you find life, the more life you'll find."

The harder you find life, the more life you'll find.

My father was a wise man. He'd inscribed those words over forty years ago in a book he had given to my sister just a few months after our brother's death.

Life was particularly hard in that moment. We spent a long time trying to find answers to unanswerable questions.

Yet, as I reflect upon my father's thoughts, I do believe we discovered a richness of life through a deepened appreciation of each other and our precious time together—time that perhaps we had taken for granted before Forest's death.

With effort, we healed and grew. Coping muscles flexed time and time again as we adjusted our daily life to include unexpected and unwanted changes. We fought for rhythms, routines, and a sense of balance that sent our roots down deep into the soil of living, looking for nourishment.

And yes, perhaps we found more life.

How about you? What hard questions have you been faced with that have pushed you to find more life?

September 13:

Getting Unstuck

Here's an exercise I use often, especially when I feel stuck in a circular thought or lingering problem.

I take a good look at the circumstance, state the reality of the situation as honestly as I can, and fill in these blanks:

> *Even though* _____,
> *I can still* _____.

This simple exercise allows me to be active within a limitation. It helps me reevaluate *what can be* within *what is*—what are the possibilities within my new reality?

It also moves me farther down the path of acceptance. The "even though" premise may prove to be temporary. Nevertheless, I've kept active—forced myself to move through it instead of festering in it.

I may even learn something and discover a new way to do an old thing.

How about you? Can the "Even though_____, I can still _____ " exercise help you get unstuck today?

September 14:

Crushing It

During my son's college years, the three-hour time-zone difference often made it hard for us to sync up our conversations. One day, after a failed FaceTime connection and three different attempts to schedule a call, I finally resorted to a text.

"Are you okay?"

As I waited for my phone to light up with his response, I thought about that simple question. I guess that's all I really wanted—scratch that, *needed*—to know. I *wanted* to know a whole lot more—his classes, schedule, workouts, how it was going with his roommates, social life—all those "annoying" details that mothers want to know.

Finally, a shrill ding interrupted my daze, lighting up more than my screen.

"Hey Ma! I'm exhausted and busy, but I'm crushing it right now!"

I was expecting "exhausted" and "busy." But the words I got, "crushing it," made me shake my head and laugh out loud.

"Great!" I texted back. Then I thought about it for a minute and added, "Me too!"

I'd finished a book proposal, queried a few literary agents, and just received two positive responses. I, too, was exhausted and busy from a breakneck pace of appointments, to-dos, and deadlines. But when I stopped long enough to take a snapshot of that moment and reflect—well, yes, I too was "crushing it"!

Our exchange reminded me of a quote that inspires me when life gets hectic and I wonder if I can possibly do one more thing. John Motley Morehead III, the original founder of the Morehead-Cain scholarships at UNC Chapel Hill, offered this challenge to graduating scholars in 1959: "Stay with it, play the game, play it according to the rules. If you get hurt, don't holler; if you lose, pay up. Nobody can win all the time. Play it hard, for any machine—electrical, human, or mechanical—shows its greatest efficiency when loaded closest to its capacity."

Perhaps that's what my son and I were experiencing. Loaded to our capacity, we were feeling that exhausted -yet-blissful moment of crushing it.

Why not admit it? Why not celebrate it? I must admit that it felt good to say it.

Who knows what tomorrow will bring. More rejections. More work. More busy-ness and exhaustion for sure. But in that moment, it felt great to simply acknowledge that well-earned success.

How about you? Have you experienced the feeling of crushing it lately? Think hard about a time when you were exhausted and if that exhaustion was worth it. Though you were tired, were you also crushing it?

September 15:

Lasting Words

As part of a two-year graduate writing program, we were required to take an elective outside our field of study. The only option available to me was a poetry class.

I was terrified.

Although I love snippets of poetry, cherish several books gifted to me by my poetry-loving father, and have tons of quotations posted around my office, I'm about as poetic as a doorknob.

My first and last attempt at poetry was when I was sixteen. Our family dog had died, and I was devastated. Dad encouraged me to write a poem about it—the first time I'd tried to express feelings through words—and then suggested I share it with my English teacher. I'll never forget (obviously) the two words she used to describe it:

"Morose" and "maudlin."

I knew what morose meant. I was gloomy and yes, it was a sad poem. But "maudlin" sent me to the dictionary. "Overly sentimental" was the definition I found. "Overly" anything wasn't good, especially for a fragile sixteen-year-old who'd just spilled her damaged heart onto the page.

However, the dismissive look my revered teacher gave me spoke just as loud as her demoralizing comment. It was one of those evaluative, "I-know-you-are-a-top-student-honey-but-this-is-not-a-strength-of-yours" looks, given with one raised eyebrow.

I'd never attempted a poem since.

But I needed to face the demon. And what a demon it was. Beyond the extensive readings, we were required to write a poem—weekly!

The professor told me not to worry. He said, "The close attention to language that poetry can develop is extremely useful for writers of all kinds."

I do love words. Always have. I didn't mind studying them more closely if it would help me with future writing.

But his last comment was what really sold me: "In my undergraduate program at Northwestern," he told me, "no one was allowed to take their first fiction writing class until they had taken an introductory poetry writing class."

A prerequisite for an intro class? Surely, I could handle that.

Inspired by my professor's encouraging words, I pressed on and passed the course. More importantly, I enjoyed learning something new, and at the end of the semester felt accomplished that I'd taken on and completed the challenging work.

❧

How about you? Have you ever had a teacher's words limit you? Or inspire you to take on a challenge?

September 16:

Holding Questions

It's a strategy I use often, especially when I'm feeling fragile: "Don't ask the question until you're ready for the answer."

No one has ever told me that this a good or healthy strategy. And I can't find a source for it anywhere. But I've lived it, many times. And it's saved me from some heartache, or at least protected me from it until I was better prepared to deal with it

Will my daughter outgrow her autism?
Can my marriage be saved?
Will I be able to walk again?

Instead of asking the question, I prepared for the answer I didn't want to hear. That way, when the answer became clear, I was ready for it.

Some questions give us information we aren't ready to deal with. We're curious beings, and curiosity can be useful; but in some cases, maybe we need to rein it in until we are secure enough or strong enough to handle the answer.

It's not "I don't want to know." Rather, it's "I don't want to know *yet*."

How about you? Have you found merit in holding questions until you were ready for the answer?

September 17:

Remembering What to Miss

⟶ ⁂ ⟵

"Where are you going?" I asked my then seventeen-year-old daughter as she grabbed her keys and headed for the door.

"I told you, Mom," she quipped with a bit of a playful smile. "Don't you listen?"

I punched the playback button in my mind and rewound. *Did she tell me already? Did I forget? What were those last mumbled words over her cell phone? Maybe she did tell me. I wish she would open her mouth more when she spoke. Maybe I should get my hearing checked.*

"I'm sorry, honey, could you remind me what you said?"

Time and place were hollered out as the back door swung open.

"Call me when you get there," I hollered back. "I love you, Brittany!"

And then she was gone and I was left sitting there, exhausted from the mental gymnastics.

I told myself, *I must remember that I am going to miss this feeling.*

For parents of high school seniors, the end of an era has begun. Next year, there'll be no schedules to double-check, no mental rewinds of mumbled conversations, and no "I love you"s hollered out the back door.

Not long before this exchange with Brittany, my friend Kim had just told me about a back-to-school conversation with her own seventeen-year-old daughter. Kim had noted their last time driving home from summer vacation, their last time buying white shirts for school, and their preparations for the last field hockey pre-season.

"And, Kaley, this will be your last first day of school," she'd concluded, snapping a photo of that very moment.

"Mom," Kaley had huffed back, "enough already! Will you please let me get through the first day of school before you start in with the 'lasts'?"

Kim and I smiled at the story, with that wise smile moms share when they know their daughters have pushed them away—but also secretly liked the attention we've given them.

We vowed to remember that we were going to miss that too.

∽❦∾

How about you? If you are approaching the end of one era, what moments will you choose to remember?

September 18:

Strong Themes

The middle-school faculty faced a stalemate. Two character themes had emerged as possibilities for the upcoming school year. "Ownership" and "civility" were vying for the yearlong honor and so far they had found equal support, the principal explained to us at our back-to-school parents' night.

"Ownership" would encourage each child to take responsibility for their actions and behaviors while nipping the tendency kids that age have to blame others. "Civility" would encourage each child to treat others with respect and courtesy.

"Amen," I said to both. No wonder the faculty couldn't decide. For kids in those middle-school years, taking ownership of their lives and minding their manners are both tall orders.

As we watch our kids leave their childhood with each additional responsibility, the infamous "fault line" sharpens its jagged edges. Kids find the most creative ways to put blame on anyone else but themselves for misplaced books, socks, athletic equipment, homework—the list goes on.

"Not my fault" is truly the archenemy of ownership.

Civility takes a healthy hit, too, during these middle-school years. Shrugs, rolling eyes, and mumbled replies often creep into even the most mannerly child's repertoire. Kids teeter between childhood and those teenage limit-testing years where being "cool" edges out being courteous, sometimes pushing civility to the side.

My father often referenced journalist Hugh Sidey's quote from late Vice President Hubert Humphrey in *Time* magazine. "The first sign of a declining civilization is bad manners," Sidey reported Humphrey as saying some thirty years ago.

Ouch.

The haunting statement challenges weary parents (and teachers) to make that extra effort to remind our children to say "please" and "thank you," and to look people in the eye when talking to them.

And these days, some adults could use that reminder as well.

That year, the faculty decided not to choose between the two values: they adopted both "ownership" and "civility" as themes.

"You know when you should take responsibility; you know how to act with civility—now just do it," one teacher told my son's class. "Own it. Act it."

Those words struck a timeless chord for me.

How about you? What positive effect has taking ownership or behaving with civility (or both) had in your life?

September 19:

Honest Emotion

Before I began my presentation, the book club host gave me the perfect gift: a "Bee Strong" charm that included a tiny bedazzled bee and matching heart.

"Be strong," it said to me. "Let your heart sparkle with love."

Just what I needed!

Only eight hours earlier, I was in tears while preparing for my reading. Thankfully, my sister Rachel was in town, so I was able to rehearse and talk through it with her.

I nailed the first practice reading, but when I began the passage about our brother's water-skiing accident, I lost it. Reliving the moments that launched our family of five into that awkward and foreign configuration of four—it was too much. The tears wouldn't stop.

"I can't do it, Sissy," I wailed. "I just can't do it."

"Then don't. You have other scenes to read," she said, then hugged me tight before leaving for her home.

I worked on other passages, but kept coming back to the difficult one. It was going to be tough, but I knew I had to share it.

On the way to the reading, my phone lit up with a call.

"How's it going?" Rachel asked.

"I'm going for it, Sissy. I want to honor these honest feelings."

And I did, reading the words I'd wanted to say to my seventeen-year-old brother:

What were you doing? Where were you looking? Why didn't you pay attention? I am angry at you—for being careless, for being thoughtless, and, yes, for leaving me here to

miss you for the rest of my life. How dare you
die on me!

I crammed tissues into the tears that
weren't what they seemed. I was supposed to
be sad and yet I was hurt and angry—and
then ashamed for feeling that way.

My voice quivered, but I shed no tears. Strangely, it felt good to share the rawness of that pain and the confusing feelings of anger and hurt I'd felt back then.

I hope it showed the depth of my love. I hope it invited others to be honest about their feelings. I know it affirmed my belief that only through expressing our pain can we begin to work through it.

We can be strong and let our hearts sparkle with love—even if that love's expression is complex and confusing.

How about you? What encouragement have you received (or can you give to others) to share honest feelings?

September 20:

Twenty-Second Fits

Standing on the football field watching the university team stretch and warm up, my father saw the players do something he'd never seen before.

At a given signal, they started jumping, hollering, and flinging themselves around on the ground. The exercise had no uniformity, symmetry, or unity to it. Every guy did his own thing. Some looked joyful. Some looked angry. Some looked relieved to finally erupt.

The assistant coach's whistle sounded; the unorthodox activity stopped. A more traditional workout program followed.

"What in the world was that all about?" Dad asked the head coach.

"That's a twenty-second fit," the coach replied, laughing, and told his assistant to do it again for my father's benefit. The players seemed delighted to do it again.

A twenty-second fit—what a concept. And what a creative method to relieve tension.

I wonder what would happen in tension-filled offices if a daily email announced, "It's time for a twenty-second fit!"

Perhaps there'd be sprints in the corridors, chair races around the desks, or even dancing on the conference room table. I'm sure some would seek the privacy of a bathroom stall to let out a muffled scream.

On the home front, parents would jump up and down on unmade beds while their children ran circles around the house, waving their arms and yelling.

When tension builds, we do "pitch fits"—one way or another. And fits are often destructive. People get hurt.

But what if we had these "organized fits?" That might be the answer. Then everyone would know what was happening.

When we throw unorganized and unscheduled fits, we leave people guessing, unsure if our behaviors are provoked or just circumstantial.

But if others know what we were doing, they could not only understand what's happening but also join us.

How about you? What would you address in a twenty-second fit—right now?

September 21:

Beauty in What's Broken

The treasured mirror hanging in my hall bath illustrates one of my favorite sayings from my father: "Some things may be broken beyond repair, but not beyond some use."

Broken dishes, pottery, jewelry, and other keepsake baubles adorn this mirror's thick frame. My friend Beth taught me the technique of arranging and gluing each layer of the masterpiece and then faithfully popped by to check my progress.

"What about these jagged edges?" I asked after the first layer of dishes. "You can see the mirror frame through the cracks."

"Don't worry about those," she told me. "We'll cover with filler."

The "filler," I discovered, was a mixture of tiny, colorful beads that would be glued between the broken edges, knitting my shards and remnants of memories into a surprising work of beauty.

But it wasn't a quick transformation. The craft took days between layers.

Yet I found the process therapeutic. At that time, I was writing my memoir about adapting to life after significant loss. So, both in word and deed, I was pulling together broken pieces and precious memories into lasting works of art. Each process seemed to fuel the other.

The filler proved to be the messiest step. Despite fresh glue and careful application, the beads scattered everywhere.

"Yep, just part of the process," Beth told me. "Paper plates underneath the frame will help. Reuse what you can."

"Always," I said, smiling back to my friend. "Always."

How about you? Have you ever found another use for, or even beauty in, something broken?

September 22:

Scary Starts

The scariest moment is always just before you start.
—Stephen King

And this guy knows a lot about scary, right? As an author who's published over fifty best-selling novels, he also knows a lot about the how difficult it is to successfully start something new.

But his message doesn't just apply to writing.

So often ideas float around in our minds, haunting us with their unspent energy. Lists help, but there's nothing like actually beginning a task. Sometimes the best way to get on our way is simply by the act of starting. Motion begets motion.

How about you? Anything "haunting" you that you need to start today?

September 23:

Helping Hands

Months before Madison's eighteenth birthday, I attended a Baltimore County Community Forum on the transition process from school to adult services for children with autism. I learned about the services she could receive, put faces to agency names, and—most importantly—met the highly regarded Forum coordinator.

With a developmental age around three, Madison required constant supervision. Crowds, waiting, and unstructured time often provoked volatile tantrums. I hoped the application process for adult services wouldn't be too demanding of her.

Even though I was better informed after the Forum, the first phone call in the screening process shook me.

"If approved, she must open a bank account," the examiner directed.

"But she can't manage that."

"Then have her sign her name. You deposit it."

"But she can't write," I tried to explain. "Or read, either."

"Oh, so she is illiterate," she said, as if enlightened.

The word stung. Never had my precious child been called illiterate. The uncaring connotation stunned me.

"But she's attended specialized schools since she was three . . . with home-based therapies . . . she just can't grasp it . . . " I stammered against the drone of her stoic typing.

"So, you are alleging that your child has a disability?"

"Alleging?" I echoed, bewildered.

"I see no recent IQ score."

"IQ? I have sixteen years of school assessments . . . medical records . . . she was diagnosed early . . ."

"One of our psychologists needs to test her IQ," she interrupted. "You'll incur no cost. I'll schedule."

She did. We went. And within fifteen seconds, their psychologist understood Madison's limitations.

"What is her IQ?" I asked.

"She cannot be tested," she replied. "That says enough."

I knew it; but it was still hard to hear. At least she wouldn't have to go through other interviews, I was told.

Then a letter came with a mandatory appointment for Madison in the social security office—where rooms are small and waiting times unknown. For three days I called, held for operators who never answered, and left unreturned messages. In desperation, I finally contacted the Forum coordinator—who, thankfully, was willing to help.

Several emails later, I got a call. "You don't need to bring Madison in," the manager said simply. "We'll do a telephone interview."

He had spared my daughter what was sure to be a stress-laden visit.

Unquestionably, life with autism is filled with obstacles. However, it's also filled with good people willing to help—if we take the time to meet them.

How about you? When has a personal connection helped you through a tough journey?

September 24:

Stabilizing Advice

I parked my wheelchair in my doctor's small exam room, pulled out my trusty pen and pad of paper, and prepared to take a long list of notes.

We'd reviewed bloodwork and all the appropriate tests. He already knew my history since he'd cared for my health through four pregnancies, two miscarriages, two kidney stones, my divorce, and my paralysis. He'd been there for me every step of the way, the solid rock among all fleeting specialists. I was ready and eager to hear his annual exam recommendations, especially since he would be retiring soon.

"Okay, Dr. Lamos," I said. "I'm ready. Tell me everything I need to do to improve my health."

"It's simple, Rebecca." (After all these years, I still couldn't get him to call me Becky.) He sat down, put both hands on his knees, and said gently, "Don't get worse."

"Excuse me?"

"Yes, I'm keeping it simple this year and just telling my patients not to get worse. If everybody would not get worse, chances are they'll have a pretty good year."

I smiled at his advice and then let its truth settle in deep. He was right. Even if I didn't improve, if I could manage to stay the same, life would be pretty good.

Sometimes stability is actually an improvement. It lets us live more confidently—and that enhances life, at least in my experience. And especially as we age, even just maintaining the status quo requires a lot of effort.

Might as well at least acknowledge prevention as a positive.

How about you? Are there areas of your life where applying Dr. Lamos's "Don't get worse" advice would be helpful?

September 25:

When Valleys Come

I love Brené Brown's insight on what to do with the inevitable valleys in life:

"The irony is that we attempt to disown our difficult stories to appear more whole or more acceptable," she says, "but our wholeness—even our wholeheartedness—actually depends on the integration of all of our experiences, including the falls."

There are no mountains without valleys, right?

But it's hard to acknowledge our valleys. We like to minimize them, even discount the lasting effects they have on us. Yet those experiences can be the very ones that help distill what's important to us and in the process connect us to others who may be struggling too.

When I was first paralyzed, I also lost vision in my left eye from a different rare inflammation process called Devic's syndrome. Since I regained sight in three days, one neuro-ophthalmologist predicted that because of the course of the Devic's in my eye, I should have recovery in my spine as well.

But after nineteen months of paralysis, I let go of that hope. I had to let go of the life I wanted in order to live fully in the life I had.

I fought hard to keep being the Becky I'd been, determined not to let paralysis define me.

Yet it did, and still does. I hate to admit it, but paralysis limits me. I have to be real about that, or I'm only setting myself up for disappointment and failure every day.

I need structure, routines, lead time, and plans that include an A, B, and C option for almost everything I do. My body requires it.

I need quiet time, down time, reflection time, and reliable folks "in the boat" with me who will support and encourage me. My mental and spiritual health require it.

I don't like it, but I've accepted my limitations. I now fight hard to keep nurturing the Becky I can still be.

Brené Brown's words ring true: *Our wholeness depends on the integration of all of our experiences.*

Whether we admit it or not, whether we like it or not, our paths through the valleys and mountains shape who we are and how we live our lives.

⁂

How about you? Has a valley redefined your life? How did you have to change to keep living fully within it?

September 26:

It's All Part of the Process

Need a little inspiration to keep trying? This one from Thomas Edison fires up my resolve every time—and even makes me smile:

"I never failed once. It just happened to be a 2,000-step process."

What a great reframe.

So often failure feels like a dead end. But the more positive—and, I think, realistic—way of looking at it is as a ruling-out of what didn't work in the pursuit of what could work.

We just have to keep going.

How about you? What has a failure taught you about how to proceed next in the process?

September 27:

Sizing Things Up

When my youngest child was leaving for college, I was reminded of a story my father once told me and found new comfort in its message.

Willie, a fictional character whose actions always had a larger meaning, wandered into a local bar. He'd had a few drinks—just enough to make him feel invincible, even though he stood barely five foot four and weighed just over a hundred pounds wringing wet.

He sat at a table and wrote on a sheet of paper for a while. Then he got up and yelled loud enough to silence the crowd. Once he had their attention, he announced, "I've got a list here of everybody in this room I can whip."

A big, 200-pound man with the body of a football linebacker strode up to Willie. "You got my name on that list?" he thundered.

Willie looked up and checked his list. "Yep. Your name is right here."

Looking down his nose at Willie, the big man said, "But you can't whip me."

Willie eyed his challenger for a long moment, taking in his full size. "Okay," he said, "then we'll just mark your name right off the list."

I still laugh at the story—but I admire Willie's insight too. Although tipsy, he sized up the situation, marked off what he couldn't master, and faced reality.

As my children grew up and out of the home, I felt a bit like Willie, sizing up my new empty-nest reality with each launch. The first round began after my eldest whipped through my house, plucking only what she needed for her new home with her husband, before moving three thousand miles away. The next round started when my youngest purged his prized belongings before heading off to college.

By that time, I knew the local consignment shop owners by their first name. I had the number for Salvation Army's pick-up service in my phone favorites. I knew every Goodwill drop-off site within a ten-mile radius.

Trash, donate, save—my obsessive three-bin battle cry—reminded me of the frenzied preparation I'd undertaken while carrying my firstborn.

Then, I had engaged in nonstop nesting. Was I now un-nesting?

Maybe, like Willie and my kids, I was simply sizing up the situation and marking off what no longer mattered so I could focus on what did. It wasn't an empty nest; it was an open nest, once again ready to receive.

How about you? What can you mark off or leave out that no longer matters to you? Does it help to view the new space as open instead of empty?

September 28:

Temperature Control

"This week we're going to be the thermostat, not the thermometer," the NFL player hollered back to the reporter as his teammates cheered.

Be a thermostat, not a thermometer? What did that mean?

Some quick research brought up mixed origins and wide-ranging uses:

- Locker room hype, boardroom mantras, and demands for peaceful protests and transformational leadership
- Anger management, de-escalation techniques, gentle parenting, and home-schooling tips
- Quotes from Martin Luther King, Seth Godin, Roger Ailes, and more . . .

The phrase had wheels! It certainly made me think.

As we know, a thermostat regulates the temperature of its environment. It is set to a certain temperature. If its surrounding area gets too hot or too cold, it kicks in and gets that temperature back to the desired level.

A thermometer, however, reacts to the temperature of its environment. If the environment changes, so does the thermometer. A thermometer merely states what is, with no capacity to change it.

A thermometer reflects its environment. A thermostat affects its environment.

Every day, we choose how we'll respond to the ups and downs of the temperatures in our environment—the people and situations we encounter. With each interaction, we decide what temperament we'll adopt.

We can choose to *reflect* what we experience or *affect* what we experience.

That's the powerful message that fired-up football player delivered.

How about you? What kind of temperature control will you use today? Will you be a thermostat or a thermometer?

September 29:

You Are Better Than This

I heard about her all my life: Claudia S. Kincaid, my father's eleventh grade English teacher. He'd been warned of her toughness before he even set foot in her classroom. Whether she was standing before a class with chalkboard at her back or sipping coffee with a troubled person who needed a listening ear and honest response, she lived and practiced the three "C's" of teaching: Comfort, Confront, Correct.

But it was the "confronting" skill that etched her role permanently in my father's life.

She'd assigned the class a research paper. She returned the papers to everyone in the class except for my father. He raised his hand to inquire.

"See me after class," she said, her stern voice sparking an *Oh my Lord what have I done now* feeling, Dad recalled.

When they were alone, she pulled out the paper, which had enough red marks on it to "flag down the local freight train," as he said. She locked my father in the grip of her tough gaze, said, "R. F. Smith, you are better than this," and shoved the paper into his hands—and then she walked out the door.

"That statement turned me around in more ways than in writing," Dad said. "Whenever I've conned myself into doing less than I'm capable of doing, I hear the distant but ever so close and present voice of my teacher saying: 'You are better than this.'"

She was a teacher bent on giving the best to her students and demanding the best from them. Stretching to learn was prelude to living, she believed. Without it, life could never be experienced to the fullest.

Her purpose in teaching was to move a person from outward stimulation to inner motivation.

Mrs. Kincaid is gone. And so is my father. The lessons written large on the old blackboard are fading as chalk turns back to dust.

But the real lessons ripple on.

Am *I* better than this? Although no one ever spoke those words directly to me, I heard my father repeat this story often enough that it became my own private litmus test. It's one I use often—and it always makes me try just a little harder.

❧

How about you? What words inspire you to find your best? Who is inspiring you to do your best?

September 30:

Momentum Advice

Don't watch the clock;
do what it does. Keep going.
—Sam Levenson

Momentum is sustained doing what the clock does—stay in motion. Don't be distracted or discouraged by the passing time. Let persistence and progress fuel your momentum.

How about you? What actions will you take to sustain your momentum today?

OCTOBER

October 1:

Simple Truths

Today's inspiration comes from a rare, special visitor—granddaughter Blakely Faye, who at fifteen months old came in for a Thanksgiving visit and left me with a timeless lesson.

At our large Thanksgiving table, filled with family and friends, each of us shared something that we were grateful for. Although I'm sure that beneath our gratitude each of us had tender places of hurt or sorrow, Thanksgiving is the time we let our best thoughts of appreciation rise to the top, so that's what we focused on.

As adults, we choose which parts of ourselves and our thoughts to show at any given moment. But Blakely Faye reminded me that young children know no such layered living.

Even though she had only a few words, when she was sad, we knew it. When she wanted something, we knew it. And when she was happy, which was most of the time, we knew it—and reveled in it. There was something about the simplicity of her life that refreshed and restored me.

Was it the doting care of everyone around her, determined to teach her only the most positive parts of life?

Or her creative play, which, in its close mimicry of real life, illustrated so clearly the power of observation?

Or was it the lesson she gave me about being fearless? Although my dog Tripp was nine years old at the time, he still jumped and barked like a puppy. Most visitors kept a distance, wary of his enthusiasm. Not Blakely

Faye. She not only petted him, she often plopped down beside him in his dog bed.

Or maybe it was her eager curiosity and willingness to learn, her pointing finger begging for more information about everything her little eyes spied.

After she left, my morning reading time offered this quote that gave me some insight:

"Iron rusts from disuse, stagnant water loses its purity, and in cold weather becomes frozen; even so does inaction sap the vigor of the mind." —Leonard da Vinci

That's it! Blakely Faye reminded me that no matter our age or situation, whether we grateful or hurting, we must keep moving and keep learning.

How about you? Have you ever been restored or refreshed by someone's simple approach to life?

October 2:

Power of the Past

Today's inspiration comes from the past and from some very special people who "knew me when."

In the span of forty-eight hours, I'd traveled to the University of North Carolina at Chapel Hill, spoken to a group of seven hundred fellow Morehead-Cain scholarship alumni, signed books at UNC's student store, and given a book talk to an audience of family and friends who'd traveled from nine different cities up to three hours away.

We laughed. We cried. We reminisced.

It was awesome.

One college roommate flew to Baltimore to drive me the six hours to UNC; another drove me home and flew back the next day. My book talk audience included my precious eighty-three-year-old uncle Bob, his wife, and their daughter; two kindergarten classmates; a grade-school buddy and subsequent IBM colleague; a high school classmate; six college friends; and an unforgettable wrestling coach (and his beautiful wife) whom I met when I was eighteen. Most knew my entire family, before we lost Forest, and remembered us as a family of five.

I was exhausted after the trip but filled with a new appreciation for the power of the past.

"Don't look back" is an oft-heard phrase. "Let the past pass," we are coached, especially when going through difficult times. "You can get stuck in your past if you keep looking back."

Maybe.

Maybe not.

Linking the past with the present can be a powerful connection, I discovered. Snippets of who we were can spark new dreams of who we still can be. The dreams you once had, the ones that didn't come true, can be safely brought back to life with people who shared your past and want to share your future, despite any setbacks you've encountered along the way. A new perspective of gratitude starts to color your outlook as you recognize that despite the years and the distance, you are not alone.

You are still remembered; you are forever connected through the power of the past.

⤙⧓⤚

How about you? Have you experienced the power of the past in a positive way?

October 3:

Craving Proprioception

Proprioception is our body's awareness of where it is in space. Sometimes referred to as our sixth sense, it's the ability to feel where your body is without seeing it. For example, even when you close your eyes, you know what to do in order to touch your nose because you can sense where your arms are in relation to your nose.

I first learned the term from a physical therapist who was helping me adjust to life without the use of my legs. Paralyzed from the waist down, my body was confused and disoriented. I felt like I was sitting in a bowl of jelly. I was seated safely in a wheelchair, but still terrified of falling forward and landing on the ground. Even though I knew I had a seatbelt around my hips and could see my lap in front of me with my feet on the footplates, I did not trust what my eyes were telling me.

It took weeks for my body's awareness to catch up with its new reality. Each day I accepted a little more of the evidence as my experience taught my mind what to trust. I was safe. I not going to fall. I could let go of that fear.

I now sit comfortably in my wheelchair—I can even close my eyes and touch my nose while in it. Yet I still think of that word, proprioception, each time a hardship comes my way and my mind becomes confused or disoriented or struggles to adjust to a new reality.

I crave the return of my mind's proprioception.

Some hardships are acute—illness, death, or even the abrupt loss of a daily living pattern. Others, like aging or the growth stages of our children, are more gradual.

Life flows. We change. We adapt and move through it. In either case, a reorientation is required. I like the way the Greek philosopher Heraclitus describes it:

"No man ever steps in the same river twice, for it's not the same river and he's not the same man."

The struggle to synch up self and circumstance is ongoing. Sometimes we have to give ourselves time to absorb, accept, and let our experiences teach our minds to trust the evidence we need to embrace.

How about you? Have you ever craved proprioception after an acute or ongoing loss? What evidence helped you adjust?

October 4:

Reorienting for Results

No problem can be solved from the
same level of consciousness that created it.
—Albert Einstein

Are you stuck in a hot mess? Consider how you got there, back out of that mindset, and change your approach. Think smaller. Or larger. Or imagine it is your best friend's problem.

A different perspective may reveal an unexpected solution.

How about you? Could a different view of a lingering problem help you solve it?

October 5:

Treading Water

I'd had one of those days.

The left front caster wheel of my wheelchair developed a strange click. It could have been a pebble, a chunk of salt, or something more serious like a damaged ball bearing (which could lock up my wheel and prevent me from moving).

Then the gel lining in my wheelchair cushion ripped, causing a pasty substance to ooze out all over my seat—and my clothing.

Later that day, it started to rain and the roof in my sunroom started leaking. Again. I'd just had it resealed two weeks earlier.

That's when a mighty migraine decided to visit me.

Yep, one of those days.

Forget any plans of swimming through the checklist of my carefully planned day; it was all I could do to tread water.

After making calls for repairs, I took my migraine medicine and tucked myself into bed. Within twenty-four hours, my migraine departed, a technician came to assess my wheel, I got a quote for my roof repair, and I found a way to temporarily repair my seat cushion with a new discovery: Gorilla Tape.

I was still treading water, but at least the pull of the deep wasn't quite so strong.

Why?

Action.

I may not always be able to go in the direction I'd planned, but taking action always helps me feel like I'm making progress. At least when I'm moving, I'm not sinking anymore.

In fact, if I look at the situation in just the right light, maybe I even grow stronger just by "swimming" in place.

Treading water is a heck of a workout. I better give myself credit!

How about you? What helps you tread water when you have one of those days? Do you find it makes you stronger?

October 6:

Load Carrying

It's not the load that breaks you down,
it's the way you carry it.
—Lena Horne

We can carry our struggles with confidence or with hesitation. With hope or with despair. With respect or fear. With grace or with blame.

We can keep our burdens from breaking us by choosing how we carry them.

How about you? How will you choose to carry your struggles today?

October 7:

The Laughter Connection

The new service coordinator wanted to meet Madison and her residential and day program staff. We met at lunchtime in the conference room. Madison kissed my cheek and then sat down beside me.

"What do you say, Madison?"

"Hi Mommy," she said softly.

At age twenty-seven, Madison was still using phrases learned from therapies or from favorite videos. Her responses were generally prompted, rarely spontaneous.

"Madison, meet your new friend." I introduced the coordinator and then prompted Madison to say each team member's name.

She complied but kept looking at the door. And when her one-on-one assistant brought in her lunch, she got up, grabbed my hand, and pulled me toward the door.

"No, Madison," I said. "It's lunchtime. Sit down."

She wouldn't.

She tried leaving with each of her team members, grabbing their hands and tugging them toward the door. Each redirected her to the table.

She resisted and became agitated.

"Let's take a walk," her assistant offered. Madison bolted out the door with her.

"Maybe she just needs a moment," I said, trying to fill the awkward silence. "Does anyone remember that show *Ally McBeal*?"

Blank stares answered.

"Well, it was a long time ago," I plowed on. "Anyway, there was this lawyer who would stop right in the middle of a courtroom proceeding and say, 'I'm sorry. I need a moment.' He'd pause, shut his eyes, and pinch the bridge of his nose to gather himself before proceeding."

The group chuckled.

Politely.

"Maybe Madison just needs a moment?" I suggested.

More polite chuckling.

Just then Madison barreled through the door, plopped down, and took a huge bite of her lunch.

"I guess she did need a moment!" I smiled tentatively.

As if she'd heard my story, Madison stopped her spoon midair and belted out, "*For sure!*"

Shocked, we all burst out laughing. Forget polite chuckles. Deep belly laughs pushed us to the verge of tears.

Where did she learn that? I wondered. *How did she learn that?* It was spot-on. I was stunned, dismayed, and encouraged, all at the same time.

I prompted her once more, and she did it again. This time, she even laughed herself!

What?!

Rarely does Madison ever give a spontaneous reaction—let alone an appropriate one! Yet in this moment it was as if she had joined our group and was enjoying making us laugh.

As I looked around the room, I realized laughter connected us in a way nothing else could. It was like electricity, both connecting and charging us.

Madison, the comedienne. Who knew?

How about you? Has laughter ever created a special moment of engagement and encouragement for you?

October 8:

Evergreen Lessons

Late one fall, I thought a beautiful pine tree in my yard was dying. I'd just finished removing a beloved red sugar maple and dogwood, both victims of a harsh winter, when I discovered a large pile of pine needles under this tower of a tree. Its mass of green had become riddled with an alarming brown.

But when I asked a professional, he told me this was a normal part of the tree's growth process. Although the pine tree is considered an evergreen, its needles do not stay alive and fresh. It sheds the needles it no longer needs.

Sure enough, weeks later I noticed the brown needles were gone. Only the luscious green greeted me, fortified and ready to endure whatever the upcoming winter had in store for it.

How envious I was of the tree! How did it know exactly what to shed? What needles to hang on to? Which ones to discard?

I wish life could be that simple for me.

As anyone who has ever dared visit me in my office knows, I tend to hang on to things too long, whether in lovely floral file folders resting patiently on my desk or in the colorful baskets, bins, and binders that are artfully tucked in, on, and under my desk.

Wouldn't it be nice if I could figure out how to be like my pine tree and simply shed what I no longer need?

Curious about how the tree knew what to do, I did some research. Here's what Michael Kuhns, Extension Forestry Specialist, has to say about the process: "As needles age, they become less efficient at producing food for the tree. They also become more shaded by newer needles. For these reasons, old needles finally turn brown and drop off."

Aha!

The tree sheds what no longer nourishes it—either what is too old to continue to produce value for it or what may have been prevented from becoming useful by newer growth that shaded it from the sun.

Perhaps that's a new way to discern what to keep and what to let go. Does a project, activity, cause, or hobby still nourish me? Or has it been overshadowed by another growing interest? If so, it may be time for me to shed it.

❧

How about you? What projects or interests still nourish you? Which ones don't?

October 9:

The Gift of Immediacy

I had not been up the stairs in my two-story house in three-and-a-half years. The last time I'd been up there, I could walk.

Now paralyzed, I feared going up my new elevator to see my old life. I was prepared to be sad, even depressed. I'd mentally toured each bedroom a thousand times. Now it was time to do it in real life.

The kids were at school. I had a fresh Starbucks cappuccino awaiting me for after my excursion—I had a feeling I'd need a pick-me-up by the time I was done.

When the elevator door opened, I realized I'd prepared for the wrong thing.

Nothing grounds you as quickly as the sight of a teenager's bedroom that has been un-mothered for three years. I couldn't have wheeled into Brittany's room if I wanted to.

Clothes were everywhere—clumped on the floor, spilling out of dresser drawers, and scattered across her unmade bed. Her large French provincial desk, stacked high with school papers, toiletries, odd dishes, and jewelry, had no visible surface. The clock beside her bed blinked the wrong time. The smell of her hamster cage filled the musty room, even though she'd promised me before she left for school that she had cleaned it.

"Oh my word," I said, gaping.

Pat, our longtime caregiver, had met me upstairs. "I've offered to help her," she said, surveying the mess and my reaction. "Many times."

Months prior, when Brittany had turned thirteen, I'd told Pat that it was time to let Brittany take care of her own room, something Mom had done with me during my teenage years. "I'm closing my eyes and closing your door," she used to tell me when the clutter was too much to bear. But I didn't think my room had ever been *this* bad—or had it?

"It's not your fault, Pat."

I scanned the room again and spied my favorite coffee mug, now half-filled with moldy hot chocolate. It sported my most hopeful motto: THE BEST IS YET TO BE.

"Not at this rate," I replied to my missing morning mug. Then, muttering to myself, I said, "Got to regroup," and I descended back to my tidy and orderly downstairs world.

An hour later, a two-page list of action items rested patiently on Brittany's dinner plate. My Starbucks was cold by the time I remembered to drink it. Its role had replaced by a more immediate need: parenting my teenaged daughter.

What I'd been sure would be a time of reflection and sadness had become a call to action and accountability.

How about you? Have you ever had a pressing issue prevent a potential sad one?

October 10:

When Words Hurt

From the very beginning of my son Matthew's seizures, I felt like I wasn't working hard enough to meet his needs. A testy exchange with the hospital social worker didn't help.

At first, as she probed for more details about Matthew's care, I thought she was just being thorough, a necessary part of the process. Then her questions sharpened, infused with a strange, almost accusatory tone. "So, you didn't do . . . you only did . . . and why didn't you think of . . . ?"

My fragile defense finally crumbled. "I'm doing the best I can," I blurted out. "You make me feel like I'm a bad mother!"

Unfazed, the woman leaned toward me from her desk. "*I* can't make *you* feel any particular way, Mrs. Galli." She paused, looking directly into my eyes. "*You* make yourself feel. Not *I*."

My hurt whitened to anger. This professional, who specialized in helping parents with critically and chronically ill children find resources, chose that moment to "educate me" on the source of my feelings instead of empathizing with me and trying to help. She was supposed to give me guidance, not send me into a deeper tailspin. I stood up, left her and her heart of steel, and made it to the car before I broke down sobbing.

I called my father as soon as I got home. He agreed that this woman was terribly insensitive and had "no business being in that profession." Then he tried to help me see the truth of her words.

"Others can give you information, BB," he said gently. "But how you feel about it and respond to it is up to you."

"So, I should just take it, let her treat me like that? She's incompetent, Dad. An embarrassment to the profession. I think I should get her fired!"

"I hear you, BB," he said, "but you need to focus on *your* needs. Don't get sidetracked. If she can be helpful to you, great. If she can't, move on and find someone who can."

It's hard to not let other's reactions create guilt, especially during times of uncertainty. From Matthew's seizures to Madison's autism to my own paralysis, I've learned to always move toward those who strengthen my pursuit of clarity and away from those who don't.

And perhaps more importantly, I've learned to trust myself—to trust that my best is enough at that moment.

How about you? How do you guard your feelings from a hurtful influence of another?

October 11:

The Power of Touch

Today's inspiration comes from the birth of my grandson, Beckett James. Arriving safely at a whopping 9 pounds 4.4 ounces, he along with his mother were doing well, my son-in-law texted me. He would let me know when I could come in to see them.

After an hour, I texted back, *What's the plan?*

He said that Brittany and Beckett needed more time for mother-child bonding.

I understood that—I thought. After each of my four children were born, they were whisked away, measured, wrapped tightly in a warm blanket, and returned to my arms. I knew the importance of holding newborns.

But this version of post-delivery period advocated for skin-to-skin care (or kangaroo care), where the naked baby (sometimes with a cap or diaper on) is placed on the mother's bare chest. If possible, mothers and babies should be in direct contact for one to two hours after birth.

Research has shown that this special time has tremendous benefits for both mother and child. It can regulate the child's breathing and body temperature, stabilize blood sugar levels, improve gut health and immunity, and reduce the baby's crying. For the mother, it can improve her sleep, reduce postpartum depression, and increase her milk supply.

But the power of touch extends beyond the birthing room, I later learned.

In her blog post "Why cuddling is good for kids' brains," Rachel Norman notes the science behind the boost we all feel after the touch of a good hug.

"When you get a loving and firm hug," she writes, "it stimulates pressure receptors under the skin, which in turn send a message to the vagus nerve in your brain. The vagus nerve takes this cue to slow down your heart rate and your blood pressure, putting you in a relaxed state. The hug even curbs stress hormones such as cortisol, facilitates food absorption and the digestion process, and stimulates the release of serotonin, which counteracts pain."

Who knew the power of touch could be so important? If you think about it, touch has the power to connect us in a way that can last far beyond the moment.

Keats may sum it up best: "Touch has a memory."

Indeed. For those who give as well as for those who receive. Thoughts of special hugs from my family and friends transport me back all sorts of beautiful memories—especially that very first one with Beckett James.

How about you? Have you felt the benefits of a good hug? Who can you hug today?

October 12:

The Unstable Scar

Fourteen years after paralysis, I sustained an injury that became a wound. Despite all the specialized care I received for it, it took over fifteen months to heal. The progress was maddening; it would close for a few days, only to reopen when I bumped it while moving my body from one surface to another.

Frustrated, I went to a plastic surgeon for another opinion.

"Yes, Ms. Galli, the wound is closed, but it has not healed properly," the young doctor explained. "You have an unstable scar."

"A what?"

"An unstable scar. It is closed for now, but it will reopen at some point because it has not healed with healthy tissue."

I shook my head. "I'm sorry. I'm just not getting this. So, my scar tissue is not healthy?"

"Yes, I know it's confusing. When a wound heals, it needs to close with good, healthy tissue. When it doesn't, it becomes unstable and at risk for reopening. Your wound has technically closed, but it closed with fibrous tissue that's created this unstable scar. It will most likely reopen."

"Oh no." I let out a long, slow sigh. *Here we go again. One more thing to learn about that I'd rather not.* "So, what do we do with this unstable scar?"

"We have to start over and debride it or cut out the fibrous tissue that's filled in the wound," he said. "Then healthy tissue can grow back in its place. We will monitor it closely to make sure the healing tissue is good tissue. Your nurse can check it with each dressing change."

"Wow. Okay."

"Do I have your permission to debride it?"

"Sure. Do what you gotta do." I sighed again, thinking about his terminology. Unstable scars—what we get when we don't heal properly.

Somehow that sounded more like a life challenge than a medical term.

Healing properly is important for long-term health; I continue to learn and experience this in more than one area of my life.

❧

How about you? Do you have any "unstable scars?"

October 13:

Inspiring Examples

Today's inspiration comes from the creative mind of a friend in a women's group I joined a few years ago. The group had invited me to speak about my book *Rethinking Possible* at their kickoff meeting, and had also asked if I could come up with a craft idea that would complement my talk. I was at a bit of a loss, but thankfully Kim, the group's craft connoisseur extraordinaire, offered her help.

I'd originally thought of my decorative mirror craft. I so enjoyed the process—gluing broken dishes, odd pieces of costume jewelry, and special trinkets and family memorabilia to a mirror's frame and create a unique family heirloom. I thought it would be the perfect complement to my book talk, since the craft itself was a hands-on version of "rethinking" what's "possible."

But the process took weeks to complete. Each layer had to dry completely before adding the next layer. I couldn't envision a version of it reduced to an hourlong activity for dozens of people in a group setting.

Still, Kim and that creative mind of hers wanted to give it a try. So, I invited both Kim and Beth, the friend who'd taught me the mirror craft to begin with, to my home so they could review the materials and talk through options.

I listened and watched the pros discuss the techniques and considerations but still couldn't fathom how this type of project could be made simple enough for a large group to complete in an hour.

"It's doable," Kim said simply after some study and reflection. "I'll make a sample."

I was both stunned and inspired by the results.

She took the concept, minimized it and simplified it, and, in the end, offered *three* versions, each of which could be done in less than an hour. I could not only see it; I could envision myself doing it. What had at first seemed unimaginable became real and possible because of the examples Kim made.

Two weeks later, with the help of Kim's expert planning and instruction, nearly a hundred women completed the craft in less than an hour—truly a testament to the power of example.

How about you? Has a teacher or expert's example ever sparked or renewed a creative pursuit for you?

October 14:

Successful Ingredients

Author James Clear's "recipe" for success offers some key ingredients for both beginning a project and assessing its progress:

Enough courage to get started
+ enough sense to focus on something you're naturally suited for
+ enough persistence to stay in the game long enough to catch a few lucky breaks
+ a lot of hard work

How about you? How can these "ingredients" help you define or measure your progress on a project?

October 15:

Mother Nature's Time

It was mid-October and my tulip tree was blooming!

Bless her heart.

She was so confused. With all the rain followed by unseasonal warmth, perhaps she thought it was spring again.

Typically, her magnificent, magnolia-like blooms sprouted in early spring from bare limbs. Only after her blossoms peaked and died did the foliage appear.

But not this time. This time she had hardy, pale pink blooms *and* green leaves. In the fifteen years I'd lived here, I'd never seen this combination.

Her timing reminded me of a conversation I often had with my father, especially when my carefully organized plans started falling apart. A lover of words and a student of the Greek etymology and exegesis in his work, he made the point that ancient Greeks had two words for time: *chronos* and *kairos*.

Chronos refers to specific, sequential, or chronological time.

Kairos means a season or an opportune time, as in the saying, "The time is ripe."

"Relax your plans, BB," I can hear him telling me. "Trust the process." Interesting advice from the man who also taught me, "What's planned is possible."

Through the years, I've learned the value of both approaches. Maybe it's growing older, but I do think I plan less and trust more these days.

Chronos can fail us. Our best schedules and plans can be delayed, derailed, or even destroyed. Yet if we keep moving through life—absorbing the conditions, growing through the process—perhaps an unexpected kairos can occur.

So, bloom little tulip tree, bloom. Take what life throws at you and find a way to flourish in your own time.

How about you? Have you ever been frustrated when things didn't turn out as you planned but gone on to find beauty in the season?

October 16:

Five Heart-Warming Words

During my son Pete's college years on the West Coast, he and I discovered the importance of a scheduled conversation. It was the only way to guarantee connection. His course load and wrestling schedule, combined with the three-hour time difference, made random phone calls futile.

After two years of regular Sunday phone calls, we switched to FaceTime. Seeing each other face to face, despite the distance, made all the difference in the world.

But one week, things got busy. We missed our regular Sunday FaceTime and struggled to find another chance to connect. I felt so lucky when I finally reached him by phone, but almost immediately, Pete cut himself short.

"I'm sorry I'm so rushed, Ma. Can we FaceTime tomorrow? I want to tell you all about what's going on . . ."

I want to tell you . . .

How those five words warmed my heart and raised my spirits! Pete had said, "I *want* to tell you," and not "I *need* to tell you." There's a vast difference between those two words.

A seismic shift occurs when your last child leaves for college. With Pete's departure, my home life morphed from hub to satellite.

It's what we're meant to do as parents: raise those chickadees so they can successfully fly the coop. I know that, but it still doesn't make the process any easier.

There are more seismic shifts ahead when they move into their own first apartment, begin that first job, and meet the person of their dreams. Their participation in our lives becomes more of a choice than a necessity. But even with all his growth and change, Pete still needed—and wanted—me in his world.

The next day, we FaceTimed, and in his own animated, passionate way, Pete described the ups and downs that had touched his world since we'd last spoken.

I loved every single minute of it.

How about you? Have your spirits ever been lifted up by the five words "I want to tell you"? Can you can use them to brighten someone else's day today?

October 17:

A Little Encouragement Goes a Long Way

When you are having trouble, which helps the most—harsh criticism or kind encouragement?

Let's say, for instance, that your stomach hurts.

A family member says, "Well, like I've told you many times before, you can't eat greasy, fried foods. But you just won't listen. Serves you right!"

Another family member says, "I have some medicine that might help. Let me get it for you. Perhaps we need to prepare less greasy foods in the future."

The first family member's criticism was on target, but odds are it did little more than cause anger juices to flow, complicating the problem. The other family member, in contrast, offered immediate help, along with plan for preventing further problems.

Most of us *know* our faults and flaws and where we have fallen short. What we need is encouragement, not criticism. We need help in moving to our strengths, not in emphasizing our weaknesses.

If you tell me long enough, "You can't ever do that right," soon I will believe you and agree with you. But if you keep encouraging me by "propping up my leaning side" as we say in our family, soon I will stand on my own feet and be grateful for your help.

When we criticize, we are judging a situation or an individual. To criticize, as Webster defines it, is "to consider the merits and demerits and judge accordingly." Since we're already in evaluation mode, considering the positives and negatives, why not pursue the plus side of situation?

Constant criticism, no matter how well-meaning, usually produces one of two results:

The person becomes disheartened and gives up.

The person hears the criticism so often that they build up an immunity to the criticizer and from then on never takes the person seriously.

As William Arthur Ward, noted American author, scholar, and teacher, reminds us:

Flatter me, and I may not believe you.
Criticize me, and I may not like you.
Ignore me, and I may not forgive you.
Encourage me, and I will not forget you.

How about you? Is it easier for you to criticize, or to encourage?

October 18:

Sleep's Secret

Don't ask how people are doing, ask how they are sleeping. You'll learn a lot more.
—Andrew Huberman

My mom was ahead of her time. Every morning, before we even made it to the breakfast table, she'd ask each child, "How did you sleep, honey?"

The answer seemed to set the tone for the rest of the morning, almost as if the day had begun the night before.

Even though my kids are grown now, I still ask that question when they visit. I ask my guests too. There's something affirming about knowing if others have slept well in my home.

The quote above from Huberman—a Stanford University neuroscientist—is right. It's a revealing question. Sleep is a powerful indicator of how we are really doing. We often don't sleep well if we have a lot on our minds, aren't feeling well, or are disturbed by our environment's noise or temperature. We can learn a lot about others (and ourselves!) when we ask that simple question.

How about you? How did you sleep last night? What does your answer reveal about you?

October 19:

Right on Time

Despite my best planning, I was late to my book talk for the Page Turners' 20th Anniversary Celebration.

I was mortified.

I'd done the prep work.

Twelve days before the event, I went to the library, met with Mr. Mike, the host librarian, and toured the event room.

Six days before the event, I revised and rehearsed my remarks.

Four days before the event, I received and reviewed the detailed agenda, which included a timeline for each section of the program.

Two days before the event, I confirmed my transportation.

The night before, I selected my outfit—gold sequin boots and a bright knit jacket that matched my nails, OPI's "Cajun Shrimp."

The day of the event, we left fifteen minutes before my scheduled 6:00 p.m. departure, as marked in my calendar. We arrived at 6:30 p.m., a half-hour early.

I thought.

But when I opened the library door, I was immediately met with a warm smile from a lovely woman sporting a silver-sequined shirt that read THE PAGE TURNERS.

"You're right on time," she said.

My eyes widened. "I thought I was early. Doesn't it start at seven?"

"No," she said. "It started at six. But you're right on time. You're up next. So glad you could come." She smiled again.

She ushered me into the presentation room, filled with an audience listening to the other guest author.

Mr. Mike came over and whispered his welcome to me.

"I'm so sorry," I whispered back. "I must've mixed up my times. I'm always early."

"You're fine," he said, resting a comforting hand on my shoulder. "You're right on time. So glad you're here."

"Thanks." I shook my head, thinking. My calendar's 6:00 p.m. must've been the event start time—*not* my departure time. Ugh!

Before those spinning thoughts could settle, I heard my name introduced. The next thing I knew my mouth was moving and words were coming out.

Strangely, I felt at ease.

Why?

Three times I'd been told I was "right on time." In my mind, I was late. Yet because these welcoming friends assured me that I was on time, my anxiety lifted.

Their kindness reshaped my expectations.

As I reflected on the evening, it occurred to me that there's great power in feeling "right on time."

Our own expectations often invite disappointment. What if, in the midst of our angst, a warm, kind voice could always assure us we were right on time?

How about you? What reassures you when you are falling short of your own expectations?

October 20:

Conversing Roles

The question was simple. My friend was telling her husband Ezra about a tough work situation. Midway into the story, Ezra stopped her and asked:

"So, Skipper, what would you like my role to be in this conversation?"

I must admit I laughed long and hard the first time Skipper told me that story. But then I considered the wisdom of Ezra's words. He asked a clarifying question—one that could help him use the right set of ears as he listened and allow him to prepare an appropriate set of responses.

Wouldn't it be nice if we always knew what storytellers wanted from us at the beginning of a conversation? Do they need our ideas? Experience? Comfort? Or maybe they need a sounding board or simply a listening ear to vent to.

Although the question may be a bit jarring to ask, it might be beneficial to ask *ourselves* from time to time: What do we want our listener's role to be when we begin a conversation?

On occasion, I've tried it, telling my listener what I need from them. *I need your opinion. I need your affirmation. I need your analysis. I need to vent.*

Each time I've felt distinctly heard and able to connect in a more satisfying way.

How about you? Could defining roles in a conversation be helpful to you today?

October 21:

Impress Yourself

Jeff was a big hunk of a guy who had just turned twenty-five yet exuded a raw energy more like that of the kids he coached. He and his lovely wife Barbara helped me with childcare and carpooling and even created and managed a therapy program for my daughter Madison during her grade school years.

That day, though, he was telling me about his first soccer season as a coach and his 7-0 record. He began to analyze his success.

"It's amazing," he said, scratching his head. "I talked to a fellow coach about a couple of plays I dreamed up. He liked them, so we shared them with the kids."

"So, how'd it go?"

"Awesome! We scored the first three goals using those plays—*bam, bam, bam!*"

"That's great, Jeff!"

"Yeah!" he exclaimed, shaking his head in disbelief. "I think I'm starting to impress myself!"

I congratulated him again, then slowly wheeled myself into my room where I met my own smiling gaze in the wall-to-wall mirror. Somehow it made me happy that Jeff had impressed himself.

Impressing yourself. How often do we try to do that? So often, we try to impress others. But do we ever consider impressing ourselves?

Years later, I still like the shift that comes with that question as I review my day's to-do list. Sometimes the effort is less—what appears herculean requires little of me. Sometimes the effort is more—what looks easy requires a herculean effort.

I alone know the value of my work.

When we push ourselves to impress ourselves, we set ourselves up for success at the most genuine level. Then, like Jeff, we should take the time to celebrate, to enjoy, and to be proud of what we've accomplished.

How about you? How have you impressed yourself lately? How will you impress yourself today?

October 22:

Gratitude's Gift

With gratitude, optimism is sustainable.
—Michael J. Fox

For over thirty years, Michael J. Fox has lived with Parkinson's. Although his mobility and lifestyle have been greatly impacted, his humor, grit, and positive outlook continue to both inspire and inform. "If you can find something to be grateful for," he's said, "then you can find something to look forward to and you carry on."

Gratitude, the confirmation of what it good in life, can become the fuel that keeps us strong and determined. We can be confident that life can still be good—we have the daily evidence.

How about you? What are you grateful for today?

October 23:

Hard-Earned Relevance

A framed photograph of my daughter Brittany, her husband, and their dog announced a new addition to our family. My child was going to have her first child.

How could that be?

My parents used to talk about time passing so quickly—how childhood disappears in a blink, how wasn't it only yesterday they brought me home from the hospital.

Was I becoming my parents? Was my daughter already becoming hers?

I must admit she made me earn my parenting stripes. Strong-willed with energy that always seemed to outlast mine, she pushed limits.

Daily.

Until she was seven, four in the morning was her routine waking time. When she was an infant, I thought she was waking up because she was hungry, so I would feed her. But the pediatrician said I was training her to get up early, like giving a kid ice cream in the middle of the night. Who wouldn't wake up for a treat?

So, I tried *not* feeding her. And she cried. And I kept on not feeding her. And she cried louder. So, I gave up. I guess I trained her to wake up early.

My bad.

I was weak and she was strong—even when the bottles were gone.

Once she sashayed up to me and asked in her famous two-year-old lisp, "Why do I have to wisten to you, Mommy?"

At age three, she cut her bangs to the root. When I scolded her, saying that she knew better, she promptly put both hands on her hips, looked me squarely in the eyes, and said, "Well you're the one that left the scissors out."

I wonder if my daughter will know how to parent that.

I teased her that in college she better take all 8:00 a.m. classes. Which she did. Later, as a young career woman, she was up at 5:00 a.m. each day for her gym's boot camp workout before heading to work.

And now my mischievous little limit-tester was going to have a baby.

Weeks into the pregnancy, a strange new pattern began to develop.

"Hold on, Sissy," I said to Rachel during one morning chat. "Brittany's calling."

"Again?"

"Yes. I know! I think I'm her new best friend." I laughed. "But it's actually kind of cool," I said quickly before clicking over.

My daughter's customary "touch base" texts and calls suddenly changed. She called me on her way to work, at lunch, and on her way home. And when her husband traveled, I heard from her at night too—up to four times a day, sometimes for over an hour. I knew more about her life than ever before—what she was doing, feeling, thinking—and every step of her pregnancy progression.

But why?

Then it dawned on me. I'd become relevant.

She was on the cusp of a new phase of her life that I'd experienced—my twenty-eight years of parenting four children suddenly mattered.

But I guess life does that to us as we move through its stages. It gives us permission to grow, to break our patterns and create new ones.

I was real-time and relevant—and I loved it.

But Brittany wasn't the only one with a perspective shift. I began to see *her* in a new light too.

She questioned honestly and thought critically. She was unafraid to challenge a line of thinking if it didn't make sense to her. And yes, four o'clock was often the starting hour of her day.

The very things that were so difficult for me to parent had turned out to be amazing strengths for her in this stage of life.

How about you? Has a new stage of life changed your relevance in a relationship or shifted your perspective?

October 24:

One Bad Moment

There is no such thing as a bad day, just bad moments that we choose to take with us all day long.
—Anonymous

It's hard to discount problems. They seem to fester and gain importance, especially when we ruminate on them.

But perhaps we can limit how long we ponder a problem by labeling it as "just a moment," letting it go, and keeping our momentum going. We can revisit it at any time when we have more information or are in a better place to address it. We don't have to let it drain all the good moments that may be ahead.

We have twenty-four hours in the day. No need to taint all of them with one bad moment.

How about you? What moments will you choose to take with you today? Which ones will you let go?

October 25:

Rough-Draft Friends

Today's inspiration comes from theologian and scholar Martin E. Marty and his response to this question, posed by playwright Stephen Dietz: "What do we affect during our lifetime? What, ultimately, is our legacy?"

Marty's response: "I believe, in most cases, our legacy is our friends. We write our history onto them, and they walk with us through our days like time capsules, filled with our mutual past, the fragments of our hearts and minds. Our friends get our uncensored questions and our yet-to-be reasoned opinions. Our friends grant us the chance to make our grand, embarrassing, contradictory pronouncements about the world. They get the very best, and are stuck with the absolute worst, we have to offer. Our friends get our rough drafts."

As I let his words roll through my mind, I considered all the "yet-to-be reasoned" opinions I've tried out on my friends, my safe place to wonder aloud about what to think, what to say, or what to do. More than once, I've asked, "Can I borrow your brain for a moment?" when I've needed to talk through a complex situation that had my mind stuck in a loop.

They've listened to half-baked ideas, absorbed ludicrous temper tantrums, and patiently gone with me down rabbit-hole pursuits that led to nowhere.

But we journeyed together, writing a shared history and creating time capsules filled with experiences that enrich and extend far beyond our time together.

How about you? What friendships do you consider legacy? Which ones get your rough drafts?

October 26:

Raising Awareness

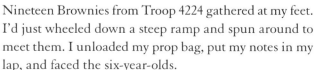

Nineteen Brownies from Troop 4224 gathered at my feet. I'd just wheeled down a steep ramp and spun around to meet them. I unloaded my prop bag, put my notes in my lap, and faced the six-year-olds.

I was terrified.

I'd politely declined the first time I was asked to speak. Although I'd been paralyzed for six years by that time, it still hurt to admit I couldn't feel or move my legs. The thought of explaining this to small children overwhelmed me.

Yet I knew eventually I wanted to face this fear.

When the leader asked again, she said she wanted to introduce me as her friend and fellow mom. She hoped I'd talk about what it's like to be in a wheelchair with the message that even though I am in a wheelchair, we are more alike than we are different.

It was a tall order, considering how often my wheelchair limited me and made me feel incredibly different. Poorly irrigated ballfields, misplaced sidewalk cutouts, and ramps too steep to navigate wreak havoc on a wheelchair. More than once, I'd become a joint project for dads who'd helped me tame the unkind terrain to see my son's lacrosse and soccer games. Then there were those unthinking motorists who use handicapped parking as loading zones or short-term parking, creating even more obstacles to overcome.

Life from a wheelchair is unquestionably different. But how could I help the girls understand what might not be obvious about people who use wheelchairs?

I first described the spinal cord and its amazing role in a person's mobility. Then we discussed who uses wheelchairs, what it's like to be in a wheelchair, and what the girls should think about when they see someone in a wheelchair.

"Just like you, I want to participate in as many fun activities as possible," I told them. "It just takes some extra effort for me to move around since I use a wheelchair. And sometimes some extra space."

For the grand finale, I demonstrated my minivan's special feature: the ramp it lowered and raised so I could get in and out of the vehicle. As the ramp unfolded into the hash-marked parking area, the girls saw firsthand the need for the extra space.

With disarming honesty, one Brownie confided, "My daddy parks there when he's in a hurry."

The Brownie leader quietly approached the young girl. "Maybe you should tell your dad how that affects someone who uses a wheelchair," she gently suggested.

I watched the leader's warm and caring manner as she, too, helped the child understand what might not be obvious. Everyone could strive to be thoughtful and kind, she was teaching her troop.

I hope that sharing my life with those children helped them learn how.

How about you? Have you ever helped raise awareness in others about a particular issue by sharing your own life experiences?

October 27:

Change of Tone

My adult children were home for a few days, working remotely. Set up in different rooms of my home, their muffled conversations created a medley of moods.

"You sound more excited, even laughed on your calls today," I said to one. "You must be having a better day than yesterday."

"Well, not really. I'm talking to my team today. They're still kids, and I'm trying to encourage them. Yesterday I was talking to my peers, and I needed to keep them accountable."

"Interesting," I said. As I wheeled back into my bedroom office, I smiled at the thought of the different audiences. The corresponding shift in tone and purpose reminded me of my own shift in parenting roles.

For the first two decades of my children's lives, I parented them to be accountable for their actions and decisions. It was a contact sport with daily workouts featuring limit-testing and boundary-setting along with that always necessary consequence-driven thinking.

It was often exhausting.

But now my role with my children has shifted. I'm more on the sidelines, mostly as an enthusiastic cheerleader. Sometimes I coach too—but only if asked.

I'll admit it; it was a tough shift. But then I remembered the advice from my wise friend Debbie that made it easier for me to adjust.

"The older we get," she said, "the more weight our words carry."

With that thought, I found it easier to measure my words. In fact, my words became less of a requirement and more of a gift I chose to give with careful thought.

Indeed, we can change our tone and role based not only on our audience but also on the goal we wish to achieve with that audience.

How about you? Do you notice yourself changing your tone and choice of words based on your audience?

October 28:

In Pursuit of Contentment

Months into the COVID-19 pandemic, I listened to a lecture that referenced *Death Be Not Proud*, a book I'd read years earlier. The author, father of Johnny Gunther (who died at age seventeen from a malignant brain tumor), noted these words his son had scribbled in a notebook:

"Contentment with the universe.
Discontentment with the world."

The lecturer contended that only by reaching and stretching toward contentment with the universe can we deal with the discontent we have with the world.

This idea gave me a new vocabulary for describing my mid-pandemic, pre-election, ever-present battle with uncertainty that resisted definition, much less management.

Discontentment permeated our world. Our adaptive skills were being tested in so many ways that it was hard to find sustained contentment in daily living.

We were tired. And tired of being tired.

Most of us were exhausted in ways we didn't even recognize until someone pointed it out—COVID exhaustion, compliance exhaustion, and even compassion exhaustion. Our stamina for enduring ongoing stress was getting fragile while the necessity to strengthen ourselves was building.

Yet, despite the worldly chaos, the sun came up. The stars shone. There was contentment beyond this world's discontent. And when I took the time to reflect on that, to engage in that, to rest in the peace of the universe, that day's discontentment became a bit more manageable.

How about you? How do you stay connected to the contentment beyond this world's discontent?

October 29:

Happy Family Secrets

I bought the book because of its title, *The Secrets of Happy Families* by Bruce Feiler, but cherish it because of his last line. I'd been preparing for a large family gathering and thought it might provide a few tips. Plus, I liked the guiding question of Feiler's research: "What do happy families do right and what can the rest of us learn to make our families happier?"

Feiler's three summary points hit home for me:

1. Adapt all the time.
2. Talk. A lot.
3. Go out and play.

But his final answer to the question of the happy family's secret proved to be both an enduring truth and a command:

"Try."

Families inhale and exhale with new relationships and circumstances from the moment they begin. Our lives are filled with unexpected events that can either bring us closer together or tear us apart.

It all depends on what we do next: try or give up.

Trying takes creativity, persistence, and a willingness to gently hold our expectations so that they don't limit our possibilities to be happy in unexpected ways.

Frustrated with a new or ongoing family issue? Maybe it's time to consider the question, "What can we try?"

How about you? When have you experienced the benefit of "trying" as you've dealt with the unexpected in your family life?

October 30:

Struggling Toward Happiness

"You're going to be happy," said life.
"But first I will make you strong."
—Anonymous

I shook my head and released a slow deep sigh when I read that statement, smiling at the words that resonated so deeply.

Is that what life is doing to me? Making me strong?

Happiness can be elusive. We think we have it in our grasp, and then something unexpected happens and it slips through our fingers. That uplifting positive spirit, the one we fight so hard to keep, evaporates.

Maybe our body misbehaves. Maybe we wince in pain from another's unthinking words or inexplicable actions. Maybe we find ourselves coping with losing when we were sure this time we should have been a winner.

We are shocked. Angry. Tired of the unexpected.

"Life is difficult," Scott Peck wrote in the opening to his classic book *The Road Less Traveled*. My father gave me a copy after my brother's death. I was twenty. I remember reading that line and thinking, *What a pessimist this guy must be*. I didn't want to be anything like him.

Now I see it differently. We all face challenges. Accepting life and all its difficulties does not mean that life isn't good. To the contrary.

Happiness will come—but not without struggles that can be used to strengthen us. Like the training before the competition. The study before the exam. The rehearsal before the performance. Or even those difficult losses that prepare us for new beginnings.

How about you? What struggles are you experiencing that could make you stronger?

October 31:

Lessons from My Cat

Solid black with a touch of white on her chest, my cat Inky had an odd morning routine that fascinated me. Daily, she would perch on top of a fish bowl that we'd covered and taped to ward off her wandering paws. Once she'd steadied herself, she would slowly bend over the side of the container to look at the fish—upside down. She would stare intently, focus, and then jab at the shadow of the fish.

The fish would dart. Inky would jab. Inky would pause, refocus, and then lunge again. The boxing match would continue until she scampered off to play with her favorite straw or a bottle cap—or her tail.

Every day, Inky would try to catch that fish; and every day, she would fail. I could interpret this activity as one that shows a lack of intellect, since she didn't seem to learn that she could not get the fish.

But I'm choosing to see it as her preparatory ritual, a morning routine that equipped her for the day.

I'm like Inky. I like routines. Routines keep me going, prompting me to keep moving even when I'd rather not. My favorites are my morning coffee and daily readings and chatting with my sister.

Inky's daily ritual inspires me. Regardless of the previous day's setbacks or failures, she lets her perching-pondering routine prepare her to meet her day with enthusiasm.

How about you? What routine could help you begin your day with enthusiasm?

NOVEMBER

November 1:

The Experience Challenge

↤⟶

No experience is wasted unless you let it be.
—Dr. R. F. Smith Jr.

My father offered these words not only as a prompt for reflection prior to his public speaking but also as a guide for living his life. He grew up in rural North Carolina, where his grandmother signed her name with an "X," his early childhood home had an outhouse, and he was the first in his family to go to college. Yet he cherished his upbringing and distilled timeless truths from his experiences that have rippled beyond his lifetime.

Dad loved to learn. He embraced a "growth mindset" long before the term was coined, using it to live his life and influence ours and others. After Forest's death, I watched him move through his own healing in an amazingly public way, preaching and writing on the lessons his grief was teaching him at the moment. He started a monthly column, "Looking Homeward," in the local newspaper to keep him connected to the community. And within months of Forest's death, he became a noted lecturer on grief.

"There is life for you after their death," he would tell parents who had lost children. "At first, you're not sure you will ever live again. You are certain you will never laugh again. But you will. You will always walk with a limp, but you will walk again."

Twenty years later, and only sixteen months after my paralysis, he was diagnosed with cancer. Days later, he wrote to me:

423

Dearest BB,

For some months, I have had this strange feeling that I had cancer. As I did various things, e.g., roofing the house here and in Lenoir, changing banks, getting "my house in order," I sensed something was afoot. Now I know what it is. But I am so glad that the future looks brighter than it could have been given other factors. I do feel this is but a detour on my journey, and I am even now asking, "What will I learn from this?"

We will make it. We are survivors.

I love you.

DAD

Even though Dad eventually lost his battle with cancer, his words have done more than survive. They have flourished, both challenging and comforting many. He both set the stage for learning and sent the message that we must take responsibility to learn from what we experience. Even now, those words remind me to keep open to the learning a situation has to offer.

We choose what do with our experiences. We can waste them, or we can learn from them.

❧

How about you? What can you learn from your experiences today?

November 2:

A Parent's Love

The second-grade classroom buzzed with anticipation. Nineteen children had prepared animal-themed presentations for an audience of their parents and peers.

From Kendall, we learned that a giraffe's heart weighs 25 pounds and has a blood pressure twice that of a human's to help pump blood up that long neck. From Peter, we learned that a newborn elephant weighs 250 pounds and a full-grown elephant eats 330 pounds of food daily.

Sam taught us that chimpanzees are social, caring creatures. They greet each other with handshakes and often eat the insects out of each other's fur. And when it comes to the nurturing of their offspring, Sam reported, "If a mother chimp isn't loved as a child, she won't love her baby chimp."

At this the parents collectively winced, and an uneasy silence settled in. Sam had hit a raw parenting nerve: *Am I teaching my child to love? Am I giving my child all that they will need to give their child?*

"You can't give what you don't have," they say. I once argued that you certainly can. You can give tickets to a concert even if you've never been. You can give trips abroad even if you've never boarded a plane. You can give a college education even if you've never finished high school.

Yet there are more important gifts to consider. Can we give our child a love of learning if we do not stretch ourselves with new information and experiences? Can we give our child a sense of worth if we do not value our own thoughts and ideas, our own time and talents? Can we give our child respect for values if we show no ethics or integrity in our personal and business lives? Can we love our children if we have not felt love?

If we dare, we can use that thought as a mirror and lift it high above our heads to see what we are giving our children.

At its best, we may see principled parenting with consistent messages. At its worst, we may view a reflection that startles us, making us wonder if perhaps all we're giving our child—in that moment, at least—is something to tell their shrink about in twenty years.

No family is perfect. And as we grow, we are occasionally confronted with memories that make us realize our parents made mistakes too.

But even though mistakes happen, love is constant. As parents, we press on, despite the highs and lows of childrearing, fueled by a desire to love our kids the best we can—and to teach them to love others too.

How about you? What love-themed lessons have you given or received?

November 3:

Pouting with Purpose

For eleven months I'd been planning the trip from Baltimore to Philadelphia for a November conference. It was the final stop of my book promotion.

I had a friend to drive me there and a caregiver for my dog. I had an accessible room booked, my conference sessions selected, and a meeting set up to reconnect with a fellow author and friend that I'd last seen forty years before. Most importantly, though, I was going to meet the publisher of my father's book at an author reception where, for the first time ever, I would have the chance to represent both Dad's book and mine.

I was beyond excited.

Then it snowed. Really snowed.

I sat there, staring at my suitcase—filled with plans that would never be. Life was not cooperating with me, and I was ticked.

A small voice tried to break through my funk: *It is not wise to go, Becky. The roads are horrible. You could get stuck. It is not safe. This is the right choice. Move on. Get over it.*

But I wasn't ready to move on or get over it. So I sat and fumed some more: *It's early November. It never snows now. Are the roads really that bad? This is crazy! I've worked so hard to make these plans . . .*

Then I caught a glimpse of myself in the mirror. Wait, was I pouting?

How childish, I scolded myself.

Then I looked up the word and found a strange relief:

When you pout, you're expressing annoyance or displeasure. It's a sulky kind of gesture, one that involves a facial expression more than words—in fact, a pout is often accompanied by a moody silence.

The definition comforted me. Pouting wasn't pointless—it was giving me time to silently absorb the situation. I couldn't push straight through to acceptance; I had to pout first.

I smiled at that thought, wheeled my unpacked suitcase into another room, and shut the door. Pout time was over, its purpose complete. I called the hotel to cancel, messaged my dear friend that I wouldn't be coming, and called my father's publisher. I was shocked at her response:

"Why don't you send me a flyer about your book and I'll share it at the author reception?"

"Oh my," I stammered. "Thank you! I'd love to."
Pout-less and with great purpose, I did.

How about you? Have you ever caught yourself pouting?
Did it prepare you to accept a disappointing situation?

November 4:

Sophomoric Challenges

Five minutes into a thirty-minute meeting with Peter's academic advisor, my phone lit up.

"Oh, it's Pete," I said. "I'll call him back."

We resumed our conversation, our first in my sixteen-year-old son's sophomore year.

Pete called again. This time he sent a message.

As we reviewed Pete's progress, my mind wandered—and worried. Pete usually texted, rarely called.

There was no school that day, so I'd allowed Pete to host a mid-week sleepover to celebrate the release of a new video game. Seven friends had been "summoned for duty" to my basement, where they'd hooked up gaming consoles and launched a war zone complete with gunfire, explosions—and hysterical laughter. That morning, I'd made pancakes for them. All had been well when I left.

After the conference, I thanked the adviser. His advice echoed in my mind as I left his office. "Often as conscientious parents, we're so busy keeping kids 'on track' that it's difficult to let their actions reveal their commitment and focus," he'd told me. "There's a time to let go a bit, to let our kids discover their own vision."

Pondering that, I retrieved my cell phone.

It's a tricky time, transitioning into that sophomore year. No longer rookies, these savvy sophomores are expected to know (better than the previous year, at least) the ins and outs of high school life.

Yet hormones rage unevenly for these kids, a group recognizable by their stair-stepped heights and octave-differing voices. Unprecedented freedoms await with the magic of the driver's license. Mobility and maturity crash head-on, launching parents into their own transitional period of consequential thinking and anticipatory parenting.

"You're just making it up as you go along, Mom," Pete's older sister told me when I crafted rules during her teenage years.

She was right.

Who knows what limits we need to set until they are tested? One kid's temptation is another kid's last thought.

Pete's video interrupted my thoughts. "So, Mom, whenever you watch this," he paused to pan the camera, "the ceiling is leaking." He zoomed in, showing water pouring from the ceiling into two coolers. "Need help," he announced, matter-of-factly.

The plumber met me at the house and quickly unclogged the upstairs toilet that had overflowed. The damage was minimal and easily remedied. This particular cry for help was clear, its remedy swift and simple.

Not always so, in that tricky sophomore year.

❧

How about you? What experiences challenged you in that tricky sophomore year?

November 5:

How to Care Better

I was honored, if a little intimidated, to be asked to participate in a panel discussion entitled, "When Life Doesn't Go as Planned." When I asked for more details, the first discussion question almost scared me off: "In what ways has life not gone as you expected?"

Gulp. Let me count the ways?

"I'm going to cheat," I later told the audience. I took a deep breath, read my list of losses, and then listened to my fellow panelists share theirs.

As I listened to our collective stories and struggles, I realized that no matter how many detours your life has taken, large or small, the hurt of life-changing loss lingers. And we all, in one way or another, have to figure out a way to recover from that hurt.

Although we'd taken different paths to healing, all of us on the panel agreed on one thing that day: it is hard to know the appropriate things to do or say when trying to comfort someone in deep grief.

"How were other people helpful during your experiences?" the moderator asked us. "In what ways were they not helpful or even hurtful?"

After a lively and robust conversation, we were all surprised to discover that we had often been both the offended and the offender—that what helped some of us hurt others. In the end, the frank discussion helped us all become more sensitive, thoughtful, and aware of other perspectives.

So, what did we learn that can help us do a better job of caring?

1. Grief can make us behave and react differently, so it's vital to be gentle in how we give support and in how we receive it.

2. Some folks are especially sensitive while experiencing grief; others appear totally unaffected.
3. Pain is hard—but feeling alone in pain can be unbearable. Whether we know it or not, whether we show it or not, we need an acknowledgment of the loss we've suffered and enough support to feel like we are not alone.
4. Cards, notes, and emails, as well as practical expressions of providing meals, transportation, or caring for children, are enormous helps. Often, we don't even know what we need, so routine check-ins can be helpful, as are other demonstrations that you are present and available.

Bottom line, there is no one-size-fits-all approach to comforting those experiencing loss. However, simply showing up in gentle ways that are sensitive to the person and the situation eases the loneliness of loss.

How about you? What kinds of helpful support have you given (or received) during times of grief or significant loss?

November 6:

Mantras That Matter

Some call them slogans. Others label them as mantras or mottos. Whatever you call them, these short, sticky sound bites are powerful, often reminding us quite succinctly what is important.

I'll never forget my first meeting with my IBM sales manager in 1982. Although my first job out of college was as a recruiter in Charlotte, when I switched to a sales position and relocated to Atlanta, I was suddenly a rookie again.

On my first day of work, I wore my best pinstripe suit, a white blouse with a floppy bowtie (all the rage in the early '80s, at least at IBM), and navy pumps. I shook my new boss's hand firmly and looked him in the eyes before sitting down in an uncomfortable chair—at which point saw the words he had on display, and began to fidget.

On his spartan, overly organized desk was a sleek brown laminated tent card sign that read simply:

THINK

A nearby bookcase hosted another laminated beauty with an equally challenging sentiment:

WE'RE AT WAR: TALK NET

Needless to say, following that meeting I only ever came into his office prepared, rehearsed, and ready to take action.

In the years since, I've always been on the lookout for new sound bites to inspire me or remind me what's important *right now.* Life continued to roll on—and so did the challenges. You'd think after all the hairpin turns I've had (sibling loss, special needs children, divorce, paralysis), I'd be used to it.

But I'm not.

Do we ever get used to life's adversities?

I don't think so.

And just because we've been in a valley or two, does it mean we're "good" at it?

Perhaps, but that doesn't mean we like it.

In the meantime, mantras help. They concentrate our focus as we move through what we must. One of my favorites continues to guide me from time to time:

ELEVATE.

It encourages me to rise up high enough above the difficulties to gain perspective, maybe even begin to see the patterns of life.

Richard Bach describes it beautifully: "But the sky knows the reasons and the patterns behind all clouds, and you will know, too, when you lift yourself high enough to see beyond horizons."

How about you? What mantras do you rely on when you find yourself in a valley?

November 7:

Healing Obstacles

The doctor gave us the bad news at the follow-up visit: my son's fractured ankle was still too swollen to cast.

He had hurt it while walking between classes, twisting the ankle on the sidewalk's edge. We'd iced, elevated, and even missed a day of school for it. But we weren't out of the woods yet.

"We need a tight fit for proper healing," the doctor reminded us. If casted while swollen, he explained, there'd be excess room between the ankle and cast when the swelling subsided. "The swelling needs to go down," he said, "so the healing can begin."

The stubbornly swollen ankle was splinted again and we returned to elevating and icing with renewed vigor. Meanwhile, I thought about this swelling business and what it tells us about injury—and life.

When an injury occurs, the fibers of the affected tissue are disrupted. Often the blood vessels in the area are broken, leaking blood and serum into the surrounding tissue, bringing on swelling and sometimes pain.

Swelling may actually impede the healing process. A study at Duke University found that two immune system proteins produced during swelling blocked healing of a damaged knee cartilage.

So swelling can be both an indicator of injury as well as a potential block to healing.

As I thought about the body's amazing response system, I wondered if the same process occurs when we experience emotional trauma.

Illness, divorce, death, and other life-changing events hit us like injuries, sending our bodies into react mode. Our minds flood with anger and grief, reacting to the disruption in our lives and the brokenness that we feel.

And there is pain.

Perhaps unresolved anger and grief impede healing. We need to find ways to cope, to work through our reactions, and adjust to the trauma as we strive to ease the pain and begin to heal.

Like my son's swollen ankle, however, we can't circumvent the process. Casting before the swelling process finishes can lead to all sorts of complications; so, too, can ignoring our anger or grief.

But can we heal at all before the inflammation subsides—before our bodies have totally adjusted to the trauma?

"Yes," our doctor told us at the follow-up exam. "He's started to heal."

Swelling or not, he was making progress—perhaps an assurance for all who are struggling to heal.

⁓§§⁓

How about you? Have you struggled with patience for a healing process of body or mind?

November 8:

Sharing Our Brains

It's the stage some of us fear as parents. Those cuddly babies toddle their way through elementary school straight into the tween and teen years, and adolescence descends upon us.

The road is long, mixed with joy and a few bumps. So arm yourself with patience, humor, and a good dose of science. Yes, science.

Through the years, I've attended many health and wellness seminars for my children—some optional, some required. For two years, my presence at one meeting was my daughter's permission to attend prom. Regardless of my motivation, I always left the seminars loaded with information and in awe of life beyond my backyard.

There's no quicker trip to reality than having a former-crack-addict-turned-counselor tell you what's out there facing your kids. Or hearing a health and wellness expert present statistics for underage drinking—from a survey at your school. Or listening to an account of the consequences of serving alcohol to underage kids—in a nearby home. Or facing a panel of kids who shared more than you were ready to hear.

"I have a friend who sells marijuana here," one student admitted.

Dumbfounded at the candor, I listened as the student explained his friend's decision. Eighty-five dollars for a small baggie of marijuana was good money compared to other jobs. If caught, it was unlikely the friend would go to jail at that age. Yes, the school would be upset, but often kids return if they're kicked out.

The logic fried my brain. The honesty both alarmed and enlightened me.

The most helpful information I found about all this came from Duke University neuropharmacologist Dr. Wilkie Wilson.

"The frontal lobes of the brain are still developing until a child reaches their early twenties," Dr. Wilson told a group of high school parents. He went on to explain that this area of the brain is responsible for executive functions such as processing complex information, reasoning, and problem-solving. It also manages impulse control and gives us the capacity to use good judgment in making decisions. During these developmental years, the wiring of the brain is not complete, which means our tools for making good decisions are not finished.

"Share your frontal lobes with your kids," Dr. Wilson advised.

In other words, we must guide them until they can gain enough growth, maturity, experiences, and, yes, brain development to make good choices on their own.

How about you? Has the (il)logic of teens ever surprised you?

November 9:

Thoughtful Clothing

"What do you think, Aunt Becky?" my niece Ashley texted me.

She'd sent a pic of her sporting a new pair of shoes, some fuzzy, on-trend Birkenstocks. Julie, her new friend, had recommended them.

"Julie wore them on Insta and I absolutely love them! But I'm not sure. Are they too big? Do they look like clown shoes?"

"Yes" was my first thought. But I resisted a quick reply.

Even though paralysis limits my wardrobe, I attempt to keep up with the latest fashions. But Ashley is in another league—*always* on point, *always* on trend. So I did some quick research.

I found Julie's post, screenshot it, and studied it. Indeed, Julie looked great in those shoes. But she wore them with a thick suede jacket and a large tote purse.

I sent the screenshot to Ashley and texted, "Shoes are so cute here, but she has a lot of heavy, chunky pieces to balance it out—the bag and the jacket. I think they look oversized on you. Draws attention to your feet in a distracting kind of way." And then added two heart emojis and a smiley face blowing a kiss.

"Thank you. You are so helpful!" she texted back.

I smiled at her words, grateful that a sixty-something aunt could still give helpful advice to her twenty-something niece.

The next day, this quote by Jonathan Swift found me:

"Words are the clothing of our thoughts."

Exactly! I was so glad I took some extra time to clothe my thoughts in that exchange with Ashley.

In fact, when you think about it, most often our "naked truths" could use some clothing.

How about you? How will you choose to clothe your thoughts today?

November 10:

What Would You Change?

For seventeen years, I had a brother on this earth. His name was Forest: Robert Forest Smith III, as he liked to sign his name. On September 3, 1978, he hit a pier while water-skiing at Lake Hickory. He never regained consciousness. Nine days later he died.

He was president of his high school's student council, an athlete, a musician, and an active leader in the church. He had his sights set on Wake Forest University, our parents' alma mater, then law school and a career in politics. He had a dream and was working hard to make it a reality.

"I would change nothing," he wrote on the last line of his college application essay—the last words he would ever write. The next day he would go water-skiing.

He was seventeen when he died. I was twenty.

Forest and I were more than siblings; we were the best of friends. We confided in one another, debated political issues, and probed deep philosophical questions about the meaning of life.

We were proud of each other and our family. One of my prize memories is the night we won the high school dance contest. I brought back all the latest dance steps from Chapel Hill and we shagged, hustled, and bopped our way through the night. He was proud to have me as his date. I was proud to be his date. We were an awesome team.

I was a junior at UNC when Forest died. I almost dropped out that semester. My mind was so consumed with grief; I had no room for learning, only pain. Somehow, I made it through.

I've come to be thankful that I had a brother. Not everyone is so lucky. But even now, decades later, revisiting that time in my life causes those embers of my love for him to burn bright with fresh hurt. I miss him every day.

But he is worth the hurt. Worth the pain. Worth remembering.

I would change nothing.

His words have become an inspiration for me, a daily mantra I aim to own before my head hits the pillow each night. About the day. About the decisions I've made. About the way I've treated the people I care about and even those whom I may have touched without even realizing it.

And in doing so I hope that, looking back, I can honestly think, *I would change nothing.*

How about you? How can you use my brother's words as inspiration today?

November 11:

Polishing Memories

It's that time of year when we are reminded to be thankful.

Some years are easier than others. Our bodies may have misbehaved or even betrayed us with illness or ailments. Our investments of time, energy, and effort may have yielded disappointing results. Or, more visibly, we may have been forced to accept an unexpected empty chair at our Thanksgiving table and then deal with its unwelcomed replacement: grief. Life may have been more difficult than we'd planned or hoped it would be.

Despite our losses, it may be time to "major on the minors." We may need to find a little something that went right instead of wrong and embellish it with all the positivity we can muster.

For me, that inspiration comes from memories. Sometimes we need to pluck a tiny memory and give it the old spit shine that my father used to talk about when he'd polish his wingtips until they glistened.

Then, to give it life, we need to share it. We need to tell that story in all its glory. We need to get out our little paintbrushes, add a little sparkle, and make that memory shine with love. Like this one:

A few years ago, my sister drove from her home in Georgia to check on our parents' home in North Carolina. She arranged to have lunch with Aunt Pearl, who lived nearby, and Aunt Pearl's daughter Robin, who drove in from South Carolina to join them. Once they settled in at their table, they noticed they all had something in common.

Cajun Shrimp nail polish!

Three women, three states apart, meeting for a rare lunch together and all wearing the exact same color. It must be in my family's DNA!

That story warms my heart every time I tell it. And when I choose that color for my nails, I think of my aunt, my cousin, and my sister, and I am grateful.

As Jean-Baptiste Massieu reminds us: "Gratitude is the memory of the heart."

How about you? What heartwarming story could you "major on" to prompt your gratitude today?

November 12:

Valley Lessons

Although I'd faced challenges before—the loss of my teenage brother, parenting my special needs children, and a painful divorce—paralysis plunged me into a radically altered lifestyle that gave me a point of view unlike no other.

"Perspective," I called it. And in the early months of my paralysis, I felt like perspective was my gift to give others, my purpose to teach, and my obligation to share.

Friends would tell me of their latest last-minute "running late" episodes, and I would find myself quipping, "At least you can run."

I would hear complaints of waiting in line for a movie or concert tickets, and I would offer, "At least you can stand."

At one wedding I attended, a friend declined a dancing invitation because he said his feet hurt. "At least you can feel your feet!" I reminded him.

Thankfully, all my friends chuckled graciously with me. And yet, I kept telling myself that I was offering these folks perspective. Given *my* circumstance, certainly their situation had to look better. My words from my valley would put their own valley "in perspective," I reasoned—make it feel smaller.

Wrong. Embarrassingly wrong.

Your valley is your valley, I've finally learned. Your pain is your pain.

Others' stories may make yours seem less important, but truthfully, it is all relative. And not relative to everyone's circumstances—only your own.

Pain is real. Disappointments are sad. Failure hurts.

"Your broken leg doesn't make my broken pinky hurt any less," my father once said.

Each of us has our own paths with our own pain. Big or small, pain hurts. To compare to others, to try to discount its effect, results in a denial of reality. One person's mountain may be another's molehill—yet each should respect the other. True perspective comes from within.

We choose our perspective in the valley by how we view both our mountains and our molehills. No one else can do that for us.

How about you? What have you learned when you've tried to compare one of your valleys to someone else's?

November 13:

The Power of Thank You

⌒⌒⌒

Next to "I love you," the three most important words we can say to another human being are, "I thank you!"

Fact is, "I thank you" is a great way to express "I love you."

Author and poet William Stidger tells of being prompted by a book he was reading to write a letter to someone who had meant a lot to him in life. He wrote two former school teachers, expressing gratitude to them for their contributions to his life.

The first replied with this:

My dear Willie,
I cannot tell you how much your note meant to me. I am in my eighties, living alone in a small room, cooking my own meals, lonely, and, like the last leaf of autumn, lingering behind. You will be interested to know that I taught in school for fifty years, and yours is the first note of appreciation I ever received. It came on a blue, cold morning and it cheered me as nothing has in many years.

The second letter came from a former teacher who had lost his wife:

My dear Will,
Your letter was so beautiful, so real, that as I sat reading it in my study, tears fell from

my eyes; tears of gratitude. Then, before I
realized what I was doing, I rose from my
chair and called her name to show it to her—
forgetting for a moment that she was gone.
You will never know how much your letter
has warmed my spirit. I have been walking
about in the glow of it all day long.

After receiving those letters, Dr. Stidger started writing letters by the handful!

In the course of a lifetime, many people touch our lives. And we're grateful—but we often don't take the time to express it.

Most of us will never be famous and touch the lives of millions, as some are privileged to do. But we each can become famous to at least one person—that person who has touched your life—if we simply take the time to say, "I thank you."

How about you? Who could you thank for their influ-
ence on your life?

November 14:

Time for Re-measure

This George Bernard Shaw quote is a favorite of mine, especially when I am reconnecting with friends or family:

> "My tailor is the wisest man I know. He's
> the only person who measures me every
> time I go in."

444 | Morning Fuel

Most of us don't extend such wise courtesy to other people or receive it from those we know. We tend to see people in the same light year in and year out, never considering that they may have grown or matured.

We categorize people by our experiences with them and the choices they've made and form opinions based on shared time together, layering those experiences to create a concrete image that's hard to change.

After all, labels save time. Plus, it's hard work to reassess a person, especially if there is no pressing need. We have to stop long enough to take in new information, analyze it, compare it to our previous perspective, and then decide whether or not to apply it.

The temptation to label people by the same size— mentally, emotionally, spiritually—is often greatest with family, despite the fact that they're the people we've lived with longest and have had the greatest opportunity to re-measure over the years. Labels like, the "baby," the "smart one," the "competitive one," the "shy one," the "risk-taking one," the "never-achieved-their-potential one"—all are difficult roles to shed.

But people do grow, change, and embrace new perspectives—even within our families.

Celebratory gatherings offer a prime time to re-measure. The evidence of change can be as simple as wish lists or gift reactions or as complex as trying to schedule a family dinner that takes into consideration each family member's physical location, work schedule, significant others, travel plans, and food preferences.

Maybe, like the tailor, we can wise up and re-measure as an ongoing caring pursuit, taking stock of our loved ones and let their growth prompt ours.

❧

How about you? What opportunities do you have to re-measure someone you care about?

November 15:

Growing Through

Nine months into the pandemic, life since March 11, 2020, seemed like one big smudge on my calendar. Yet January 2021 had arrived, demanding a theme word per my New Year's tradition. Perched on the cusp of a year that held so much promise, I chose:

Meanwhile.

To some it was an odd choice. Finally, there was light at the end of the pandemic tunnel—or so it seemed—and yet I was choosing to focus not on the tunnel's end but on living fully in the meanwhile moments. It's an approach that continues to serve me well when I'm facing tunnels of uncertainty.

We can look at our tunnels in two ways: dark with dread or green with an opportunity for growth. Uncertainty fills both, but we can choose our meanwhile mindset.

As we wait for the tunnel's light to clarify the reality ahead, we can consider:

- What can we do in the meantime that will allow us to grow?
- What can we learn about ourselves and others?
- What new perspectives can we gain that will allow us to live in a more meaningful way?

The light at the end of the tunnel is the same, but the path through it is lived differently. We can go through it or grow through it.

I must admit, "meanwhile" was not the first word I chose. Initially, I considered defiant words like "despite" or "nevertheless"—words that exuded grit and resolve.

But the fatigue of pandemic living had begun to settle in deep. I didn't want to spend my remaining energy gearing up again and again for battle with an elusive enemy. The better approach, I decided, was to hold life lightly.

When we squeeze life too tightly, we often choke out our possibilities—the very things that allow us to rethink and adapt. A meanwhile mindset that holds life lightly allows us to be open and receptive, to breathe through the difficulties instead of holding our breath and shutting our eyes until it's safe to come out again.

How about you? Could a shift in mindset from going to growing help you through a tunnel of uncertainty?

November 16:

How Many Stars?

One morning, my dad walked through the church office reception area and greeted the gentleman waiting to see another staff member with a quick, "Good morning."

Dad continued down the hall, where a staff member who'd overheard the brief conversation whispered, "I see you met a one-star person."

"A one-star what?"

"A one-star person," she repeated. "You decided that person was only one star."

"What do you mean?"

"Well," she replied, "we *star* people based on how you engage with them: A one-star person only gets a good morning. A two-star person gets a good morning *and* a how-are-you-today. A three-star person gets a good morning, a how-are-you, *and* an inquiry about his family or an interest."

Dad listened, intrigued.

"With a four-star person," she continued, "you greet him, ask how he is, inquire about an interest, and then say, 'what do you think about' a topic, soliciting an opinion. Beyond the usual chit-chat, you acknowledge that you value his judgment and recognize his worth."

It was a startling point for my father then, decades ago, that's even more complex now.

Granted, our responses may sometimes be situation-based, influenced by time and circumstance. We may value a given person but not have time for a four-star exchange with them. Nevertheless, how we interact with people does reflect how we value them. And in this age of interruption-driven conversations, having real conversations is more challenging than ever.

Beeps, buzzes, and the glow of mobile devices have practically fostered a self-made attention deficit syndrome. Multitasking rules. Instant updates are not only accepted, but often expected, somehow giving permission to carry on two private conversations at once.

One gifted family member can buffer an entire paragraph of conversation while wrapping up a text, tweet, or Facebook post before responding to me when I am sitting right in front of the darling.

Hello?

Forget stars; I feel like a footnoted asterisk!

Being present no longer guarantees our full presence, as we grant those absent the same attention as those who have made the effort to show up in person.

But whether stars or asterisks, it's still about worth. How do we value others? Undivided attention helps.

As does that powerful question, "What do you think?"

How about you? How would you star the last conversation you had?

November 17:

A Vocabulary for Grief

Several months after my father's death, I called Mom and could tell she'd been crying. She couldn't seem to quiet herself as she usually did. After several denials, she finally acknowledged what was bothering her.

"I can't believe the questions people ask me," she said.

"I'm so sorry, Mom. What happened?"

"Well, people keep asking me, 'How are you?'" The emotion rose in her trembling voice. "How do they think I am?" she said as tears thickened her words. "I am devastated. I am sad. I have lost my husband, and I miss him terribly. How do they think I am?!" she said, sobbing.

"Oh, Mom." I felt helpless.

I listened some more and then joined her in reminiscing about Dad—how much we missed him, what a special man he was, and how it was tough to live without him.

"You know, Mom," I said after all that, taking some extra time to put as much tenderness as I could I my voice, "I am sure those folks did not mean to upset you by asking how you are."

Her breathing steadied.

"When you think about it, it's a greeting most of us use from time to time," I continued, choosing each word and tone with care. "I can see how it would be upsetting to you, but I think any hurt that you felt was unintentional. They just care about you."

Days later, I slipped and asked, "How are you?" in one of our own conversations. I cringed at the thought of what flood of grief I might have inadvertently set off for my fragile Mom. But she surprised me.

"I'm a-doin', BB," she said simply. "I'm a-doin'."

And she was. She was not "fine," and did not want to say so. She was "a-doin'"—moving forward as best she could.

Go, Mom! I thought to myself as I realized how she'd triumphed over one part of the victimhood of grief, finding her own way to cope.

How about you? When you are fragile, what phrase can you use to more accurately state how you feel?

November 18:

Undelivered Gratitude

Gratitude opens us up for connection. We aren't focusing on the past or the future but rather on the best of what we have in that very moment.

But to be fully experienced, gratitude must be delivered. As William Arthur Ward says:

> "Feeling gratitude and not expressing it is
> like wrapping a present and not giving it."

Armed with this new mentality, I began making an extra effort to express gratitude—with words, a gesture, or even a smile:

- To the clerk who picked up an extra shift so I could shop early when it was less crowded.
- To the person in line behind me who was patient with me as I fumbled for my wallet.
- To the delivery man who followed my instructions and didn't ring the doorbell since it upsets my dog.
- To the driver who slowed down so I could make that left turn out of my neighborhood.

- To my trash collector, who not only put the lid back on my emptied trash can but also retrieved my newspaper from the mulch.

Gratitude has the power to renew in us the best of what our shared humanity offers: kindness, understanding, and love.

⤳⚮⤳

How about you? Have you had the chance to express gratitude and felt the warmth of the connection it offers lately?

November 19:

Which Tooth?

My parents were preparing to come from West Virginia to Baltimore for Thanksgiving. Two days before their departure, Dad developed a severe toothache. Fortunately, he was able to see his dentist and get a prescription to treat the infection. However, the trip was in jeopardy for a day or two.

During this time my sister Rachel called me from Dallas, where she lived at the time. I updated her on the trip plans and told her about Dad's lingering toothache.

She listened intently, absorbing all the facts. After I finished, she asked, "Which tooth?"

I paused, smiled, and replied, "Well, Sissy, I don't know that detail. But I can find out!"

We laughed and finished our conversation. I eventually talked to Mom and Dad, identified the tooth (upper left bicuspid) and conveyed the information back to Rachel. The trip proceeded without a hitch; the medication did its job to relieve the pain and restore health to Dad's tooth.

Yet Rachel's question lingered— "Which tooth?"

Why would it matter which tooth was affected? How could that detail possibly benefit my sister, who was 1,500 miles away?

It's the connection, I reasoned. Details define us. They separate the uncommon from the ordinary. They give our world color and contrast. They give us hooks to link us to each other's worlds.

As you may recall, my father playfully called this "using a little paintbrush," particularly when describing my mother's detailed accounts of events. Although he'd sometimes encourage her to "big-brush it" to move her story along, there were benefits to those little paintbrushes. Their dabs of color offer more than just glossy paint. They fill in connections with color.

"Which tooth" translates to "What are you doing?" when I call my family or friends now. Those details connect my world to theirs. Each time we talk I try to place myself in their world, even if only for a moment.

A defined, detailed moment. A moment colored with the smallest of paintbrushes.

How about you? What detail can you ask about today to connect your world to another's?

November 20:

Turkey Disaster

The star of the Thanksgiving table that year was Chef Tyler Florence's maple-roasted, bacon-topped turkey.

My children Peter and Brittany and Brittany's then-boyfriend Brian joined me in watching the four-minute, thirty-seven-second recipe video that morning. We took notes, and then executed each step to perfection.

Our table setting included special wineglasses for the teens' sparkling apple cider. After four hours and thirty-five minutes of basting, the table welcomed the beautiful bird.

"It's amazing, Sissy!" Rachel exclaimed.

"Wow, Aunt Becky!" her daughter Ashley added. "You outdid yourself."

Next all six feet of my nephew Adam grabbed his glass, thrust it into the air, and bellowed, "Cheers everyone!"

And the unthinkable happened.

Beneath his thundering voice, there must have been a faint crashing sound. But at the time, our first clue of the disaster was Adam's bewildered face as he slowly lowered his hand, now holding only the stem of the glass.

"Uh-oh," he whispered.

"Adam, what happened?" I stammered, rolling my wheelchair closer to the table.

"Watch out!" Brian said. "Glass is everywhere."

Everyone froze as we realized what had happened. Adam's exuberant toast had crashed into the low beam of my vaulted ceiling, shattering his glass into hundreds of slivers.

My prize turkey glistened with more than a maple glaze. It was covered in glass.

My mind joined my paralyzed legs as the shock shut it down.

Adam's face fell. "I'm so sorry, Aunt Becky."

"It's okay, Adam," I managed to reply, trying to absorb the scene. But it didn't feel okay.

My family quietly began the clean-up of the blanket of glass while the turkey sparkled.

"Maybe we can clean it off," someone suggested.

But a closer look revealed embedded glass.

I moved the wounded bird to the top of my washing machine, and then pulled out lunchmeat trays I'd prepared for the next meal.

Somberly, we began our hodgepodge dinner.

"Someday, we'll laugh about this," someone said.

I nodded and smiled, knowing it would not be this day.

After dessert, we wandered back to the laundry room and gave that glorious bird one last look before we bade it farewell and dumped it in the trash can.

I haven't looked at that turkey recipe since that day, but I must admit that story is now family folklore—and sharing it brings an odd but special joy.

How about you? Do you have a Thanksgiving dinner disaster that is now family folklore?

November 21:

Little Ears

Lindsey was nine years old, the same age my daughter was when I was paralyzed by transverse myelitis. Her mom, Robin, was one of my best friends in college. Apparently, Lindsey had heard her mom talking to me through the years, so when she needed to write an essay for her fifth-grade class, she wrote this:

> *Becky Galli is my mom's very good friend. She is my good friend too.*
>
> *These are ways why she should be honored.*
>
> *First, her brother was water skiing and he ran into a pole. He died from this. Then after he ran into a pole, her dad wrote a book about him. It is called* Sit Down God, I Am Angry. *This book is about him.*
>
> *Then she got divorced in January. She has two handicapped children. In February, she*

*got a bad cough, then she got very sick. After
that, a bacteria got in her body and attacked
her spinal cord. The bacteria made her not be
able to walk.*

*I feel very bad for her and I think she
should be honored and be on a stamp.*

When Robin sent me this essay, I cried, overcome
with what this child had pieced together from overheard
conversations. Beyond the facts (and the details!), what
struck me most was the heart in her words—to "feel very
bad" for me, and yet want to "honor" me by being on
a stamp.

And I wondered: Is this the beginning of compassion? To want to honor those struggling instead of pitying
or judging them?

Perhaps she learned it from her mom and the
caring way she spoke to me and about my situation. Not
as someone to be pitied but as someone to be lifted up
and respected.

I can think of no finer thing to give a child than the
gift of compassion.

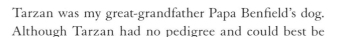

*How about you? How can you describe the struggles
of others in ways that can teach compassion? And
when you speak, do you always consider who might
be listening?*

November 22:

Dog Tales

Tarzan was my great-grandfather Papa Benfield's dog.
Although Tarzan had no pedigree and could best be

described as a "duke's mixture," he was a storied dog who loved and was loved by the family.

A small fellow clothed in a brown and white coat, Tarzan carried his tail in a question mark, wagging it constantly as he went about his dog life. He was known by just about everybody in the small town where my father grew up. Tarzan's appearance downtown immediately cleaned up conversations, I was told, because everyone knew he was "Preacher Benfield's dog." When he showed up, the beloved and respected pastor could not be too far behind.

My great-grandparents had a family ritual they observed every night: Just before bedtime, Papa Benfield read the Bible and the family knelt for prayer. Tarzan was always there. After the evening devotions, they would lead him to the basement door and he would go down to his sleeping quarters.

But there was another part of the family ritual. Just for fun, my father would try to get Tarzan to go downstairs *before* devotions—and every time, the dog wouldn't budge, no matter how intensely he was called. If Dad tried to pick him up, the usually nonviolent little dog would growl in a tone that showed he meant business.

Only after Papa Benfield read and prayed would Tarzan get up, stretch, and go to the basement door. He had done his family duty and knew it was now time for bed.

Tarzan was seventeen when a car struck him. My father's family cried when their dog's lifeless little body was placed tenderly in the garden ground. And tears came again, many times, I was told, when family devotions were over and Tarzan was no longer there to stretch and go to the basement.

Our pets become part of our family. They not only enrich our lives, they also punctuate our lives with their routines—and, in doing so, sometimes remind us of our own rituals. Rituals that matter.

How about you? Have you had a pet whose steadfast routines reminded you of yours?

November 23:

Thanksgiving Firsts

I knew I wouldn't be with my family on Thanksgiving, but I'd prepared for it. I'd accepted an invitation to a Thanksgiving meal with a dear friend and her lovely family and was looking forward to it.

But early on that Thanksgiving morning, when I realized that for the first time in my life I wouldn't be seeing any family on Thanksgiving, a sinking feeling grabbed me. Suddenly, I found my face wet with tears.

Each family member checked in first thing that day with texts, photos, and good wishes. But I could not get myself in gear to move through the hours ahead.

I'd made great plans. I was supposed to make Aunt Pearl's famous squash casserole. But when her hand-written notes set off another bout of tears, I decided that memory wasn't a good one to recall—at least not that day.

Hoping caffeine would help, I made an extra strong cup of coffee and wheeled into my bedroom, where I was greeted by the outfit I'd planned to wear that day. *Keep moving*, I kept telling myself. *It's a great outfit, good colors, on trend. Move into your plans, Becky. Let's go.*

So I did—but my pace was off.

Slow start this morning, I texted my friend. *Can you come for me an hour later?*

No problem, she wrote back.

By the time she arrived, I was ready. And when I wheeled into her home, the smells of Thanksgiving over-whelmed me. No tears this time; just a strange relief. The energy of her family, their helpfulness, and their caring ways for each other was like a massive, warm, invisible hug. They made room for me in their home, in their family celebration, and in their hearts.

I tried to make conversation, but everything that came out seemed trite. I couldn't get my words to match my thoughts. Then I couldn't get my brain to hold on to what had been said.

Stop trying to engage, I told myself. *Just enjoy the day.* And I did.

I learned so much from that hard day:

- Even when we know what's coming and prepare for it, the firsts are hard. Change is hard.
- You cannot plan away pain; sometimes the best you can do is to keep moving.
- Don't dismiss reality. If it's too hard to engage, go with the flow and enjoy being a part of someone else's plan. Let their opened hearts warm yours.

How about you? Did you have any firsts this Thanksgiving?

November 24:

Out of Character

It's an interesting exercise. The results can be fascinating—and revealing!

Ask a few people to give you three words that describe you.

A writing instructor gave my class that assignment as way for us to develop ourselves as characters in our own books, since most of us were writing memoirs.

We had to look at ourselves as characters in our own lives. Our task as writers was to create scenes and interactions that would reveal these character traits to the point the reader could anticipate what the character would do in a situation.

Through my writing, they would come to know "Character Becky" well enough to predict my behavior. They would also know if Character Becky's behavior was "out of character" and suspect that something was up.

My therapist at the time, Dr. Lucco, loved this idea. What if we all could see ourselves as characters in our own lives? Insights about ourselves—our temperament, our patterns, or our expectations of ourselves and others—could be tremendously helpful in maintaining good mental health.

We can also use this character definition exercise to reframe the way we look at the behavior of our friends and family. Maybe we can assure ourselves that a temper flare-up, unkind word, or judgmental comment is "out of character" for this person and let go of it a little more quickly.

How about you? Ask a few people to give you three words to describe you. How does that compare to the three words you would you use to describe yourself?

November 25:

Love Perseveres

The statement startled me. I pushed my popcorn bowl to the side, paused the remote, and replayed the words three times. I was deep in the COVID-living bubble, grateful for the escape into the light-hearted world of Marvel Comics Universe, when a character in

WandaVision—a robot, no less—redefined grief for me in a way I'll never forget:

"What is grief," he asked, "if not love persevering?"

Even now, reading those word, tears come. I think of my seventeen-year-old brother, my fifteen-year-old son, my parents—all leaving this world far too soon.

But when I think about grief as my love for them that's still here, still active, still persevering, it is redefined in a way that both explains and honors its presence.

So often we try to avoid grief, to discount it, to become impervious to its effect on us. We just want the pain of loss to stop.

But if our grief is actually one more expression of the love we felt, then to feel that grief deeply and often is but an expression of the depth of our love.

We are not weak; we have simply loved deeply.

When grief visits me now, I can see it in a new, less painful way. My love for my lost beloveds is strong, vibrant, and perseveres—as must I.

How about you? Does thinking about grief as love persevering help you experience grief in a less painful way?

November 26:

Half of a Fall

In one winter, my father fell twice on the ice. Although he was not hurt, he enjoyed embellishing the tale by saying that he had experienced one and one-half falls.

Of course, he was asked, "What's a half of a fall?"

"A half of a fall is when you fall and no one sees you," Dad explained. He went on to conclude that everything in life is only half until you share it.

You see a beautiful sunset, and immediately you call someone to come and look at it with you. It's more beautiful when you share it.

Or you spy the season's first snowflake and phone a loved one, as my mother did each winter, to share the wonder and promise of it all.

And there's the drive in the mountains—only half as inspiring if you are alone.

As a youngster, I recall traveling through the snowy mountains of Virginia on Interstate 77. We were listening to the then-popular CB radio for weather and traffic information.

Suddenly an excited voice broke in. "Breaker one-nine," he called out. "Look at that family of deer!"

The two-way radios came alive with people asking for the location of the deer. People all along the interstate chimed in, discussing the beautiful animals standing like a Currier & Ives card, backdropped by the rolling hills.

The driver's experience became full when he shared it.

No longer a half, but a whole.

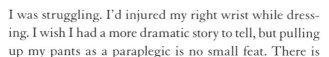

How about you? What "half" experience could you make full by sharing it?

November 27:

Unexpected Joy

I was struggling. I'd injured my right wrist while dressing. I wish I had a more dramatic story to tell, but pulling up my pants as a paraplegic is no small feat. There is twisting and turning and pulling and tugging and pivoting and rolling so that I can inch my pants and unmentionables into their proper places.

It's a workout!

But in one evening's routine pivot and pull motion, my wrist popped and searing pain ripped through to my three outer fingers. I could not move them. Already in bed for the night, I shut my eyes and prayed.

The next day, the hand specialist said I had a partial TFCC (triangular fibrocartilage complex) tear. It was life-altering, affecting my ability to transfer to my wheelchair and shower/toileting chair. I couldn't type on a computer or use a mouse. That side-to-side motion was painful for my wrist.

Our arms are not meant to be weight-bearing, they told me in my rehabilitation program after becoming paralyzed. And yet my arms are what I must rely on to be as independent as possible.

Total healing may not come for six months, the specialist told me. And the way I used my wrist made reinjury likely. As I worked to absorb this information, Mark Nepo both challenged and sustained me with this thought:

> "To be accepting of life that comes our
> way does not mean denying its difficulties
> and disappointments. Rather it means
> that joy can be found even in hardship,
> not by demanding that we be treated as
> special at every turn, but through accepting
> the demand of the sacred that we treat
> everything that comes our way as special."

Indeed, this was a special season. I had to accept my new limitations, their ripples through every part of my life, and address them. It was exhausting, yet in a strange way, fulfilling.

Although I struggled in the process, I must admit I found joy along the way as I engaged with people who could help me—doctors, nurses, therapists, and caregivers. Their expertise unexpectedly eased my angst. Their willingness to help me yielded special, even lasting relationships.

⊱⊰

How about you? Have you ever found unexpected joy in a season of hardship?

November 28:

A Humble Foundation

Tom H. Broyhill cofounded Broyhill Industries, a major furniture manufacturer headquartered near my North Carolina roots.

My grandfather worked for him during the struggling years of the company's infancy. Mr. Tom, as he was affectionately called, was a fine man, sensitive to the needs of people and the community.

My favorite Mr. Tom story happened on a college campus after a trustee meeting. He was seen talking with a man whose clothes and general appearance indicated a modest background and means.

The men conversed briefly, and then the stranger asked, "What do you do for a living?"

Mr. Tom sputtered a bit, shifted his weight, and said, "My family makes a little furniture."

"I fool with furniture some," the stranger replied. "I made two split-cane rocking chairs last month. Sell 'em to tourists coming through."

They continued talking about furniture. But not one time did Mr. Tom ever indicate who he was or what kind of furniture enterprise he had. The stranger never knew he was standing in the presence of one of the world's foremost furniture manufacturers at that time.

When someone asks for a definition of humility, I think of Mr. Tom. He did not make the other man feel badly or inferior by reciting statistics about his company's success. Nor did he put the less-fortunate person at a personal or professional disadvantage. He didn't make him feel stupid or less important.

In fact, Mr. Tom asked for details about making split-cane rockers.

"Just how," he asked the stranger, "do you go about making that wood bend to suit you?"

The man told him—just one furniture maker talking to another. And Mr. Tom listened intently.

Humility is being open to what another person can teach you, and respecting that potential in every person. Even with his great success, Mr. Tom remained open for input. He was teachable.

The season of Thanksgiving invites humility to dine with us at our table. When we are thankful, life becomes less about what we have done and more about what we have been given. And when we approach things this way, we become open to the gifts that others may have to share.

Gratitude breeds humility. Humility keeps us open to the lessons ahead and receptive to new people, new ideas, and new experiences.

How about you? When was the last time you actively practiced humility—perhaps downplayed your expertise and learned from someone with less experience? How did it feel?

November 29:

Getting Real

~⌒~

Willie was a substitute quarterback on the football team, my father's story goes. He was fourth, maybe third string at best. But every day, he showed up for practice, being hit, taking blocks, and generally letting the star players and their satellites rehearse at his expense. Seldom, if ever, did he get a chance to take the field during a real Saturday afternoon battle. But he dressed for every game.

One day during a big game the coach sat down beside him on the bench. "Willie, if the ball was on the four-yard line with fourth down and goal to go and we were losing by three points—what would you do?"

Willie thought for a moment. "Well, Coach, I guess I'd move down to the other end of the bench where I could get a better look."

I like this story. Willie is a realist. He faces the facts of the situation and accepts his role.

I also admire Willie. He represents the unsung heroes who work behind the scenes. They may never make the headlines, but they are there, in the trenches, laboring diligently and faithfully. They have no interest in the limelight; they simply find fulfillment in the role they know they can play.

The Willies of the world are not to be discounted, however. They matter. More importantly, they know they matter, and that assurance is enough for them. In fact, they may not be "Willie" in every part of their life. They may have a starring role on another playing field—in the community, office, church, or in family life. They wisely know their strengths, limitations, and interests, and they choose to play a given role.

Perhaps there's a little "Willie" in all of us. We may have discovered a role we can't master but want to support. We've spent enough time and effort to know our limits. Or perhaps we've simply learned that we have no interest in being a star and have willfully embraced a supporting role.

Whether starring or supporting, the key to enjoying life is to embrace reality, find a meaningful role in it, and give it all you've got.

How about you? Do you find fulfillment in a starring or a supporting role—or perhaps both?

November 30:

De-stressing in Real Time

Looking for a quick way to de-stress this morning? Neuro-scientist Andrew Huberman offers this suggestion:

> "One physiological sigh—a big inhale through the nose and then a second sharp inhalation through the nose, in order to maximally inflate the alveoli of the lungs, and then a long, extended exhale until the lungs are empty—is the fastest way to de-stress in real time."

Even one can be effective.

How about you? Could a de-stressing sigh benefit you today?

DECEMBER

December 1:

Confidently Imperfect

I was at a holiday lunch with friends, most of whom were mothers of children with autism.

"You have two kids on the West Coast now?" one mom asked. "Are they coming home for Christmas?"

"Yes! Brittany is flying from Seattle; Pete from Palo Alto, and my sister and family are driving from Georgia too. I'm so excited!"

"And when does Madison arrive?" another mom asked. She knew Madison had just started another adult residential and day program.

I stopped short, that deer-in-the-headlights feeling draining my enthusiasm as I tried to form a response that another mother of a child with autism would understand.

"Well, she doesn't come home with the rest of the family. It's too much activity, not enough structure," I said, shifting in my wheelchair, my palms beginning to sweat. "We have a 'floating holiday'"—I gestured quote marks—"celebrating Christmas when she returns from her holiday camp program. Madison rarely talks, but does say, 'I want camp please.' She adores that camp . . ." I babbled on, flashing a smile.

The mom nodded, her expression unreadable. Other moms were talking about the extraordinary ways they were able to include their children with autism in the holiday.

After all these years of thinking and rethinking what's best for Madison, my family, and for me, why wasn't I more confident of my answer to a simple question?

Then again, are we ever one hundred percent confident we're doing the best thing for our child, that we've made the right decision?

"You may make the right decision, Becky," a wise friend later consoled me. "But it may not be perfect."

That brought relief. I'd made sure Madison received good care, I continued to see her regularly, and I cherished each "floating holiday."

This insight from Rosalynn Carter helped even more: "Once you accept the fact that you're not perfect, then you develop some confidence."

I may not be perfect. My decisions may not be perfect. But I'm perfectly confident that I always put in my best effort to make the right choices.

How about you? Have you second-guessed yourself about the choices you've made for a loved one? Does it help to embrace that idea that it may be right, but not perfect?

December 2:

Better, Not Bitter

While waiting for my divorce to be finalized, I went back to work as an outplacement career consultant where I counseled clients who had just lost their jobs about how to approach the next steps in their lives. I discovered that the words I spoke to them also applied to me:

- Assess your strengths and move toward them.
- Become a free agent, knowledgeable of what you have to offer beyond the confines of your job (marriage).

- Recognize the different facets of your life that may have been dormant in your last work experience (marriage), and include those in your plans.
- Reflect and create your "what happened" story and practice it. The more comfortable you are with your explanation, the more at ease others will be.
- Stay away from anger-tinged comments about your former employer (spouse). Bitterness can adversely color your qualifications (and is unattractive!).

"It's hard to speak positively about a negative experience," I coached my clients and reminded myself. "But an objective look at the situation, yourselves, and what's in your best interests will help you make your next step a better one."

We may not be able to choose what happens to us, but we always get to choose how we speak of it. We can let that experience make us bitter—or better.

How about you? How can you prevent bitterness from affecting your next steps—and what words can you choose to reflect this positive approach?

December 3:

Blakely Faye's Wisdom

My daughter Brittany and granddaughter Blakely Faye (age three at the time) had flown in for a special girls' weekend. Our plans for our days together included shopping, crafting, and visits with friends and family.

Like her mom, Blakely doesn't require much sleep. After the first night, a late one that was well past her bedtime, she woke up earlier than usual.

"Blakely," Brittany said, "I thought you were going to sleep in today."

"No, Mama, I didn't." She paused to give us both her cherubic (impish?) grin. "I didn't sleep in. I slept out!"

Brittany and I laughed hard as I shot her that *I-feel-your-pain* look since in her own toddler years she routinely woke up at four in the morning. Then, just as I had nearly three decades earlier, we took advantage of that early start and were the first to arrive at a local Sip-and-Shop celebration.

Blakely made it through lunch and then promptly crashed in her stroller during shoe shopping. She woke recharged from her nap, and we returned home and began arts and crafts. We started a sticker project but soon needed colored pencils. I showed her how to use my handy-dandy battery-operated pencil sharpener.

She succeeded with two pencils, but with the third changed her hand position and the sharpener toppled to the floor, crashing hard. Pencils, batteries, and shavings flew everywhere.

I braced myself for tears, hysterics, or a frantic run to her mom for comfort.

Instead, she just looked at me and said softly, "It was an accident, Nana. An accident."

No drama. No tears. No hysterics.

She carefully picked up the pieces, handed them to me, and resumed the sticker project while I put the sharpener back together. Later I showed her how to hold on to the sharpener with one hand while inserting the pencil with the other. We finished the pack with no more accidents.

I loved the way she dealt with her mishap—a lesson in resilience. She accurately assessed the situation, did what she could to address it, moved on to accomplishing other tasks (while others more skilled solved the problem), was receptive to learning from it, and, most importantly, was willing to try again.

Oh, if we could only learn to view our failures so crisply, so simply! So often we can let the drama of a misstep overpower the simple reality. We let feelings amplify the facts, "awfulizing" what's happened into a larger issue.

So thank you, Blakely Faye, for reminding us to simplify our setbacks and keep moving through them so we can learn what they have to teach us.

How about you? How have others' approaches to failure or setbacks inspired you?

December 4:

Four Word Reset

A friend had passed along an email that contained a short list of "tweets" for the advent season. Most of them resonated with me, but the one that really made me think was this one from writer Steve Scoggin:

"Lower expectations, heighten relationships."

Wow.

I know that expectations can be a tricky endeavor, especially during the holidays. Traditions can comfort us—or trap us. Grand plans can become unrealistic expectations. And as sister Rachel has told me more than once, high expectations are sometimes simply resentments-in-waiting.

Yikes!

Lower expectations, heighten relationships—yep, that sounded good to me!

What matters most—really? The gifts given, or what we learn about preferences as we shop for or with one another? Specific menu selections, or what we discover about each other in discussing what to serve? An exquisitely prepared meal, or the revealing conversations around the table? The on-point holiday outfit, or the opinion-sharing about which one to choose? Snapping that perfect holiday photo, or laughing through the drama and antics we use to get everyone to smile?

Holidays give us the unique opportunity to get to know more about each other. We can focus on our expectations or choose to let the time together heighten our relationships.

This holiday season, I'm going to let the experiences matter more than expectations.

How about you? How can you lower your expectations and heighten your relationships this holiday season?

December 5:

One Right Thing

Even on our worst days we can find one thing we did right.
—Melanie Beatty

On those days where we've fallen short of our own expectations, it's sometimes helpful to take a personal inventory and give ourselves credit for what we've done right.

Did you say a hard thing in a soft way? Lead with love instead of anger? Behave with kindness when it was unmerited?

Depending on the situation, our "right" thing could vary. We could have:

- Spoken out—or kept silent.
- Said yes—or said no.
- Made a commitment or deferred a decision.
- Taken a risk or played it safe.
- Accepted a situation or decided to let denial help us get through it a little longer.

Giving yourself credit for at least one right thing is a great way to start your day—or reset a bad one.

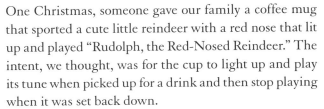

How about you? What compliment can you give yourself today?

December 6:

Living with Questions

One Christmas, someone gave our family a coffee mug that sported a cute little reindeer with a red nose that lit up and played "Rudolph, the Red-Nosed Reindeer." The intent, we thought, was for the cup to light up and play its tune when picked up for a drink and then stop playing when it was set back down.

But that's not the way it worked at our house. Mr. Cup played his tunes randomly—when picked up, when left alone, in the middle of the day or night—and for no apparent reason.

At first, we thought we'd figured it out. The cup's home was on a glass shelf that held all our coffee mugs, perched just above the coffee maker. One morning, we switched on the light over the coffee maker and Mr. Cup started playing. He stopped when we turned the light off.

The light must have activated the battery, we thought. So my father tested the theory, slipping quietly up to the coffee maker in the morning's darkness. But before he could turn the light on, Mr. Cup lit up and starting playing his tune. He refused to be understood or managed.

We studied and tested Mr. Cup with other theories—heat activation, motion detectors—but to no avail. There was no pattern, no trend, and no answer for Mr. Cup's mysterious behavior. In time, he endeared himself to our family to the point where we found ourselves talking to him, even admiring his strong will and steadfast commitment to joyful spontaneity.

We decided to accept what we couldn't understand. In fact, we thanked the little fellow for reminding us that Christmas is not a one-day event but an experience that sings at the most unexpected times during the year.

We also learned an important lesson from Mr. Cup: sometimes our obsessive pursuit of answers clouds the joy right in front of us. Our best option may be to learn to live with the questions and to seek the peace that comes with an acceptance that we cannot understand everything that life presents to us.

⤙⧖⤚

How about you? Have you ever found unexpected delight (or peace) once you accepted something you couldn't understand?

December 7:

Curling Ribbons

As a child, it fascinated me to watch my mother put her thumb on the sharp edge of the scissors with only a thin strand of ribbon sandwiched between the two. With one swift tug, the unsuspecting strand bounced to life in a perfect ringlet, the ideal adornment for a holiday gift.

I quickly learned that there was an art to the tug—too slow or not enough pressure, and the curl would not appear. And heaven forbid you curl the "wrong side." It'd ruin the ribbon, producing a permanent limp that could never recover.

But with a little practice, curling ribbon was a satisfying endeavor, one of those tangible "effort-in" and "results-out" activities that can be so elusive during the holidays.

At their best, holidays are a chosen series of traditions architected to merge family, friends, and the spirit of the giving and gratitude with our religious beliefs and practices. But sometimes our prepackaged plans splinter under the weight of the changes the year has bestowed.

Nothing is more special than a toddler's first Christmas. Often the little ones play more with the bows and boxes than with the contents, but their wonder refreshes and inspires the wonder of the child inside each of us, even the oldest among us.

For many of us, though, the holidays bring a different family configuration—one that is often not of our choosing. Separation and divorce are among the toughest alterations to manage, especially with children.

I recall how, the first year after my separation, a divorced friend consoled me about my concerns about getting through Christmas Day. I can still hear her words now: "Remember, it's only twenty-four hours."

Ironically, that statement both comforts and energizes. It both relieves the pressure to make the season so perfect—it's just another day—and remind us that we have choices about how we define each hour of our day.

When necessary, we can take the sharp edges of life and run our ribbons of traditions through them to create something new and alive in a different way. Although never the same, we can artfully define the moments we now have. We can rediscover simple joys that can restore our child-like wonder.

How about you? What simple joys have you discovered (or rediscovered) this Christmas?

December 8:

Ties That Bind

We packed the pew. I parked my wheelchair as close as I could, bookending a collection of folks never before assembled. Snippets of my life's chapters, filled with both pleasure and pain, scooted and scrunched together, beautifully coifed and clothed, as we all faced the same direction and waited for the Christmas pageant to begin.

My former father-in-law and mother-in-law sat beside me, the first time we'd been in church together since I married their son twenty years ago. On the other end of the pew sat their son (my former husband), and his new wife. Her parents joined us as did mine, all at my invitation. Products of that marriage—our lovely children, some of our best work together—were sprinkled in between.

Holidays pose some of the greatest challenges when it comes to family gatherings. Traditions that once celebrated family ties often trap our new lives with painful memories of what once was but can never be again.

With no pattern to guide us, we piece together remnants of our past with the new fabric of our present.

Taking a child's view helps. As I watched my children talk to each member of their family, old and new, I realized their circle of relationships had grown. Their so-called nuclear family had divided but also multiplied, putting new people in their lives.

Yet that perspective did not come readily or naturally for me. Like many, my first reaction to divorce was self-preservation, complete with boundaries and walls to limit painful interactions.

After a while, though, I learned that I needed to look closely at that wall to make sure it wasn't a contrived obstacle to moving forward. That judgment, of course, is clearly individualized and clearly subjective. Only in our hearts do we know the true nature of our boundaries and the spirit in which we use them.

Holidays provide a unique opportunity to be inclusive—and creative. They give us a reason to rise above the past to create new patterns for the future as we face the same direction—forward—and wait for life's new pageant to begin.

$\rightsquigarrow$

How about you? Have you found creative ways to strengthen family ties during the holidays?

December 9:

Keep on Thrilling

"I was just sitting here thrilling," one of Dad's parishioners told him during a visit in her home, adorned with antiques and mementos of the past.

"Excuse me, you were doing what?" he asked her.

"Just sitting here thrilling," she repeated, and then explained by showing him what the tattered folder on her lap held: mementos of an ocean cruise that she had taken decades earlier.

Memories are wonderful, but fickle. Bad memories can haunt, sometimes re-traumatizing us. And good memories can hurt even while warming us with past joys.

Christmas and New Year's kick up many memories. These two days are markers, standing like tall towers above the skyline of all the days and experiences that preceded them.

My mind wanders back to my childhood. Thanksgiving was hardly "turkeyed" away, as Dad used to say, before my siblings and I were scampering up the attic stairs to pull out all the Christmas trappings.

Then came the big day for trimming the tree. Furniture was rearranged or moved out for the season. The fireplace was loaded up with logs that later filled the room with warmth and brilliance. With Christmas music playing, Dad would drag the tree into the front hall, trunk first. We helped carry it, we thought—but mostly we got in the way.

Mom would organize the ornaments by child. Dad would test and string the lights. His work complete, he would get a cup of coffee and sit back in his favorite wingback chair and watch our ritual of placing favorite ornaments in special places. Mom then garnished with garland and icicles.

Ah, those memories! So fickle—fickle as a fumbled football, as Dad used to say. Past joys stir deeply in an empty spot down inside, churning warmness but also sadness over what was and can never be again.

Memories, so precious and powerful. We may not be able to recreate the past, but if we "sit there thrilling," perhaps those same memories can inspire us to be grateful for what we've had and excited about what is yet to come.

How about you? What special memories prompt grati-tude for the past or excitement about the future for you?

December 10:

Sweet Persistence

I still can't believe I won.

Home from college for the holidays, twenty-year-old Brittany had encouraged me to participate in a cookie exchange. I'd made my holiday M&M cookies but come up short of the required six-dozen cookies.

"Make candy cane cookies," she suggested.

Ironically, I'd just seen one Food Network star spend most of her show demonstrating how "simple" it was to make those tricky cookies—two colored batters were pre-pared, refrigerated, rolled, measured, braided together, and finished with precision hooks and snipped ends.

It looked challenging—and I don't even like pepper-mint.

I shared my reservations.

"But Mom, I'm into candy canes this year," she pressed. "Don't you think it'd be cool? I've always wanted to make those cookies. Can't you try?"

Before I could raise any more objections, a recipe appeared in front of me, complete with a color photo. The ingredients soon joined the instructions, and I yielded to my daughter's tender but strong-willed request.

With Christmas music and evergreen candles, we baked the afternoon away. Brittany finished her snowball cookies long before my candy canes touched the oven racks, but she stayed with me, and we chatted about her life, my life, and our plans for the months ahead.

But I did complain. The mess of red food coloring. The brittleness of the dough. The difficulty of uniformly twisting and braiding the two colors together.

"Can you help me twist these?"

"No, Mom, you're doing great."

"But these are for you," I reminded her. "Can't you help?"

"I didn't say *I* wanted to make them," she clarified. "I said I wanted *you* to make them,"

Exasperated, I kept braiding the delicate dough—a chore for anyone lacking good abdominal balance. Paralysis often steals trunk control when it permanently relaxes stomach muscles. The simplest midline activities can be a challenge.

Brittany cheered me on. "It's a good workout for you, Mom."

I smiled, choosing to be charmed instead of annoyed by the mess my daughter had gotten me into. After all, it was Christmas.

When fourteen women gathered around twenty-six varieties of cookies, I was shocked to learn I won "most festive" cookie.

Brittany beamed.

My heart warmed. Grateful for the experience, even the unassisted process and unintended workout, I was proud of my cookies and the gift of my daughter's persistent encouragement.

How about you? Have you experienced an unexpected success because of a loved one's persistent encouragement?

December 11:

Meeting Grief with Grace

Although the topic intrigued me, the seminar's title sealed my attendance: "Meeting Grief with Grace."

Grief and grace—I would have never put those two words in the same sentence. Grief is a painful, disruptive force. Grace is a welcomed, comforting kindness.

Could one possibly help us get through the other?

As I wheeled through the maze of literature and support offerings, I realized I'd never attended a lecture on grief. The presenter's advanced degrees, her twenty-year career in hospice and bereavement management, and her organization's record of serving seven hundred and fifty patients daily was impressive. So was the popularity of her topic, one she'd lectured on dozens of times.

Suddenly, I began to feel awkwardly naïve.

Although I'd experienced tough losses, grief was apparently far more than a personal journey. It was its own entity—licensed, lectured on, and serviced.

Had I done it right?

At age twenty, after Forest's death, I learned about Elizabeth Kübler-Ross's stages of grief—denial, anger, bargaining, depression, and acceptance. But I had trouble remembering what each one meant, much less assessing my progress.

I slogged through that valley, clueless and uncaring about the stages. And when I was paralyzed by an illness that affects one in a million, my daughter was diagnosed with autism when, at that time, autism affected males five time more than females, and my second son developed a condition typically seen in first-born males, I started to think that life's rules didn't apply to me anyway.

So when the slide "Beyond Elisabeth Kubler-Ross—How We Move Through Grief" flashed onto the screen, I cringed.

484 | Morning Fuel

What did I miss by ignoring those stages?
Would paying attention to them have made
grief easier?

The answer was swift:

"Grief is not linear—there are
no checkboxes."

Then the presenter began describing my experience:

"We move slowly and tenderly. . . .
"We feel the reality and pain. . . .
"We manage to adjust and move forward
while still honoring our loved one."

Today marks the anniversary of my mother's death. I'm never sure how grief will visit. Some years I cry remembering our last conversation. Other years I laugh recalling her tickle-box meltdowns at Dad's jokes. Most years I vow to tell my kids one more story about her.

But every year, I grieve in my own way.

No right. No wrong. Just mine.

Maybe that's how we meet grief with grace. Maybe we accept that painful foe and its unexpected visits, meeting it with tender kindness for our loved ones and ourselves.

❧

How about you? Could meeting grief with grace ease the pain of a loss you've experienced?

December 12:

Eight Day-Making Words

Sometimes I think of the holidays as the season of family. It is a time of high expectations, steadfast traditions, and hopscotch travel plans that often yield a unique togetherness only experienced during that time of year.

Some of us vow to simplify the sure-to-be chaos. But often it is the very rarity of the gathering that sends us seeking out new ways to "make it special" and therefore even more complex.

One Christmas, twenty-seven people floated in and out of my home in fifteen days. Despite last-minute plan changes, miscommunications, forgotten gifts, and even illness, hearing these eight little words made my day every time they were spoken:

"Is there anything I can do to help?"

Better than dark chocolate, a fine Cabernet, or even my new favorite Starbucks sweet cream cold brew, those words lightened my load and lifted my heart each time I heard them from so many of my family members.

The extra help showed a special kind of caring and consideration, an encompassing kind of love that knitted us all even closer together. From taking out the trash to washing pots and pans to walking the dog and even to offering to make my favorite afternoon tea (green tea with a slice of lemon) in my new favorite Christmas mug, the helpfulness that surrounded me made that holiday even more special.

How about you? What words have helped you get through a holiday season?

December 13:

Lighthouse Lessons

—⁓—

Lighthouses don't go running all over an island looking for boats to save; they just stand there, shining.
—Anne Lamott

There is merit in standing still and being. We don't have to "do" to be useful, helpful, or brighten the darkness.

We can let who we are shine through exactly where we are.

⤳⧓⤳

How about you? How can you shine today?

December 14:

Grateful Pauses

—⁓—

Thankfulness is not some sort of magic formula; it is the language of love.
—Sarah Young

So often, we're instructed to be grateful, to begin each day with gratitude, to make lists of what we're thankful for, and to even strive to adopt a "gratitude attitude."

But why?

Pausing to be grateful equips us with a loving mindset. It can also defuse frustration, I learned during an early round of food shopping one morning as I was heading warp-speed into the home stretch of a holiday season.

Power wheelchairs and crowded aisles don't mix well, so I like to shop early. A young couple had done the same, but they were struggling to keep up with their two rambunctious preschoolers.

One child was fascinated by the wheels of my wheel-chair. More than once, he ran beside me and then darted in front of me, making me stop abruptly. Each time, his father retrieved him and apologized. About the third time it happened, I was beginning to lose my patience and thought about shooting that dad one of those *can't-you-control-your-kid* looks, but I took a deep breath and didn't. He again apologized, grabbed his son's hand, and led him back to the cart. After a few steps, the weary dad turned around and waved, mouthing the words, "Thank you."

I smiled and waved back, so very glad I'd kept that admonishing look to myself. Memories suddenly flooded back as I recalled the antics of my own preschoolers and our storied grocery shopping jaunts.

His simple "thank you" melted my frustration and connected our worlds.

When we pause to be grateful, we are taking the time to acknowledge a gift that we've been given, whether it's a compliment, assistance, or even a tolerant response.

How about you? What expressions of gratitude can you pause to give today?

December 15:

Good Enough

It's a comment my sister and I rarely make:

"That's good enough."

We're not sure why, but we tend to be driven—always focused on finding our best and delivering it. We like to think it is our commitment to the pursuit of excellence. But one day Rachel shared this nugget of wisdom: "In this quest for excellence, we can sometimes act as if our own personal mantra is: 'If it's worth doing, it's worth making a major project out of it.'"

Yikes!

These lines made us laugh long and hard at ourselves. Both of us routinely find ourselves expanding our efforts at what could be simple projects, especially when it comes to family celebrations, holidays, milestones, and matters of the heart.

We want what we do to reflect how deeply we feel. Why?

Perhaps we don't know how to shut down our creativity. Or we tire easily of cookie-cutter approaches. Or we find the search for a unique addition to be an exciting challenge. Or it's simply an inherited family value.

Or maybe, just maybe, we are perfectionists underneath it all.

Yikes again!

So Rachel and I made a pledge. We vowed to stress less, do less, and say more often, "That's good enough."

True to my pledge, I've tried to be more self-aware during the holidays in recent years. My favorite example is my treat-making mishap.

Every year I make a huge batch of a sweet and salty snack mix, Texas Snow, to give to family and friends. One year, one of my helpers mistakenly purchased chocolate almond bark instead of vanilla.

Was it worth the effort to return and repurchase?

Or was it time to implement the "good enough" mantra?

Good enough, I decided. Meanwhile, instead of being stressed about getting it just right, I began to feel more like a foodie-entrepreneur on an adventure to see if something new and delicious could come from being "good enough."

It tasted great but definitely needed a new name. Not much is "snowy" about dark chocolate!

How about you? Do you have trouble stopping at "good enough"?

December 16:

Ornamental Visitors

Today's inspiration comes from a dear friend's Christmas card. I love Ralph Waldo Emerson, but this was the first time I'd read this quote from him:

> "The ornament of a house is the people who frequent it."

Isn't that so true?

Folks breeze in and out, each leaving their own imprint.

We prepare. We experience. We create memories. In the process, our homes are touched and transformed by each visitor. Daily routines shift into new rhythms and moods depending on those who join us and the energy they bring.

Just like each ornament on our Christmas tree gives it personality so do the guests who visit our homes.

Some sparkle with an upbeat attitude and can-do spirit. Others add depth and texture, sharing family stories and traditions. A few may bring a bit of drama and stir up a little chaos, while others, especially little ones, may create a whole new vibe.

How about you? How has your home been "decorated" by its guests this year?

December 17:

Friendship's Surprising Gifts

My niece Ashley sent me a screenshot of a quote from her Chinese fortune cookie: "A friend is a present you give yourself."

"What do you think this means, Aunt B?" she texted.

I told her I thought friendship offers us a gift by giving back to us another's perspective on life. Our lives are enriched because we get to share in someone else's life experience.

But author Melody Beattie offers another insight on the gifts that relationships offer. In her meditation "Relationships," she describes them as a form of teaching. Relationships, she believes, help us acquire new behaviors—things like detachment, self-esteem, becoming confident enough to set a boundary, or owning our power in another way.

Although it wouldn't be the first way I'd describe the gifts in my friendships, I see her point. After some reflection, I thought of several behaviors my friends have helped me strengthen:

- Watching others say no when they mean it has helped me set boundaries more confidently.
- Seeing others refuse to engage in useless arguments while still being respectful has helped me detach from prickly conversations more comfortably.

- Having others be honest with me about their limitations has helped me be more honest in stating mine, making it easier to make decisions that are in my own best interests.

Indeed, our relationships can nurture us into our own maturity—one gift at a time.

How about you? What gifts have your relationships given you?

December 18:

The Sting of Joy

Today's inspiration comes from a reference to C. S. Lewis, one of my favorite writers and thinkers. In the weeks before Christmas, Pastor Andy reminded us about Lewis's writings on the sting of joy—the bittersweet nature of those complex moments that evoke a supreme happiness even as they are marked by tears and even melancholy.

He noted that sometimes our joy falls short because the celebrations are *far different* from last year. Perhaps someone we love is no longer with us and we are struggling to meet grief with grace.

Then again, sometimes our joy falls short because the celebrations will be *exactly the same.* We hoped to be at a different place in our lives or with different people or with a heart a little fuller than the year before, but life has stalled.

Despite all the joy around us, it may be lacking within us.

And that stings.

But why?

According to scholar and theologian Dr. Jerry Root, Lewis defines joy as a deep longing that is embedded in each of us the is questing for its proper object. For example, we may long to go back to the place where we grew up, but when we do, it's not the same. Writer and philosopher G. K. Chesterton says, "It's like being home-sick in your own home." We long for what we cannot have or for what we experience but know we cannot sustain.

So perhaps we approach this season acknowledging the "sting of joy," should it arrive, by celebrating both the memories of what can no longer be and our dreams of what we hope will come.

How about you? When have you experienced the sting of joy?

December 19:

Traditional Breaks

"Are we having Chinese food on Christmas Eve again?" the youngster asked his mom.

"Why yes, honey," she replied. "It's a tradition."

Tradition. I love that word. I've discovered a new use for it lately. It gives those of us short on creativity or time a break.

Debating whether or not to wear the same festive sweater you wore last year for the Christmas Eve service? Do it and call it a tradition.

Can't think of anything new for the kids' stockings? Could be a tradition-in-waiting.

Tired of searching online or leafing through the latest magazines to update your New Year's meal? Repeat last year's menu and start a tradition.

Reduce your stress by having to make one less decision can save your creative juices to do something extraordinary for yourself, your family, or your friends.

At its best, tradition not only gives our creativity a break but also breeds a comfort zone of familiarity that gently ushers in a season. Festive lights brighten our homes and our moods as the holidays approach. Evergreen and balsam, cinnamon and eggnog, and gingerbread and sugar cookies prick our senses, alerting us of the good times ahead.

Traditions, old and new, await.

How about you? Do you have any traditions-in-waiting?

December 20:

In-Person Inspiration

Neither one of us was overly enthused about going—but my friend Kim and I thought we might be able to knock out the remainder of our Christmas list at the local Nordstrom shopping event.

We began by grabbing a bite to eat in the café and reviewing our detailed notes. Soon the lights flickered and the live music began—and so did our missions-drive shopping. We parted ways and agreed to meet after forty-five minutes.

During our rendezvous, we told each other about our discoveries. We described the recipient of each gift, how the gift would be used, and why it was the perfect gift for that person. Shopping became more than just checking the box; it became a time of sharing family personalities, stories, and traditions. It was energizing to think through the festivities ahead and then envision a gift that would make the experience even more special or memorable.

Happiness expert Gretchen Rubin may sum it up best:

> To eke out the most happiness from an experience:
> anticipate it,
> savor it as it unfolds,
> express happiness,
> and recall a happy memory.

That's exactly what we did!

And yet I still was surprised at my sudden vigor. I'd been cyber-shopping for weeks. What was it about this round of shopping that invited me to experience gift-giving in a different way?

My mind rewound to the words I'd just heard from the director of our Christmas pageant. He'd asked us to recall our own pageant memories.

"Were you an animal?" he asked. "Anyone ever promoted to a human?'

I chuckled at my own memory of being a sheep and then an angel.

But his next words gave me pause.

Citing the tremendous popularity of the Christmas Eve pageant, he noted that live performances, even if on the same subject matter, hit our brains in a different way.

Wow.

Maybe it was the talented musician behind the piano or the fabulous Christmas decorations or the artful displays of merchandise or the stellar sales people who not only helped me shop but took the packages to my van. Or maybe it was simply the opportunity to deepen a friendship with so many shared recollections. But there was no question that this live experience helped me shift into a more earnest and reflective gear, becoming more open to all this season of love, joy, and hope has to offer.

How about you? Have you had a live experience that reenergized your holiday spirits?

December 21:

Unmerited Kindness

My son and I had signed up to give a child an Angel Tree gift for Christmas. I had the best of intentions, purchasing the specified gift for the correct gender and age of the child. My son picked the Angel tag, approved our gift choice, and even reminded me of the due date.

But something had gone awry. A gentle but firm phone message alerted me that our gift was missing, late, and in fact, holding up the delivery process.

Mortified at my oversight, my mind raced with the guilt. *Did I over-commit again? Was it a mistake to take on this responsibility? Perhaps I need to rethink doing anything like this next year.*

"It's my fault," I told my son when we arrived at the church. "I'll take the gift inside. If there are any harsh words, they will land on me."

I straightened my Christmas sweater, plumped my hair to reveal my snowflake earrings, and sported the merriest smile I could muster as I approached the doorway. After all, how angry could they be with such a festive lady in a wheelchair?

Two men greeted me.

Great, I thought. *Now I've got a committee to charm.*

But before I could apologize, they introduced themselves and thanked me.

"Your gift is making a difference," one said warmly.

My mind's pace slowed to a comfortable idle as I realized our gift was still worthy. These gentlemen could have justifiably been upset with me, yet they were kind. I'd experienced my father's favorite definition of grace: unmerited kindness.

Grace can be hard to find during the holiday season. Schedules jam, plans change, and unexpected events thwart the most organized souls. Amongst of all the celebratory chaos, we can lose our ability to be kind and forgiving, especially to strangers.

"I do not at all understand the mystery of grace," Anne Lamott writes. "Only that it meets us where we are but does not leave us where it found us."

A kind word, merited or not, can soften harshness, relieve stress, and even restore our sense of worthiness. That day, I left the church refocused on the important thing: we were helping a family in need at a special time of year. And I was already thinking about the next year. Perhaps I should sign up for more Angel gifts—and mark the due date in red.

How about you? Have you given or received unmerited kindness during the holidays? How did it make you feel?

December 22:

Imagination Gear

Logic will get you from A to B.
Imagination will take you everywhere.
—Albert Einstein

Sometimes we need to give ourselves a break from planning, structure, and to-do lists to give our minds a chance to wander and create. Logic can thwart the brain's creativity, funneling its power into linear reasoning and problem-solving.

Imagination expands thinking beyond the problem. Although the problem may be solved along the way, shifting into imagination gear unleashes the full power of the mind to discover more than one answer. And probably more questions too.

How about you? Do you need to shift into imagination gear today?

December 23:

A Rockin' Holiday

It was the number one item on my son Peter's Christmas wish list in 2007. But I had no idea it would become *my* favorite too. The music video game Rock Band made an impressive entrance, energizing Pete, then fourteen, as he snatched his Xbox 360 from the depths of our basement and placed it squarely in the center of our family room.

I'd played Pac-Man in the '70s and been hooked on Tetris for a while. But as the buttons seemed to shrink and the games grew more complex, video games became a pastime for my kids.

Then Rock Band appeared. Gone were those intricate controllers, replaced by life-size band instruments. Four drumheads, two guitars, and a karaoke-style microphone filled my family room.

After selecting a song, the music's track appeared on the screen, where colored notes matched the colors on the instruments. I watched my son strike the drum in rhythm to the moving notes. With an accurate hit, the note splashed and played the drum sound missing from the background song. A missed hit yielded no splash and, more importantly, no sound, leaving the song void of that instrument.

The more accurately you played, the more complete the song.

I tried and was even more amazed. I could do it!

That Christmas afternoon, my son, my daughter, her boyfriend, and I rocked on, nonstop, for four hours.

We received points for accurate hits, the longest streaks of accuracy, and extra points for solos, where every keystroke is counted. Believe me, there's nothing finer than scoring a 100 percent on your solo—which I did, more than once.

Perhaps it's a good time of year to ask, "When is the last time you did something for the first time?"

What experiences can we snatch from the basement, shine up, and place squarely in the center of our lives?

What possibilities can we revisit, overcoming the fear of complexity that stalled our once-loved pursuits?

What harmony can we find if we reframe our interests and talents with new approaches?

My absolute favorite part of this whole experience was the transformation of my family room during the rest of the holidays. We created bands from ages eleven to fifty-four with singers, drummers, and guitar players ranging from beginners to experts.

My world was enlarged because I dared to try something new.

⚘

How about you? What holiday gifts have challenged you to new experiences?

December 24:

A Single Candle

Although I can't find a source to credit, these words have helped guide me through more than one holiday season:

> "Love is like a candle, shining in a
> dark place."

Those words touch a special place in my heart. For me, Christmas is all about love. It's about sharing gifts and time and creating experiences and memories that have the capacity to last a lifetime.

It's often a joyous season. Some of us will welcome new family members to our traditions. Others of us will creatively modify our traditions to accommodate changes within our family.

Yet it can also be a season of longing and hurt for those of us who must rework all traditions because we've lost someone dear to us. Despite our best efforts, grief—that strange companion—reminds us of the love that we have lost.

Yet the candle shines on. Love can pierce through the darkness.

Through the years, I've learned that when I can focus on the light instead of the dark, it's a little easier to navigate the holidays. The love of those who have passed—my parents, my brother, my son—all those memories shine brighter when I focus on the good things that they taught me and the meaningful experiences we shared. The love I still feel for them still burns brightly.

Anne Frank may have said it best:

> "Look at how a single candle can both defy
> and define the darkness."

This season, light a candle and place it somewhere prominent. Shine on, candle of love. Illuminate for us all the best this season of love has to offer.

How about you? Could your holidays be enriched by the lighting of a single candle?

December 25:

A Little Understanding

It was the first time in thirty-three years I hadn't been with my daughter at Christmas, thanks to COVID-19. I wanted to accomplish one thing that would make this Christmas feel more like a normal one.

I was excited about my idea—sending a crab cake dinner to my daughter and her family for their Christmas Eve dinner—and was ready to place the order.

Alicia, my kind and patient order-taker, helped as I rattled off my daughter's name, address, and other pertinent info.

"And what would you like to say on the note?" she asked.

"Merry Christmas . . ." I began. But the rest of the words stuck in my throat. Out of nowhere, my voice thickened. I couldn't speak. "I'm sorry," I finally stammered, my breathing labored, tears blistering my eyes. The awkward silent space between us grew.

"It's okay," Alicia said. "Take your time. I understand." She paused. "I do."

Something about her tone unexpectedly connected us; it was as if she were joining me in my struggle—perhaps with one of her own.

"Thank you." I exhaled. "I don't know where that came from. I'm so sorry." After a few deep breaths, I finally finished the thought that was so hard for me to say: "Merry Christmas! I love you and miss you so much."

"Yes, of course. I've got it," she said softly. After we finished the phone call, I sat for a while thinking about those words:

I love you and miss you so much.

Oh how those words pierced my heart. They were so personal, and yet were profoundly universal and inclusive too! How many others would be saying those very words on this Christmas Day?

Did you?

We all had lost so much, some much more than others. And yet those words had the power to connect us, creating a safe place where tears could help ease our pain while still expressing our love.

How about you? Have you experienced an unexpected kindness or connection that helped you express your love to someone you missed?

December 26:

Catching the Good

To improve the golden moment of opportunity, and catch the good that is within our reach, is the great art of life.
—Samuel Johnson

When life gets full and threatens to overwhelm, I try remember to "catch the good" within reach by taking some small action to make life better.

Maybe I'll text a friend I haven't seen in a while. Or water my thirsty houseplants. Or start reading a new book. Or pick up a sidetracked project or start a new one that I've been hesitant to try. Or even do something special or unexpected for someone else.

We don't have to wait for good things to happen to us. We can find small actions to take today to make life better.

How about you? What small action can you take today to make your life better?

December 27:

Listening Power

I value good listeners and try hard to be one myself. But these words from my father's writings reoriented me to the skill in a new way:

"Listening is healing."

I'd never considered that by listening to someone, I could be helping them heal. But when I thought about it, it made sense. Sharing what's on our minds is a clarifying process. It forces us to funnel thoughts into words and words into conversation.

We choose what we say, when we say it, and how we say it.

It can be a status update. Or a mood dump. Or a very long story laced with layers of subtle points.

It can be hard for us to listen sometimes. Too long. Too frequent. Too negative. Too rambling.

But what if by offering a listening ear, we were

helping our friend or loved one to heal? What a powerful way to rethink our roles in conversation and invite compassion and empathy to join us in the process.

How about you? How would you change your approach to listening if you thought it could also be healing?

December 28:

Taking Stock

Holiday visits and family celebrations are winding down. Some traditions may have been a carbon copy of last year's; others may have had to adapt.

Some changes were likely welcomed; others not.

The birth of a baby quickly reconfigures family celebrations. With chaos spilling into every minute of once steadfast rituals, "Baby's First Christmas" opens a new era with its firsts shining expectantly into the future.

But the death of a loved one casts a shadow over the firsts, causing them to pale. Families move numbly through traditions that can no longer be the same.

Even in these years, however, we can still find joy. Memories give our minds a context for the firsts ahead, anchoring our new experiences in the richness of our past. We can look back and measure the fullness of our lives by what we have experienced.

So how can we measure this year? My father once offered these criteria.

It has been a good year if:

- You knew the warmth of just one person loving you—and loving them back.

- You felt the snuggling touch of one child.
- You sat and listened patiently while a friend poured out their troubles.
- You laughed when you felt like crying because laughter lightened your load.
- You reached out to others when you were afraid or lonely, and they reached back and held you tight.
- You renewed an old friendship or made a new friend.
- You let go of some part of your past that kept you from moving forward in your present.
- You released a grudge that marred your thinking.
- You made amends to one person you have wronged.
- You allowed people to pray for you when you were too weak to pray for yourself.
- You saw a loved one facing eternity with faith and grace.

If your year included any of these experiences, he concluded, it has been a good year.

Taking stock can help us cherish what we have had while helping us embrace more fully what is ahead—both the firsts and the lasts.

How about you? How does your year measure up?

December 29:

I Appreciate You

My father once sent a birthday card to a man who attended his church and signed it simply, "I appreciate you."

Twenty-five years later, Dad revisited the church for a homecoming celebration. The man sought him out, gripped his hand firmly, and with a tear in his eye, said, "Years ago you wrote 'I appreciate you' on my birthday card. You'll never know how much that meant to me. I've still got the card."

He went on to tell my father how that one phrase inspired him in his job and his work with Boy Scouts in the church.

Although the phrase "thank you" is important, "I appreciate you" strikes a different chord.

Gratitude tends to be transactional, specific to a particular gift or experience that was given. Appreciation, however, is broader, more relational in nature. It includes not only the experience but also the person.

Gratitude is being thankful. Appreciation is seeing the good.

Nothing can be more encouraging than to feel appreciated. It's a powerful force—a resilience-fortifying source, in my experience.

Through the ups and downs of paralysis, I've learned the value of encouragement, even asking for it when recovery from one ailment or another has put me in a funk. Like my father's friend, I've kept cards and special notes for years, often rereading them when I'm struggling to stay positive.

In turn, I've tried to be more appreciative of others, letting them know that I see the good in who they are or what they do. It may take extra effort to tease out the positives of an experience, but it's worth the effort. The process itself can shift a critical mindset into a benevolent one.

We aren't meant to struggle alone. Appreciation helps us connect with one another, highlighting the positives we see in others with words that last far longer than the time it takes to write them.

How about you? What good quality can you appreci-ate in someone today?

December 30:

Settling In

"He has never settled down."

It's an indicting remark, a phrase we use to describe a person who appears to lack maturity. Perhaps this individual is not dependable, struggles with commitments, and is generally unfocused in most pursuits.

It's a negative evaluation, to say the least.

But it can be a positive statement. The unsettled person can also be one who is constantly growing, learning, and refusing to allow daily living to stagnate into the mundane.

In fact, we're encouraged to not "settle on our lees." Wine, we're told, loses its taste and strength, turning to dregs, when it loses the necessary motion in its making and settles on the lees. We settle on the lees when we no longer allow life to move through us. We lose our dreams and settle for less without taking our best shot, wherever we are in life's process.

We, too, need to stay in motion.

The unsettled person is not always dissatisfied with life. Quite the opposite, in fact—sometimes they are unsettled because they know they have so much more left to do. They live expectantly, looking forward to the future like a gift, a time to (like the kid on Christmas morning) tear off the ribbons, rip apart the paper, and discover what new talent life has revealed for them to develop.

Three years into retirement, my father suggested adding one last "R" to that life stage's traditional R&R

(rest and relaxation): redirection. With redirection included, he contended, we put motion back into life.

He noted several unsettled friends, including: Mr. Joe, that eighty-year-old friend who learned to use a typewriter and at eighty-one got his first typing job; Jim, who worked for the railroad almost sixty-five years and, upon retirement at eighty-five, started painting trains from memory and became a celebrated artist.

Dad also admired the spirit of Chief Justice Holmes, who, after having his pension cut by Congress at age ninety-one, reportedly said, "The cut doesn't bother me now, but I won't have as much to put up for old age!"

Perhaps we shouldn't settle *down*, but rather settle *in* for life's long ride. If we stay in motion and let life keep moving through us, it may help us discover what is in us.

How about you? What gifts are you discovering today as you settle into this stage of your life?

December 31:

Making the Old Year New

It's a magical time—December 31, about midnight, only a few minutes before January 1. In those crucial seconds, tax deductions hang on clock strokes and calendars, quotas, and fiscal years come to a hard stop.

The old year is dying. A new year is being born. That's what we say; that's what tradition teaches us.

But is that the only way to look at it?

During those crucial seconds when one year replaces another numerically, perhaps it's actually the *old year* that's dawning.

The new year makes the old year new by permitting commentaries on events, people, and circumstances that are possible only after the passage of time and travels through space.

How did we spend the last twelve months? Where were we and what did we do?

We often show our priorities by building physical or even emotional monuments to those things that matter to us. We crown our work's importance by the sweat of our brows. We enlarge our family dwellings, schedules, and circles to encompass our growth. We fill our coffers with newly discovered treasures.

All provide a yardstick to measure not so much our *worth* as the spot we were in at that point in time—a physical immortality.

Instead of focusing on the clean slate of the new year, a peek back at the cluttered one we're leaving behind could enlighten, even enrich the journey ahead. We can look at the evidences of our lives—our calendars, emails, journals, or even Christmas newsletters—and see that some issues grew while others dissolved.

"What is not performance is preparation," Emerson reminds us.

We can admit some failures and claim some successes, and consider that both may be preparation for what's ahead.

❧

How about you? What insights from last year can dawn on you today and prepare you for the new year ahead?

FROM WHERE I SIT

@CHAIRWRITER

1978: Becky and Forest   *1998: Mom, Dad, and Becky*

2018: Becky and Tripp   *2019: Becky and Rachel*

2022: Family Christmas

Acknowledgments

Pulling together 366 stories was a feat I could not have accomplished without the steadfast guidance of Stanford's Anne Zimmerman and the expertise of She Writes Press's publisher, Brooke Warner along with her team, Lauren, Krissa, and Laura. Thank you for keeping me focused and moving forward in this publishing journey.

For the content of the book, I am also deeply grateful to my friends who have enriched my life by both including me in theirs and letting me write about the experience.

Finally, a special thank you must go to my amazing family who has given me so many of these timeless stories and abiding messages that still fuel me daily: Mom, Dad, Forest, Rachel and her family (David, Ashley, Alex, Adam, Maggie), Brittany and her family (Brian, Blakely Faye, Beckett, and Baxter) Peter and his family (Meredith and Sofia), Matthew, Madison, Joe, Cindy, Zander, and of course my precious puggle Tripp. I love you all—always and forever.

2019: "FamBam" Family Gathering

About the Author

Photo © Rachel Rock Photography

Rebecca (Becky) Faye Smith Galli is an author and columnist who writes about love, loss, and healing. Surviving significant losses—her seventeen-year-old brother's death; her son's degenerative disease and subsequent death; her daughter's autism; her divorce; and nine days later, her paralysis from transverse myelitis, a rare spinal cord inflammation that began as the flu—has fostered an unexpected but prolific writing career. In 2000, The Baltimore Sun published her first column about playing soccer with her son—from the wheelchair that launched her *From Where I Sit* newspaper column. Her website (BeckyGalli.com) houses over 400 published columns. Her books, *Rethinking Possible—A Memoir of Resilience* (2017) and *Morning Fuel—Daily Inspirations to Stretch Your Mind Before Starting Your Day* (2024) reflect what she believes: "Life can be good—no matter what." She continues to write *Thoughtful Thursdays—Lessons from a Resilient Heart*, a column for her subscriber family that shares what's inspired her to stay positive. A Morehead-Cain Scholar at the University of North Carolina at Chapel Hill, she was formerly employed by IBM, where she was the recipient of the Golden Circle award for marketing excellence. Becky resides in Lutherville, Maryland, outside of Baltimore.

Join her Thoughtful Thursdays family at BeckyGalli.com/signup and follow her on Instagram, Facebook, and Twitter at @Chairwriter.

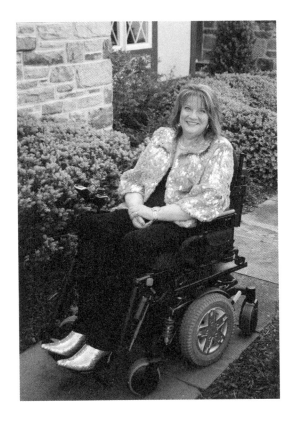

Topic References

Some of Morning Fuel's recurring themes are listed below along with a few favorite entries. There's space to add your own. Share with me on BeckyGalli.com, too!

Living With Uncertainty: January 6 *Living into the Unknown*, January 16 *The Denial Blanket*, January 29 *Who's in Your Boat?* February 28 *Parallel Paths*, April 24 *Suffering is Optional*

_____

_____

_____

_____

_____

_____

_____

_____

_____

_____

_____

_____

Staying Positive: April 22 *Once Only Hoped For*, June 30 *Let Love Be Larger*, July 6 *Moment by Moment*, July 31 *The Power of Put*, August 26 *The Milkshake Method*

_____

_____

_____

_____

_____

Letting Go: January 23 *The Art of an Empty Shelf*, January 27 *My Oprah Dilemma*, February 15 *Big Toe Moments*, June 25 *Letting Life Unravel*, September 10 *Letting Go Without Falling Apart*

Holiday Coping: February 14 *The Shape of Love*, July 3 *Easily Pleased*, November 20 *Turkey Disaster*, December 15 *Good Enough*, December 20 *In-Person Inspiration*

_____

_____

_____

_____

_____

_____

_____

_____

_____

_____

_____

Acceptance: March 10 *Light Bulb Moments*, April 16: *Expectancy vs. Expectations*, July 8 *Grabbing Life by the Lapels*, September 13 *Getting Unstuck*, November 3 *Pouting with Purpose*

_____

_____

_____

_____

_____

_____

_____

_____

_____

_____

_____

Grief: November 1: *The Experience Challenge*, November 23: *Thanksgiving Firsts*, November 25 *Love Perseveres*, December 12 *Meeting Grief with Grace*, December 24 *A Single Candle*

Laughing Matters: January 2 *Stuck or Struck*, April 30 *Letting Laughter Overcome*, July 16 *Winning Against Whining*, August 1 *Expanding Comfort*, October 7 *The Laughter Connection*

On Anger: March 27 *Making Your Problems Your Friends*, May 21 *The Law of Averages*, May 27 *Pulling Out the Pin*, November 7 *Healing Obstacles*, December 2 *Better, Not Bitter*

Looking for your next great read?

We can help!

Visit www.shewritespress.com/next-read
or scan the QR code below for a list
of our recommended titles.

She Writes Press is an award-winning
independent publishing company founded to
serve women writers everywhere.